The autobiography of Mr. Frick

By Werner Groebli

Imprint

Thomas Foeldi
Villa Victoria
Nairs 502
PO Box 22
CH-7550 Scuol
Switzerland

mrfrick@bluewin.ch

Initial Issue: October 2016 | Update: July 2018
© 2016 Author | Editor - Werner Groebli | Thomas Foeldi

Front Cover:
Mr. Frick's Cantilever Spread Eagle (70s)
Back Cover:
Mr. Frick with Swiss (Appenzeller) costume
(Oil painting: 14x18 in. | 35,6x45,6 cm)

Peanuts by Charles M. Schulz
© 2016 Peanuts Worldwide, LLC

Swiss Movements special edition
Paperback
ISBN 978-3-9524638-2-6

SWISS MOVEMENTS
An American Dream

Mr. Frick's world-famous Cantilever Spread Eagle
The autobiography of Mr. Frick
Of the legendary Comedy Ice Skating Team of Frick and Frack
By Werner Groebli

special edition

Introduction

Dear reader,

The till now unpublished autobiography of "Mr. Frick," written by Werner Groebli in the 1980s, was left in the original state for the present book. Only the black and white pictures were carefully refreshed and some square brackets were added by me to supply more useful information, when needed. All <u>underlined</u> words are in German.

"Swiss Movements special edition" contains lots of performance photos, pictures taken with celebrities, as well as personal portraits. Original newspaper clippings, honors, Peanuts Snoopy and cartoons complete the special edition.

After Werner Groebli's retirement in 1980, it was always his greatest wish to get "The autobiography of Mr. Frick" published. Even his friend "Sparky" (Charles M. Schulz) was witness to this desire and sent him a letter in 1987 concerning the last Chapter 13, which he appreciated being part of.

Therefore, this book is in honor of Werner Groebli's 101st birthday, to keep his extraordinary career of more than forty years in the Ice Follies, as an outstandingly funny ice comedian in our lasting memory.

Our little native Switzerland certainly was not ready for the huge arena of America, within which to display his remarkable talent, with which Mr. Frick was so evidently blessed.

I am glad to finally see the publishing of this entertaining book, which will give a profound and visual overview of Mr. Frick's life as one of the leading ice comedians of the world.

To watch Frick and Frack in motion was an incredible experience in my opinion. To do so I can recommend the movies "Silver Skates" (1943) and "Lady, Let's Dance" (1944), which now are available on DVD in reasonable quality.

The entire autobiography, all documents and pictures are part of Werner Groebli's estate.

In memory of Werner Fritz Groebli (April 21, 1915 - †April 14, 2008), better known as "Mr. Frick"

Thomas Foeldi

Acknowledgement

First of all, I would like to express my gratitude to Mrs. Jean Schulz, who gave to me the permission to print and publish the "Peanuts Snoopy" in all four editions of "Swiss Movements."

Many thanks as well to Kitty de Brauwere, who gave me all the assistance I needed with the Peanuts.

It was consistently funny to hear Werner pronouncing "Schnuupy" (Snoopy) in Swiss German, when he showed us the Peanuts he had.

Many thanks to my beloved life partner Carola Klinkert-Huegin, who was so patient with me and cheered me on in my work of two years to finish "Swiss Movements."

Furthermore, I want to mention and express my regards to all the professional figure skaters, assistants and staff, who supported "Mr. Frick" in his memorable and unforgettably funny ice shows (Ice Follies) as "Mr. Frick & Company."

Especially the highly talented Hansruedi Mauch (Frack), who sadly had to finish his career way too early because of his bone disease, contributed a great amount to Mr. Frick's success (Frick and Frack).

Last but not least many thanks to "Werner," who looked over my shoulder from heaven sometimes to assure himself that my work, corresponded with his ideas. I hope in the end he will be satisfied with my effort and the outcome of his oeuvre.

About Mr. Frick

Werner Groebli's story of his life as the world-famous comedian on ice

Mr. Frick (Werner Groebli) was among the enduring phenomena of the world of figure skating: an exceptional athlete, a comic genius on skates, an audience pleaser for more than four decades in major ice shows, on television, on film, and in special appearances around the United States and the world.

For a number of years, he was teamed with his original partner Frack and together their act became a part of the language -- "Frick and Frack." They found fame with the Ice Follies. Frick and Frack were known for performing eccentric tricks on ice, including the world-famous "Cantilever Spread Eagle," created by Werner Groebli, and Hansruedi Mauch's "Rubber Legs," twisting and bending his legs while skating in a spread eagle position. They also reached a worldwide audience when they began appearing in films, including the two Monogram Pictures productions (1943) "Silver Skates" and (1944) "Lady, Let's Dance."

Beloved of ice figure skating devotee Charles M. Schulz, Mr. Frick had not only performed with Snoopy and the rest of the Peanuts gang on ice, he had been a continuing reference point in the comic strip.

Mr. Frick's long career was a remarkable one, purely with regard to his success in the unique arena of professional ice skating, and he was able to provide a very concentrated and special look at this form of "show business." The rise of the great shows, life on the road with a hectic round of performances at the end of each plane, train or bus trip, celebrities in the audience eager to meet the performers, the new stars and the old ones.

On deeper level, however, the world of professional figure skating was the background for the life of a complex individual, whose will to succeed and devoted professionalism would had stood him well in any endeavor.

Although Mr. Frick eventually found himself in the company of a younger generation, he never allowed mere years to affect his art and athleticism. Although his long and contented marriage was touched by the illness of his wife Yvonne, he did not waver in his devotion to either his work or his personal concerns. Through all his career, too, Mr. Frick has had a good time -- whether it is the exhilaration of performing well, living well, conquering the stock market, seeing talented young skaters succeed, getting publicity for himself and the whole ice skating profession, facing professional setbacks and overcoming them, finding new challenges and meeting them, and making his audiences laugh.

Mr. Frick has been called one of the greatest athletes of our time, and his inventive acts were founded on his ability. He was a unique human being, whose story will touch a far wider audience than those who regularly attend ice Shows. Indeed, anyone who has dreamt of coming out of himself and finding the true person he will be fascinated by this life.

There are very few books which are centered on the world of professional skating, and certainly none with the range of Mr. Frick's experience. It is sometimes forgotten in this time of Olympic champions signing huge contracts to star in ice shows that this form of entertainment has been with us for many years, and has filled its ranks with superb athletes who were born long before television brought them into our homes. Mr. Frick was an outstanding example.

Mr. Frick's professional life was well recorded in publicity and newspaper photos and in the entertainment and Sports pages of newspapers across the country. He was an informative and interesting speaker, having appeared on major talk shows during his performing career, and before audiences of many kinds.

Contents

Prologue		9
Chapter 1		11
Chapter 2		27
Picture 1:	1938 - Frick and Frack-Ice Comedians-Tropical Ice Gardens	42
Picture 2:	1938 - Frick and Frack-Ice Comedians-Tropical Ice Gardens-Sally Eilers	43
Picture 3:	1939 - Frick and Frack-Ice Follies	44
Picture 4:	1940 - Frick and Frack-Ice Follies-Baseball Legend Babe Ruth	45
Picture 5:	1940 - Frick and Frack-Ice Follies	46
Picture 6:	1940 - Frick and Frack-Ice Follies	47
Picture 7:	1941 - Frick and Frack-Ice Follies	48
Picture 8:	1941 - Frick and Frack-Ice Follies	49
Picture 9:	1942 - Frick and Frack-Ice Follies	50
Picture 10:	1942 - Frick and Frack-Ice Follies	51
Picture 11:	1943 - Frick and Frack-Silver Skates	52
Picture 12:	1943 - Frick and Frack-Silver Skates	53
Picture 13:	1944 - Frick and Frack-Lady, Let's Dance	54
Picture 14:	1944 - Frick and Frack-Lady, Let's Dance	55
Picture 15:	1944 - Frick and Frack-Lady, Let's Dance-"Belita"	56
Picture 16:	1944 - Frick and Frack-Lady, Let's Dance	57
Picture 17:	1945 - Frick and Frack-Ice Follies	58
Picture 18:	1945 - Frick and Frack-Ice Follies	59
Picture 19:	1946 - Frick and Frack-Ice Follie-"Get in the Driver's Seat"	60
Picture 20:	1946 - Frick and Frack-Ice Follies	61
Picture 21:	1946 - Mr. Frick-"The Admiral and His Aides"	62
Picture 22:	1946 - Mr. Frick & Rita Peake-Life Magazine	63
Picture 23:	1947 - Frick and Frack-Ice Follies	64
Picture 24:	1947 - Frick and Frack-Ice Follies	65
Picture 25:	1948 - Frick and Frack-Ice Follies-"Sea Foot"	66
Picture 26:	1948 - Frick and Frack-Ice Follies	67
Picture 27:	1949 - Frick and Frack-Ice Follies	68
Picture 28:	1949 - Frick and Frack-Ice Follies-Madison Square Garden	69
Picture 29:	1950 - Frick and Frack-Ice Follies-"In The Bahamas"	70
Picture 30:	1950 - Frick and Frack-Ice Follies	71
Picture 31:	1951 - Frick and Frack-Ice Follies	72
Picture 32:	1951 - Frick and Frack-Ice Follies	73
Picture 33:	1951 - Frick and Frack-Ice Follies	74
Chapter 3		75
Picture 34:	1939 - Frick and Frack-Ice Follies-New York Herald Tribune	89
Picture 35:	Mr. Frick & Celebrities-Maurice and Nita Chevalier	90
Picture 36:	Mr. Frick & Celebrities-James and Gloria Stewart	91
Picture 37:	Mr. Frick & Celebrities-Lawrence Welk	92
Picture 38:	Mr. Frick & Celebrities-T. Bennett, R. Dwyer, W. Groebli & F. Astaire	93
Picture 39:	1940 - Frick and Frack from Switzerland-Life Magazine	94
Picture 40:	1940 - Frick and Frack from Switzerland-Life Magazine	95
Picture 41:	1940 - Frick and Frack from Switzerland-Life Magazine	96

Chapter 4 97
    Picture 42: 1969 - Mr. Frick & Mrs. Peggy Fleming-Ice Follies 113
    Picture 43: 1954 - Werner & Yvonne Groebli-The Conrad Hilton Chicago 114
    Picture 44: 1951 - Mr. Frick is boarding the airplane by snow shoes 115
    Picture 45: 1969 - Mr. Frick, wife Yvonne and poodle Lulu 116

Chapter 5 117
    Picture 46: 1953 - Mr. Frick & Ray Armstrong-Ice Follies 122

Chapter 6 123
    Picture 47: 1966 - Mr. Frick hauls fellow Ice Follies to work at Madison Square Garden ... 131
    Picture 48: Mr. Frick is reading The Wall Street Journal 132

Chapter 7 133
    Picture 49: Ice Follies Mr. Frick's Cantilever Spread Eagle-Amazed Kids 138

Chapter 8 139
    Picture 50: 1972 - Ice Follies-Mr. Frick & Karen Kresge 149
    Picture 51: 1973 - Ice Follies-Mr. Frick & Karen Kresge 150

Chapter 9 151
    Picture 52: 1974 - Mr. Frick and Swiss school children 154

Chapter 10 155

Chapter 11 159
    Picture 53: 1954 - Ice Follies-Mr. Frick's Cantilever Spread Eagle 169
    Picture 54: 1954 - Ice Follies-Mr. Frick & Nancy Travis 170
    Picture 55: 1954 - Ice Follies-Mr. Frick & Nancy Travis 171
    Picture 56: 1955 - Ice Follies-Mr. Frick & Nancy Travis-"Antarctic Adventurer" 172
    Picture 57: 1955 - Ice Follies-Mr. Frick Ice Comedian 173
    Picture 58: 1955 - Ice Follies-Mr. Frick's Cantilever Spread Eagle-"Antarctic Adventurer" . 174
    Picture 59: 1956 - Ice Follies-Mr. Frick, creator of laughs-"Park Bench Ambassador" 175
    Picture 60: 1957 - Ice Follies-Mr. Frick & Doris Meyers 176
    Picture 61: 1957 - Ice Follies-Mr. Frick-"Geiger Counter Capers" 177
    Picture 62: 1958 - Ice Follies-Mr. Frick & Gail Foster-"Alpine Antics" 178
    Picture 63: 1958 - Ice Follies-Mr. Frick-The best in ice comedy-"Alpine Antics" 179
    Picture 64: 1958 - Ice Follies-Mr. Frick-USS Nautilus SSN - 571 180
    Picture 65: 1959 - Ice Follies-Mr. Frick & Gail Foster-"Antarctic Scientist" 181
    Picture 66: 1959 - Ice Follies-Mr. Frick's Cantilever Spread Eagle-"Top Banana" 182
    Picture 67: 1959 - Ice Follies-Mr. Frick-Makeup Backstage 183
    Picture 68: 1960 - Ice Follies-Werner Groebli-Businessman 184
    Picture 69: 1960 - Ice Follies-Mr. Frick-Ice Comedian 185
    Picture 70: 1961 - Ice Follies-Mr. Frick & Doris Skillings-"Traveling Light" 186
    Picture 71: 1961 - Ice Follies-Mr. Frick & Doris Skillings-"Traveling Light" 187
    Picture 72: 1962 - Ice Follies-Mr. Frick's Nine Thousandth Performance 188
    Picture 73: 1962 - Ice Follies-Mr. Frick-Backstage 189
    Picture 74: 1963 - Ice Follies-Mr. Frick's Cantilever Spread Eagle looks so easy 190
    Picture 75: 1964 - Ice Follies-Mr. Frick & Ina Bauer 191
    Picture 76: 1965 - Ice Follies-Mr. Frick 192
    Picture 77: 1966 - Ice Follies-Mr. Frick & Ina Bauer 193
    Picture 78: 1967 - Ice Follies-Mr. Frick on the Tramp 194
    Picture 79: 1968 - Ice Follies-Mr. Frick's Cantilever Spread Eagle 195
    Picture 80: 1969 - Ice Follies-Mr. Frick & Susan Berens-"The Ice Follies Ranch" 196

Picture	81: 1969 - Ice Follies-Mr. Frick still performs his incredible Cantilever Spread Eagle	197
Picture	82: 1970 - Ice Follies-Mr. Frick-"Frozen Arctic"	198
Picture	83: 1971 - Ice Follies-Werner Groebli-Walter Matthau & Elaine May	199
Picture	84: 1971 - Ice Follies-Mr. Frick's Cantilever Spread Eagle-"The new Ice Age"	200
Picture	85: 1971 - Ice Follies-Mr. Frick & Jill Shipstad	201
Picture	86: 1972 - Ice Follies-Mr. Frick & Richard Dwyer ("Mr. Debonair")	202
Picture	87: 1972 - Ice Follies-Mr. Frick saluting	203
Picture	88: 1972 - Ice Follies-Mr. Frick & Snoopy	204
Picture	89: 1973 - Ice Follies-Mr. Frick hands over a bouquet to Janet Lynn	205
Picture	90: 1974 - Ice Follies-Mr. Frick's Cantilever Spread Eagle	206
Picture	91: 1974 - Ice Follies-Mr. Frick-Thirty-five years with the Ice Follies	207
Picture	92: 1975 - Ice Follies-Swiss Jewel Mr. Frick	208
Picture	93: 1976 - Ice Follies-Mr. Frick's Cantilever Spread Eagle	209
Picture	94: 1977 - Ice Follies-Mr. Frick-Attention Please!	210
Picture	95: 1978 - Ice Follies-Mr. Frick-Ice Comedian	211
Picture	96: 1979 - Ice Follies-Mr. Frick and Sesame Street's Big Bird	212
Picture	97: 1980 - Ice Follies-Mr. Frick-"The most enduring comic on ice"	213
Picture	98: 1980 - Ice Follies-Mr. Frick-"Funnier than ever"	214

Chapter 12 215
Picture	99: Werner Fritz Groebli retired in the 1990s	218

Chapter 13 219
Honor	1: 1978 - Frick and Frack-Ice Skating Hall Of Fame	226
Honor	2: 1962 - Mr. Frick's Nine Thousandth Performance	227
Honor	3: 1978 - Proclamation-Office of the Mayor San Francisco	228
Honor	4: 1978 - Proclamation-City of Los Angeles-Mr. Frick Day	229
Picture	100: 1972 - Ice Follies-Mr. Frick, Karen Kresge & Snoopy	230
Picture	101: 1973 - Ice Follies-Mr. Frick & Snoopy	231
Peanuts	1: 1975 - Snoopy-Charles M. Schulz-"I'll disguise myself as Mr. Frick"	232
Peanuts	2: 1977 - Snoopy-Charles M. Schulz-"For a moment there I had Mr. Frick worried"	232
Peanuts	3: 1978 - Snoopy-Charles M. Schulz-"I'd even introduce you to Mr. Frick"	232
Peanuts	4: 1980 - Snoopy-Charles M. Schulz-"I should be in an ice show"	233
Cartoon	1: Mr. Frick the most imitated comic on ice	234
Cartoon	2: Mr. Frick performs one of the most difficult and imitated skating tricks	235
Cartoon:	3: 1946 - Mr. Frick-"Helvetian Ambassador of fun to patrons of the Ice Follies"	236

Epilogue 237
Index 239
Appendix 251
Editions 253
Signs and Symbols
- Pictures
- Pages
- Honors
- Cartoons
- Peanuts

PROLOGUE

It was November, late in November or perhaps early in December. The first hint of approaching winter came to Switzerland, dusting the mountains with the first coating of snow, kissing the cheeks of the housewives with a dab of red, exciting the children with thoughts of the joys of winter soon to appear.

One of those excited children was a young boy who was thrilled at the prospect of the coming winter season.

"Muti [mom]," he said, "is it all right if I spray the yard today? Do you think it is cold enough for the water to freeze? Do you think the neighbors would mind? Will you tell father that it is all right for me to do it? Would you help me find the nozzle for the hose?"

All day, the flaxen-haired little boy -- he was five that winter of 1920 -- plucked at his mother's sleeve, pestering her with pleas and questions and offers to do extra chores if she would only let him spray the yard so he could skate.

The house at number 77 Frobenstrasse was like thousands of other houses in Basel. Grey brick, four stories high, attached on both sides to other identical houses, row upon row of houses, street after street of row after row of houses, block after block of street after street of row after row of houses, all neat and clean, and all the same.

But in the back of the house at number 77 Frobenstrasse, there was a difference. This house had a large, flat, level area -- the little boy's yard -- which, come winter, he would spray with water until he achieved his own private ice-skating rink -- small -- but serviceable.

It might seem odd to us today to realize that Switzerland, the capital of the kingdom of winter, had no ice skating rinks in 1920. But there was none in Basel, not until the mid-'30s. Winter sports in 1920 were not the well-organized, commercial, ragingly popular ventures they are today. Skiers had to fend for themselves -- no lifts, no carefully manicured slopes -- and so did skaters.

The little boy got his wish. His mother bowed to the juvenile pressure and said, "All right, Werner, you can spray the yard and skate for a little while."

He rushed outside and began spraying. It took some time, and several coats, but eventually he had his ice.

He went up to his room then and rummaged in his closet and found his skates -- metal ones that clamped to the bottom of his shoes.

And then, with his woolen cap pulled down over his ears and his red muffler wrapped around his neck, he went outside and skated. Round and round the makeshift rink he went, dreaming whatever dreams a young boy dreams, slipping and falling and picking himself up and going around some more.

Basel is on the northern edge of Switzerland. A few miles away there is a spot where Germany, France and Switzerland come together. People like to have their pictures taken there, standing with one foot in one country, the other foot in another country and an arm extending into a third.

Less than a hundred miles to the east, just across the beautiful blue Lake Constance, is Friedrichshafen in Germany. This City was the home port, in those days soon after World War I, of the great German airships.

The pilots of the LZ3 and LZ4 -- the models for the great Graf Zeppelin which was to come a few years later -- used to fly from Friedrichshafen due west to Basel, on the first leg of their trans-Atlantic crossings to South America. They would fly low during that leg of their journey, probably to give their passengers time to get their air legs, or whatever it is that airship passengers have to get, and to see the lovely scenery of the Alps and the surrounding countryside.

On this particular day, when dusk descended on Basel, one of the great airships came droning out of the eastern sky. The boys of Basel could always tell when it was coming near, because of what they called the brummen -- the dull, deep-throated hum of the airship's powerful engines.

But the little boy, skating on his own rink behind his house at number 77 Frobenstrasse, was too busy with his own daydreams, or dusk dreams, even to hear the <u>brummen</u> that evening.

He was trying something new trying to master a jump he had seen one of the better skaters in Basel do the previous winter. All summer long he had thought about that jump and he couldn't wait until the next winter to try it himself.

He skated and jumped -- and fell. And then he tried it again. He tried it a dozen times, maybe more. He tried it until he got it right.

Overhead, the great airship shoved its steady, graceless way through the twilight sky. Then suddenly, from the cabin that hung below the cigar-shaped framework, a spotlight sliced through the dusk.

Nobody will ever know whether the man operating that spotlight had seen the little boy skating in his back yard and decided it would be fun to pick him out with his searchlight, or whether he had turned the light on for some sort of practice and coincidentally picked out that small figure.

But it happened. The young skater was in a golden shower of light before he realized it. All the passengers on the airship looked down at the impromptu, unexpected show and smiled and applauded.

The little boy seemed to understand that he was on stage, that he had an audience. He doffed his woolen cape in a polite bow and waved to the audience who floated above him. Then he put his cap back on his head and proceeded to give them the best show he could possibly do. He twirled and spun and then he did his new jump -- and it was, for the first time, a perfect execution of that tricky maneuver.

Long after the airship had flown off to the west and the <u>brummen</u> had faded into the silence of the Swiss winter night, the little boy stood there on his private rink, still warmed by the excited glow of his first solo and his first spotlight and his first applause, which he imagined he had heard.

He was warm inside. He had had his first taste of the ecstasy of performing for an appreciative audience. It had been a thrilling experience.

Now, even though he didn't have the words to express it, he knew that he had lived through a profound moment, one which he would never forget and which quite possibly could change his life.

Werner Groebli -- who was destined to become perhaps one of the greatest comedy ice skater who ever lived -- had performed for his first audience. He enjoyed it that evening, and he enjoyed it for the next sixty-six years.

CHAPTER 1

The world has strange ideas about the Swiss. They think of them as sober, serious, industrious, hard-working, humorless, money-grubbing -- and other words conveying the same general impression.

Strange ideas indeed, strangest of all had been that it is pretty much the way we Swiss are.

So, take pity on me, the exception. Werner Groebli is my name, and I started in Basel with the orthodox Swiss ambitions and destinations. My parents fully expected me to grow into something sober, serious, industrious, hard-working, humorless and money-grubbing. Perhaps an accountant, perhaps an architect, perhaps a railroad man like my father and grandfather had been. But, inside little Werner Groebli, there was a clown waiting to break out.

A Swiss clown? That's a contradiction in terms, rather like saying an Irish teetotaler or a woman-hating Frenchman. The two things would appear to be mutually exclusive. There have been a few funny Swiss in our history, but not many. There's really nothing funny about a man sticking an apple on his head and letting somebody shoot an arrow at it.

The funniest thing about me, and the clown who was lurking inside me, is that I didn't know he was there, either. I grew up as a very shy young fellow, typically Swiss in my attitude toward money and work and humor. That, of course, was as it should be. A child automatically reflects the attitudes he sees around him as he grows.

Basel is a peculiar City in many ways. For one thing, it is so close to both Germany and France that it is almost an open city. There are French and German railroad stations on Swiss soil in Basel. You can buy a streetcar pass that is good in three nations. The Basel airport is actually located in France and is reached via a neutral, fenced-in freeway.

Basel is also the site of a good many large and flourishing chemical plants. It likes to joke -- this is as funny as it gets in Switzerland -- about being "the world's largest pharmacy." There are the plants of Ciba-Geigy, Hoffman-LaRoche and Sandoz (site of the disaster in 1986 which led to the contamination of the Rhine) and several other big chemical manufacturing companies [1996 Ciba-Geigy and Sandoz merged into Novartis].

No chocolate. No watches. Those are elsewhere. We just have chemicals. So, it happened often, if the wind was blowing in the right (or wrong) direction, the acrid sweetish smell of chemicals in the air. Today, I am sure they are saying that is injurious to your health, but I grew up with that smell in my nostrils and it didn't seem to hurt me.

The Groebli house was at number 77 Frobenstrasse. A large house attached on both sides, one of a string of similar houses that lined both sides of that narrow street.

They were all the same color -- a dull grey white -- with only an occasional splash of color (dark green shutters here, a pot of geraniums on a window sill there, an occasional tree) to brighten the endless parade of dull grey white houses.

Inside, I imagine they were also similar. The ones I saw were pretty much like our house. The same dark furniture rugs pictures lamps -- all things that had been in the Groebli family for several generations. (If I had them now, I could probably live lavishly from the proceeds of selling them to Beverly Hills or New York matrons as antiques, which, of course, they already were when I was a boy.)

As the youngest child in the family, and the only boy besides, I was relegated to a little room on the topmost floor, the fourth floor, under the tin mansard roof. My grandparents lived in the ground floor apartment in what was called the Parterre.

My parents, Fritz and Gertrude (I called my father Bappe [dad] and my mother Mamme [mom] or, occasionally, Muti [mom], like all good little Swiss boys did), lived on the second floor. And my sister, Gertrude or Trudy, who was two years older than me, lived on the third floor.

I didn't mind being on the top floor, except on those very rare days in mid-summer when it got very hot up there. Ordinarily, however, it was comfortable and had the very valuable virtue of privacy. For a boy, especially a shy boy, who I was, privacy is a quality desperately to be desired.

My room also had a window overlooking Frobenstrasse. You have to understand how it is with the Swiss and their windows. Windows play a very important role in the daily life of Swiss people, particularly the ladies of the house. Just inside the window, on a nearby ledge, they always keep a pillow. Where Americans take a coffee break, Swiss take a window break. Every so often, they take their pillow, throw open the window, place the pillow on the sill, lean on it, and look out the window to see what is going on.

From that vantage point, they can observe the hustle and bustle (generally, more bustle than hustle) of the passers-by on Frobenstrasse. The front window permits a view of the street and its traffic. The rear windows allow them the vista of the trees and flowers and the row of houses on Gempenstrasse, the next street over. Mamme [mom] and Trudy were particularly adept at leaning out the windows and gossiping with neighbors on the street below, in windows across the street, or, by some acrobatic stretching and craning, in windows in houses next to ours.

I used my window for more constructive purposes. A friend and I rigged up a wire from my window to his running across Frobenstrasse. We were able to transport various items along this makeshift funicular. Our crowning achievement came one morning when, by dint of extreme caution and even more extreme good luck, we were able to transport a pail of water part way from my house to his, and then, as an unsuspecting bakery peddler walked beneath us, we tipped the pail over and doused him totally -- thereby soaking his array of buns, rolls and bread.

We thought that was very funny -- but only for a short while. His anger (understandable) was ultimately translated into severe discipline for me and, I imagine, for my co-conspirator as well. I don't remember my sentence -- my parents were not addicted to beating children -- but I am certain it was justified. After all, my mother had to pay the bakery peddler for his ruined products.

He was hardly the only peddler to hawk his wares along Frobenstrasse. The milkman, with his horse and cart, was a daily visitor. There were people selling fruits and vegetables on a seasonal basis -- Italian strawberries in the spring, French grapes in the summer, German apples and peaches in the fall. Each time one of them came through, the housewives would descend on him, not only to buy but also for the opportunity to meet the other ladies and exchange chit chat.

The world thinks of all of Switzerland as Alpine, a land of perpetual snow and ice. But Basel actually has a relatively mild climate. Ordinarily, our winters are short and not too severe. So, there are thousands of Basel children who grew up in my era without ever having skated or skied today, some eighty percent ski. In fact, the Basel school system builds a two-week ski vacation into the school schedule each February.

Not so when I was a boy. And I and my contemporaries had no ice skating rink. Later, one would be built when I was a teenager -- just in the nick of time for me as it turned out -- but when I was small, there wasn't a single artificial rink in the entire City of Basel.

Somehow, despite that, I grew up with a great love of ice skating. And so, I took to spraying our back yard with water whenever it was cold enough for the water to freeze. There was also the tennis court area in the park. Just a few houses down Frobenstrasse was that corner -- the big cross street, Gundeldingerstrasse -- and across on the other side was Margarethenpark, where there were two tennis courts. The park people would spray them in the winter, resulting in a makeshift rink.

I skated in our backyard and I skated on the frozen tennis courts but even so, the skating season was short, perhaps a few weeks, maybe a month if the winter was particularly severe.

So, I did other things. I did the things boys did everywhere, except perhaps we Swiss boys didn't do as many of them as, say, American boys. We were too preoccupied with our plans -- or, more appropriately, our parents' plans for us -- for the many frivolous things American boys do.

Still, we had our fun. We improvised a sort of soccer on the Frobenstrasse pavement. We had rubber balls, smaller than regulation soccer balls, but a bit larger than today's soft balls, which we kicked around with youthful abandon. In fact, all too often our soccer ball would land in somebody's front garden, a result which was generally unappreciated by the home owner. Once, I recall with pain, my ball landed in the garden of number 75 Frobenstrasse, the home of our neighbor, a man named Biefert. He was furious when my ball decapitated one of his begonias, or some such botanical beauty, and he grabbed the ball, whipped out his trusty Swiss Army knife and proceeded to hack the ball into a thousand (give or take a few hundred) pieces.

We also played a little tennis in the park -- not on the tennis courts, that would have been too sensible. We had a favorite place, a gravel-covered area, and we would string a net -- really just a rope -- and bat a ball back and forth.

For a few years, I was totally absorbed by my Goppel -- my Bugatti soap box racer. In Margarethenpark, there was a soap box racing course, a slope of perhaps 150 yards, and the trick was to stop without crashing into the large oak tree at the base of the slope. I don't know if the person who decided to put the course there, with that menacing tree at the bottom, hated children or was just stupid, but kids crashed into that tree with alarming regularity. Luckily, I only hit it once, but that once was bad enough -- an assortment of bruises and cuts and, what was worse, a wrecked Goppel.

Like every good Swiss boy, I wore short pants until I was twelve. Between wrecking my Goppel in the summer and falling down on my skates in the winter, my poor knees were a constant mass of cuts, bruises and scabs throughout my early childhood. Not until I graduated to knickers at thirteen did my knees completely heal.

I was born in 1915, and so I have no memories -- only the distant echoing of heavy cannons -- of World War I. That war had almost no impact on the Groebli family at all, certainly nothing compared with World War II, when Allied bombers accidentally dropped bombs on Basel -- some only two blocks from my parents' home.

At seven, I started school -- Primarschule -- which was perhaps a year later than I should have started. My mother used to sneer at the other mothers who, with typical Swiss focus on financial considerations, told her they put their sons into school at six "so he can begin earning money a year sooner." My mother felt that giving me another year of pre-school lack of responsibility was more important to me than hastening my earning years by one.

I suppose most people would consider me a strange child. I had friends but I much preferred my own company. After school or on weekends, I often wandered aimlessly through Margarethenpark. I had a favorite tree and I would sit under it, leaning against its rough, yet familiar and therefore comfortable, bark. I would read books, books that told of heroic actions, romantic adventures and exciting deeds, and I would read them with envy and respect. Then I would wander slowly back to the reality of Number 77 Frobenstrasse, where life was always easy to predict. It was a pleasant sort of life, but hardly heroic or romantic or exciting.

About the only figures of my youth who were even remotely touched with romanticism were my grandfather -- because of his scarred hand, which gave him a touch of the mysterious and the mysterious is often mistaken for romantic -- and my rich Onkel [uncle] Ruedi.

Onkel [uncle] Ruedi and Tante [aunt] Emmy had lived for some years in Alexandria in Egypt. That, in and of itself, was enough to make them the most romantic couple in my entire circle of relatives and acquaintances. Later on, of course, I would far exceed their comparatively slight travels; perhaps because of that, Onkel [uncle] Ruedi, with what must be considered an air of truculence, was once heard to complain: "I have never quite understood why anyone would pay good money to watch what my nephew Werner does on the ice."

If I had known he was going to say that, I wouldn't have wasted all that good envy on him.

But I did envy him, all through my early years. One reason may have been that his was the first wedding I was invited to attend and, even as an eight-year-old boy, I think I was attracted to the concept of love. When Onkel [uncle] Ruedi -- he was my mother's younger brother -- married Tante [aunt] Emmy, I was naturally invited. The wedding was to be held at Bad Ragaz, an exclusive and ritzy resort near Lichtenstein. Eight-year-old boys, no matter how much they loved the idea of love in their secret hearts, shun public affairs and I was a particularly shy eight-year-old boy. So, I prevailed on my parents to let me stay home. I think my shyness forced me to miss many good times as a boy.

Later, Onkel [uncle] Ruedi and Tante [aunt] Emmy built a villa not far from our home. I would often go over there, ostensibly to "help" them -- I raked some leaves and did similar minor chores and got a few francs for my trouble -- but really just to see how the other half lived.

Not that we were in any way deprived or underprivileged in our stone-and-stucco home on Frobenstrasse. Far from it! My father was a respected and respectable member of the petite bourgeoisie, with his respected and respectable position on the railroad's supervisory staff.

He walked to work every morning -- a walk of a bit less than twenty minutes -- and walked home for lunch. Having the entire family for the midday meal was the norm in Switzerland in that era and still is, far more than in other western countries. My father would walk home at noon, take off his shoes, put on his slippers, read the paper, eat his lunch, then put his shoes back on and walk down the street and back to his desk. As far as I ever learned, his area of responsibility with the railroad was the procurement and control of supplies the railroad needed. It was, I suspect, an important post and one he performed skillfully but to a small boy infatuated with the romance and heroism of novels, it seemed very dull.

We lived very comfortable, as I view my childhood from the cold and sometimes harsh light of retrospect.

The street was narrow -- I don't know how it is managing in these days of heavy automobile traffic; in my youth, of course, the appearance of a car was a major event.

We ate well in our tall, narrow house. I look back longingly on the family breakfasts -- hot chocolate, dark bread, heavy butter bought from a street vendor who brought it straight from an outlying farm, and a variety of thick, fruity jams. Sometimes, for a change of breakfast pace, we would have Müesli, the Swiss cereal mixture that has lately become popular in ski resorts all over the world. On Sundays, we might top the Müesli with strawberries and whipped cream, or, for an even rarer treat, a sliced banana.

Between breakfast and lunch there was what we called Z'nüny, which I have often thought might have inspired the good new American brunch. Z'nüny was a mid-morning snack -- bread and rolls and a sausage and some ham. My mother washed hers down with what today we could call a cooler -- red wine diluted with some water. Trudy, my sister, and I had hot chocolate in winter, milk in summer.

Lunch was the main meal. The whole family would be there. Bappe [dad] would come home for it as most Swiss men did. He would leave his office at noon, briskly walk for twenty minutes, have lunch, then read the paper and take a brief nap and be back in his office by two. Many Swiss men would even take commuter trains home to be with their families for the important noon meal. (On today's Swiss commuter trains, incidentally, and even on today's Swiss streetcars, there are no conductors. Passengers pay via an honor system.)

We would linger over our noon meal because, like most Europeans, ours was a lengthy midday break. We didn't go to the extremes of the Spaniards or Portuguese, who take a midday break that lasts all day, but we did have a two-hour respite in the day's activities from about noon until about two o'clock.

On school days, I would make my own Z'nüny, Butterbrot. That was simply a thick slice of dark bread spread with a thick coating of butter. Often, I would sprinkle cocoa powder over it and a glass of milk to wash it down. I have had a lifelong love affair with milk, and even though the Swiss are remarkably efficient dairy men, I think American milk -- especially milk I have tasted in Wisconsin -- is the finest in the world.

No snacks. There was always a barrel of apples in the basement and I could get one whenever I wished. That was the extent of my snacking. No soft drinks. If we were thirsty, there was always Mineralwasser [mineral water], a huge bottle of which was a permanent fixture in the kitchen ice box. (Actually, the ice box only made its appearance in the Tate '30s; before then, things that needed to be kept cool were kept outside.)

It was that bottle of Mineralwasser [mineral water] that made our shopping basket so heavy. One of my youthful duties was to accompany my mother to the grocery store because she needed help in lugging that infernal bottle home.

The Swiss grocery store had a touch of Swiss economics to it. Swiss economics touched everything and it was certainly a part of my mother's grocery shopping procedure. The proprietor entered every purchase by my mother -- and, of course, every purchase by every other family, as well. Each family was given a little book, like a bank passbook, and each purchase was duly entered -- date, amount, every pertinent detail. At the end of the year, those purchases were totaled and the proprietor gave a dividend of, if I remember correctly, six percent. It was traditional in Swiss families that the mother got that money and kept it. It was something like a bonus for her, and for many Swiss housewives that annual windfall from the grocery dividend was the only money they got to call their own from one year to the next.

Still, for the sake of convenience, my mother and the other Frobenstrasse Hausfrauen [housewives] would patronize the steady stream of peddlers who paraded up the street. Most had handcarts they pushed, displaying their wares -- and they were arranged tastefully and temptingly. The milk wagon was a daily visitor and the butter-and-egg man, in season, the strawberry vendor, the banana man. The bakery boy (the poor fellow I dumped water on, to my life-long shame).

I imagine in today's terminology I would be called a loner. That concept didn't exist in my youth. Perhaps some of the neighbors looked on me as a bit strange since I preferred my own company to that of the other boys my age. But maybe we Swiss -- tolerant in so many other ways -- were also tolerant when it came to a strange, shy young fellow like me. I was allowed to go my own way and if people thought me strange, they kept their opinion to themselves as far as I knew.

I would walk into the countryside for hours just to be by myself. I craved solitude and, fortunately, the countryside was not far away. Within a few blocks of my home, I could be out in the fields. One of my frequent paths took me across St. Jakob's Field where, in 1444, the Swiss Army defeated some five thousand French Armaniacs.

As I grew older, my walks became longer. If I continued on, past St. Jakob's Field, and walked another hour or so, I would come to Gempenfluh (Gempen Summit), some 1,200 feet [366 m] above the Basel plateau. My destination was a six-story-high metal observation tower. Not only did this afford me -- or anyone who ventured to the top -- a truly magnificent view of that part of Switzerland, but sometimes it also afforded me the chance to make a few francs. Theoretically, there was a fee to enter the tower and climb to the top and, in fact, there was a turnstile at the base where a toll collector was supposed to be on duty. But I had discovered that, more often than not, he was absent from his station. So, on those occasions, I would take his place -- unofficially, of course -- and collect the twenty centimes (about a quarter) admission fee from the very rare patrons.

It was I like to think, an example of Swiss ingenuity and seizing Swiss fiscal opportunities.

Walking long distances was a very Swiss trait and our family was especially given to hiking. When I, the youngest in the family, matured to the point where I could keep up, we would frequently hike as a family group. We would start out on the train -- as a railroad man, my father got passes -- and ride off into the hills for ten or twenty miles or so. Then we would get off and begin hiking up into the hills -- the foothills of the Alps, and Switzerland has more Alpine foothills than you can possibly imagine. The Swiss government has been very good about marking hiking trails; these Wanderwege were everywhere. We really didn't have to plan or research these adventures; just hop off the train when the spirit moved us and we were certain to find a well-marked hiking trail. They were called "Wanderer Trails."

We all had good, sturdy hiking boots. My mother and father had boots with nails studded into them so they could attack steep grades -- anything less than the Matterhorn [14,692 feet/ 4478 m] was easy going for them -- and they would help Trudy and me along. My father and mother each carried rucksacks. In his were his field glasses, his "photo apparatus" -- I don't think the word "camera" had come to Switzerland yet -- and his maps. In hers was lunch.

We would very frequently get lost, but that

was half the fun. Then my father would dig out a map, spread it on a rock and spend a half-hour determining where we were, and in which direction we would have to go to get back to the railroad station. Then, that having been established, he would point with his walking stick and off we would go. I would estimate that in approximately three-quarters of the cases he would be right. In the other cases, my mother would give him a hard look and begin walking and inevitably she would lead us to the safety of the railroad station without even glancing at a map.

We would find a nice spot to picnic and have our lunch. Usually, it would be at the side of a rushing mountain stream, and we would wash our hard-boiled eggs and bread and cheese down with that marvelous, crystal-clear mountain stream water. Sometimes, on a good day, we would stop off before we boarded the homeward bound train at a little garden restaurant for a soft drink and a piece of pastry.

Occasionally, the four of us were augmented on these outings by another uncle, Heini, and his family. When I was about twelve, Uncle Heini bought a car. It was the first automobile in the family, and so it was an exciting treat for me to ride with Uncle Heini and my cousins in his open English Sports touring car, as he called it.

My grandparents -- my father's parents, Emil and Ida -- lived on the ground floor. I called them Grossvater [grandfather] and Grossmutter [grandmother]. Their room was something of a refuge for me. I would often visit them, where I knew I would find tranquility and a kind word. Grossmutter [grandmother] would be sitting by the window doing needlework of some kind. She and Grossvater [grandfather] stayed by the window until it was dark, I suppose in an effort to conserve on gas and, later, electricity.

Grossmutter [grandmother] encouraged me when I expressed an interest in the stage. With her directing me, I built a miniature theater out of a shoe box. There was a stage at one end, lit by a flashlight, and tiny actors and a tiny audience. I spent many happy hours playing with that theater and it is possible it had something to do with my ultimate love of performing.

It was my grandfather's mangled hand that evoked in me a great curiosity. My imagination led me to create all kinds of scenarios for the cause of that injury -- the attack of a rogue lion or a pirate or a jealous rival for Grossmutter's [grandmother's] affections who flung acid at his face and missed. Later, of course, I learned that the explanation was far from romantic -- he had been an engineer on a steam locomotive and the glass covering a steam gauge had somehow ruptured and shards had been flung off, slashing his hand. Attempts at surgery had been badly botched and that was how his hand had been so badly mangled.

He could no longer perform his duties as an engineer and retired because of that. I have no idea what sort of pension he received -- if any -- and so I don't know if the grandparents' presence in our home was a financial boom or burden to my mother and father. But I know that I enjoyed the fact that they were there. Grossmutter [grandmother] was always good for a cookie or two and Grossvater [grandfather] would always help me doing whatever it was I was supposed to be doing.

Later, when I became interested in building my soap box racer, it was Grossvater [grandfather] who helped me. Maimed though his hand was, he was a good man with a hammer and a screwdriver.

My sister and I had a childhood that seemed to consist of one long truce. There was the normal brother-sister inclination to battle, but European children are encouraged (a polite way of saying we had better do as we were told) to control ourselves. So, we controlled ourselves. She was two years older and, in children's terms, two years translates into domination. Like most girls, she matured earlier than I did, and so she was always, through our mutual childhood, bigger and more self-secure. So, she bossed me around, who I resented, but there was very little that I could do about it. The result is that Trudy and I have never been close. I respected her and I suppose, in my fashion, I loved her -- perhaps I still do -- but we have never had much in common. Where I believe, I grew, intellectually and socially, she remained insular; she studied in Zurich's Haushaltungsschule -- Domestic Science School -- and went on to run a restaurant for many years in a co-op village, Freidorf, not far from Basel.

When I was very young, our home was still lit

by gaslight. I think I must have been around eight years old when that glorious day came and we first snapped on the electricity and the house burst into brilliant light. I remember that while my parents and my sister and I all adapted quickly and happily to this new miracle, my grandparents resisted it in the way of older people everywhere who cling to the customs they know and understand. I can still see the two of them gingerly touching the button that lit their room, seemingly afraid that it could do them some harm. They would wait until it was totally dark and necessity demanded it before they would touch that fearsome switch.

My major excitement as a boy was, of course, ice skating. I really don't remember how it all began. As I have already written, there were no rinks, as such, and so ice skating was never a terribly popular Sport in Basel. Certainly, we had no frozen canals and, hence, no Hans Brinkers.

Somehow, nevertheless, I learned to skate. My skates were merely blades that clamped over my shoes. I never had a proper pair of ice skates until I was much, much older. But when the weather turned cold enough so I could freeze water in the backyard, or when they froze the surface of the tennis courts in Margarethenpark, I was always out there giving it my best.

I never had any instruction. I taught myself to skate and I taught myself to do fancy and funny steps. I saw no ice shows to spark my inventiveness. I watched no ice skaters on television to give me role models to emulate. There were a few fairly good skaters at the park and I would watch them, but with the enthusiasm of youth, I did it mostly all myself.

I fell a lot. I never broke anything, but I had bruises and bumps and contusions and cuts and scrapes over every part of my poor little body. But, battered and bloodied though I was, I would pick myself up, wipe away the gore and get back on my feet and try again.

It was something I was good at. Instinctively, I knew that. I saw the others skating and knew that I was already as good as they were and better than most. Children always like to do what they have a gift for doing. If they find that writing comes easily, they like to write; if they draw well, they like to draw; if they have a gift for music, then they enjoy playing the piano or the violin or singing. I skated well, so I skated as much and as often as I could.

I know that Americans think of the Swiss as a particularly religious people. And, in certain parts of Switzerland, that is true. There are twenty-two cantons (the Swiss equivalent of states [2016 twenty-six cantons]), and many of those are predominately Catholic, and their religion is very important. But in other cantons -- notably Geneva, Basel and Zurich -- which tend toward various Protestant churches, sadly the churches are frequently close to empty.

Swiss citizens pay a small tax to organized religion, which results in the fact that the Pfarrer, or priest, earns a comfortable salary -- some 140,000 Swiss francs [1980s], which is in excess of $85,000, and generally he gets an expense account on top of that.

Every Saturday, at seven in the evening, all of Switzerland's church bells ring for ten minutes. If you position yourself properly -- say, on a hill above Zurich -- that concert of bells can be a magnificent sound. You hear first the Zurich church bells -- big, booming burly -- and then gradually the smaller churches in the smaller cities. Invariably at the end, someone -- Senn or farmer -- high up in the Alps will blow his long Alphorn, signaling an end to that week's concert.

If you are in the heart of downtown Zurich during those Saturday bell bombasts, you will know how loud bells can be. They even drown out the sound of jets flying into the airport.

Our family was not regular church-goers. I seldom saw my mother go at all. Bappe [dad] and Trudy went to the Reformierte Kirche -- the Reformed Church -- very often. I think Trudy went primarily to see the boys and be seen by them, and father was her willing escort. Sometimes, we would go to the old Münster, the Basel Cathedral that had been partially destroyed when a devastating earthquake hit that part of Switzerland in 1356.

My main religious exposure came through Onkel [uncle] Heini and Tante [aunt] Celly. My aunt was very active in Christian Science and for a few years -- I think from the time I was twelve until I became fourteen -- I went to a Christian Science Sunday School fairly regularly.

Uncle Heini was what in today's vernacular would be called a character. He was a textile manufacturer, and I believe was reasonably successful. When he got his car, he raced it and often boasted that he had gone seventy-five miles an hour. Considering the fact that there are no straightaways on Swiss roads -- the mountains prevented any such luxury -- that was very swift, indeed, if true.

When the Kunsteisbahn [artificial ice rink] -- the first Basel skating rink -- opened in 1934, Uncle Heini was a regular visitor. He always wore his skating costume, which consisted of tights, a pair of bizarre shorts over them and a fur hat. He knew one fancy figure -- a spiral -- and over and over again, he spiraled and, as a result, he made a very comical figure. We boys would call him Ras Gugas, which was what the Swiss called Haile Selassie, the emperor of Ethiopia. I think the nickname was apt.

There was tragedy in the lives of Onkel [uncle] Heini and Tante [aunt] Celly, however. Their daughter, my cousin, Elisabeth, was a teenage suicide. She shot herself in bed. Nobody knew where she got the gun, or why she did it. I had always liked Elisabeth, and her sister, Rosemarie. Both were attractive girls, intelligent and sweet-natured. I had often talked to them, and somehow, I could talk to them about serious things where I could never talk to my own sister, who was roughly their age.

Celly, who was my mother's sister, had been a merry woman before Elisabeth killed herself. But that terrible event took the laughter from her eyes forever after, and she became morose and gloomy. My mother also had three brothers, Ruedi, Max and Richard. Another sister had died when she was a child. My mother had been the one called on to help her parents do the housework and she had really raised Celly, Ruedi, Max and Richard.

She grew up on Solothurnerstrasse, only about four blocks from Frobenstrasse, where we lived. Her whole life was that small corner of Basel.

Onkel [uncle] Ruedi had been the one to escape, the one who had lived what I construed to be a romantic life. He had gotten a job in a firm in Basel that imported Egyptian cotton and they had eventually sent him to Alexandria. He lived well there, I imagine; he was president of the Swiss Club of Alexandria and was an intimate of King Farouk. That large, economy-sized monarch had a weak spot in his heart for the Swiss, I was told, and often invited the members of the Swiss Club of Alexandria -- including my uncle -- to his palace for an afternoon of bowling and champagne, and possibly other treats.

Onkel [uncle] Ruedi, while still in Egypt, asked my father to buy a farm for him back home in Switzerland. He told my father that he wanted to have the farm as an anchor in case anything went wrong with the Swiss-Egypt cotton trade. So, my father, acting as his agent, bought a farm for Onkel [uncle] Ruedi, Tante [aunt] Emmy and my cousin, Hans-Peter.

They also had a villa in an area of Basel where the affluent lived. Uncle Heini and his family lived there, but the upper story -- what we would today call the penthouse -- was reserved for Ruedi, Emmy and Hans-Peter. When they came back from Egypt that is where they lived. I don't know whatever happened to their anchor, the farm, but I never saw it. I did, however, frequently visit them at their Basel villa.

During World War II, my father modernized the top floor of the house on Frobenstrasse. I had long ago left and it had been empty and uninhabited for years. For whatever reason, Ruedi sold the villa and moved in to the newly-renovated upper floor of number 77 Frobenstrasse.

I believe that I inherited much of my athletic ability from my father. As a businessman, he had little opportunity to utilize his athletic prowess, however. He worked long hours, six days a week. Frivolity was not part of the Swiss work ethic and Sports were considered the ultimate in useless frivolity.

Still, he was a member of the Turnverein Gundeldingen, the men's Sports club. Most of his time there, however, was spent in coaching the ladies' gymnasium section, rather than in doing anything himself. I remember how on Sunday mornings when the weather was favorable, Bappe [dad] would lead his ladies out into Margarethenpark, where they did exercises in their jerseys that extended almost to the knee.

Across the park, the male members of the Turnverein would be doing their exercises. They wore heavy shoes, not sneakers; I believe that was so when, they clomped their feet, they made a satisfactorily loud noise. Clomp, clomp, they went, as they did their exercises in unison.

Then, they would all -- men and women -- clomp off to the Wirtschaft [inn] where the Stammtisch (the regulars) had an aperitif. My father would toss his down then clomp his way home with a stop-off at the bakery to pick up some pastries for us at home. We would all have a lovely piece of pastry and coffee or hot chocolate, a Sunday treat.

The Rhine, which bisected Basel, was the artery that brought everything to the City. In the era before trucks became so important, food and fuel and virtually every sort of goods came to us via Basel Porte. (People say that Switzerland is landlocked, and technically it is, but Basel is a very busy port, because of the river. Some ten million tons of freight annually arrives in our city on the barges and the boats.)

The Rhine was more than a commercial waterway, however. It was widely used for excursions. I made several trips downstream, paddling with a friend ten miles or so in a faltboat, a German-made collapsible boat.

There was -- and still is -- a ferry across the river. That centuries-old ferry crossing has inspired a saying in Basel. Instead of the Americanism, "Tell it to the Marines," Baselers say, "Sag das im Fahrima," or "Tell it to the Ferryman."

Once, when I was twelve or so [1927], my parents, Trudy and I were walking along the banks of the Rhine a little upstream from the heart of the city. We heard somebody yelling and looked out into the river and we saw a swimmer who was obviously in trouble. I jumped in, clothes and all, and helped him to shore. I had become a Strong swimmer so it was something I did without thinking twice about it.

I often swam in the Rhine on less adventurous missions. Bappe [dad] had taught me to swim when I was six or thereabouts in a smaller river. From then on, I swam whenever I could. Built along the edges of the Rhine were several bathhouses -- huge, roofless structures -- that served somehow to slow down the big river's ordinarily rapid currents. So, we swam there frequently. It had its drawbacks, however -- mostly, the fact that the river was not the cleanest body of water in the world. It began in the mountains, crystal clear, but the pollution began somewhere in Lichtenstein and the Germans added more and by the time it reached the Basel Knee, where it turned abruptly, it was dirty.

In fact, on several occasions I would have to avoid a clump of human waste floating majestically downstream. We called that material Schiss Kaigelli and, by extension, the Baselers often referred to the Rhine as the Schiss Kaigelli Mississippi.

We boys, to show off our bravery, would swim across the Rhine, which was no easy feat because of the swiftness of the current. The river was also wide enough so that if the winds were right, there were waves. Sometimes the combination of the current and the waves made the crossing treacherous. More than one reckless youth has been lost in the attempt to swim across the Rhine. I was always cautious enough and smart enough to plot my route carefully so that I swam in a direction that brought me to the stone pilings of the railroad bridge about halfway across, which gave me the chance to catch my breath momentarily before continuing on.

Once, I remember, I was swimming with a younger boy -- his name was Hansruedi Mauch, and you will be hearing more about him shortly -- and he tired quickly. The two of us got to the bridge piling and I could see he was totally out of breath, gasping and rolling his eyes. There was a fishing boat tied up to the piling, and I grabbed a rubber hose that was dangling from the boat and threw it to Hansruedi. But the hose missed -- either my aim was bad or he was too weak to catch it -- and it fell into the water and was quickly carried away. I managed to help Hansruedi back to shore, but my exploit with the hose had been seen by the boat owner who knew me. My father had to pay for the hose and I was told, quite forcefully, to stay out of the river for the time being.

That event only served to increase the hero worship Hansruedi had for me. In the first place, I was four years older, and that, in itself, was enough to make me very important in his eyes. But we also shared some common interests -- swimming and ice skating -- and since I was far better than he was in both those activities, he was my constant shadow.

He lived next door to me at 79 Frobenstrasse.

And when I skated on my makeshift backyard rink, he would watch me, hour after hour, day after day. I knew him, of course, and had known him all my life. In a tight-knit neighborhood such as ours, you necessarily know your next door neighbors. We Groeblis knew the Mauchs and had probably known them for several generations back.

Frau [Mrs.] Mauch was considered a solid citizen -- she was a widow and worked long hours in an office to provide for her family. Her sister, Hansruedi's aunt, lived with them and was considered a little strange in the neighborhood.

She belonged to some off-beat religious cult -- it might have been Jehovah's Witnesses or the equivalent -- and she was constantly hosting meetings of her sect at the house. They were loud and noisy gatherings with much raucous hymn-singing and the neighborhood was scandalized. Hansruedi's Gotte -- godmother -- lived nearby where she took in laundry and she thought it was all absurd. She would always threaten to call the Fire Department when Hansruedi's aunt had her friends over to shout and sing -- "Maybe they can brace the house so it doesn't collapse," she would say.

The neighbors knew everybody's business. Most of them felt that Frau [Mrs.] Mauch worked too hard and the consensus of neighborhood wisdom was that she should remarry. She was supporting her sister, the hymn-singer, and then there was her brother, Hansruedi's uncle, who lived on the top floor in a room similar to the one where I spent my youth.

So, we all knew what went on and we all, collectively and individually, would tsk-tsk for poor Frau [Mrs.] Mauch who had to work so hard to support her no-good relatives. Everybody loved little Hansruedi, perhaps because of that feeling of pity for his mother.

To me, however, he was more of a nuisance than anything else. He was too many years younger for me to think of him as a friend. I tolerated him tagging along after me out of a sense of Frobenstrasse loyalty and because I had been taught to feel sorry for his mother, so, by extension, I felt sorry for him, too. But we could never be buddies. When I was eight, for example, he was four, and at that age four years is an insurmountable barrier to bosom buddy ship. I suppose I was flattered by the obvious fact that he idolized me and thought I was a truly heroic figure, and that also contributed to my tolerating his presence. I was, I am sure, always pleased to see him watching me skating; innately, most of us enjoy having an audience.

Later, that audience doubled -- from one to two. A pretty little girl from a few houses down the block began watching me, too. I knew her, naturally. She was Inge Manger and, emboldened by the fact that our parents were friends, she asked me to help her with some skating tips. I did and I could see that she had a great natural ability. I am pleased to say that I recognized her talent at once and encouraged it. And even more pleased to report that, in 1938, Inge Manger became the Swiss skating champion. I was as proud as though I had won the title myself.

Basically, my childhood was serene and peaceful. I had the security of a good, warm, loving home. Further, I had the security of growing up in a time and a place when childhood was easy. We had no distractions or temptations -- no drugs, very little liquor (a glass of wine was permitted after a certain age) and sex was most definitely to be withheld until a larger age. And there was virtually no crime in Basel.

In fact, when I think back on my childhood, the one single most exciting event involves the exception to that statement about no crime in Basel.

In 1934, the biggest crime in Basel's history -- up to that point -- culminated in Margarethenpark, only a few hundred yards or so from my house. Two German criminals -- Kurt Sandweg and Waldemar Velte -- had escaped and were being hunted all over. They had killed six during their bank robbing career. That evening, I had gone skating on a frozen puddle in the park. I wandered over to see where the rink was being built and then went back and skated on my little frozen puddle some more.

Innocently, I think I must have passed Sandweg and Velte, who were it later came out, also in the park at that precise moment -- about nine in the evening. They broke into the hut the men who were building the rink were using, where they found a telephone. They called a girlfriend and asked her to bring them some food. She said she would and she did, but she also told the police.

Within twenty minutes, two hundred policemen were in the park, surrounding the area I had left only a half-hour before. They quickly captured the two criminals, who surrendered without a fight. It was the biggest thing that happened in Basel since they invented numbered accounts.

They still talk about it there -- "Where were you the night they captured Sandweg and Velte?" It's like Americans saying, "Where were you when Kennedy was shot?"

But there was much more to my boyhood life than swimming, skating, family outings and criminals in the park. There was school to attend.

School in Switzerland is mandatory for twelve years and then a student must take an examination -- the dreaded Maturität [higher education entrance qualification] -- after which, if he passes, he goes on to university. About half of the students who take that exam pass; the rest are, rightly or wrongly, considered failures and must make their way in the world the best they can without a higher education.

I had a difficult time in school at first. A Swiss child first attends Primarschule [primary school] and my innate shyness held me back terribly there. I was afraid to say anything in school, afraid of my teachers and afraid of anything and everything that would thrust me into the public notice. (Only on the ice could I tolerate anyone watching me. Perhaps that was because only on the ice I was sure of myself, confident of my own ability.)

Still, I managed to keep my grade up above average. I could do all right on anything written -- written exams did not require me to stand up in front of the class and recite -- so my grades on my written tests were fine.

That continued through Realschule -- the equivalent of the American high school. Then followed the Mathematisch Naturwissenschaftliches Gymnasium, where I studied a heavy curriculum of science, higher mathematics, economics and other serious matters. Among my classmates -- and friends -- were young men who later went on to important positions, such as Albert Businger, who became a director of the huge pharmaceutical firm, Hoffman LaRoche, and Werner Wirz, who invented the by-pass jet and was invited to join Werner von Braun in the U.S. after World War II (I know, because a government official contacted me and asked me to give Wirz a reference, which I was very happy to do).

My own business career began rather more modestly. After graduation, in 1937, I found an office job with the Swiss co-op organization in their insurance department. A friend of my father had suggested that this would be a good place for me because the head of the department was planning to retire soon, so there might be a rapid advancement for me there. I took the job and I did well enough so I could see I was in line for that gentleman's position upon his soon-to-be retirement.

I was paid one hundred francs a month -- not much, but they held out the carrot of the boss' job in a year or two at the most. At first, that sounded good to me, but the more I observed that worthy fellow at work, the less good it looked. My poor boss sat day in, day out, stooped over his desk, eating his lunch at his desk, seldom speaking to anybody, seldom stopping even to smile. As he munched his midday meal, I always got the mental picture of a squirrel. Be hunched over his food, ate quickly and earnestly, and the combination of the hunch and munch was, to me, very squirrel-like.

We all worked hard -- there were two others in the office, besides myself -- but he worked the hardest of all. I was at that time unfamiliar with the expression "eager beaver," but, in retrospect, he was the epitome of the eager beaver. Even with retirement looming in his life, he worked as though he had something to prove, as though people were looking over his shoulder all the time. I got the distinct impression that he was working, at the time I knew him, the same way he had been working for his entire career, more than forty years.

I visualized myself forty years from then, a carbon copy of Herr [Mr.] Fluegl, the boss, a squirrel, a beaver a little mouse of a man. I had no desire to be a rodent for four decades. I worked there for about two months, I think -- sitting on a high stool, bringing the employees' premium records up to date, comparing my data with that of the two other clerks, a tedious, dull, dry, monotonous job. Fit for a squirrel or a beaver, or a mouse, but not a young man with still some hope in his soul that life had something more romantic and exciting to offer.

I lived for the church chimes -- in Basel, life itself was regulated by the chiming of the church bells every quarter hour -- to tell me it was the hour of release. Then I dashed out of the office, hopped on my bike and rode home swiftly.

After those two dreary months, I confided in my Onkel [uncle] Ruedi -- I knew he had an adventurous soul and would sympathize with me. I poured out my plight to him. I couldn't tell my father because he was something of a squirrel-beaver-mouse himself and wouldn't understand my soul's craving for romance and adventure. My father's job, I think, offered a bit more variety and challenge than Herr [Mr.] Fluegl had ever faced, but still he was desk-bound. And I knew he felt that was a man's fate and not an unkind one.

But Onkel [uncle] Ruedi had, after all, been to Egypt, so he would understand what I was going through. I think, in my efforts to convey the depth of my feelings to him, I shed a few honest, frustrated tears. I poured out to him my fears of living the next forty years on that stool in that office.

"I would be little more than a prisoner there, Onkel [uncle]," I believe I said, or sentiments to that effect. "I know my father is right in that I will have security, always a weekly pay enough money to live on and support a family. But I want something more out of my life."

"Do you know just what it is you really want," Onkel [uncle] Ruedi asked, and in retrospect, it was a fair question? So, was his next: "Or how you are going to go about getting it?"

I had to admit that I had no positive answer to either question. I suppose that somewhere, hidden deep and silent in a remote and dusty corner of my mind, there was the notion that I should do what I do best and enjoy most. To wit: ice skating. But at that time, the idea of professional ice skating had never been heard of. At least, I had not heard of it. So, no, I cannot say that the reason I didn't want to stay in my office job was so I could go out and be an ice skating star. In fact, I had no alternative to suggest to Onkel [uncle] Ruedi.

He lit a fresh cigar, poured himself a little sherry, and studied me and my problem. He had a habit of puffing on the end of his cigar and watching the embers flame up to a brilliant, fiery orange.

"Werner," he said, "you are my sister's son and I love you like my own. I wish I could tell you to go off and be a pirate or a lion tamer or join the French Foreign Legion. But my best advice to you is -- stick to your job, at least until something better, something concrete, comes along."

That was certainly not what I wanted to hear, nor what I had expected to hear. I went home, dejected and definitely not happy. My father asked me why I was depressed -- obviously, my depression must have been plain to see -- and I passed it off as nothing of consequence.

"Is it your job?" Bappe [dad] asked me. I said no, it wasn't. "You know son," he went on, completely ignoring my denial, "I have been thinking that perhaps that isn't the right job for you. Oh, I know it has its advantages -- security and a safe future and all that -- but it offers no excitement. And I know you well enough to realize that you are the kind of man who needs a little excitement in your life from time to time."

So, it turned out to be my stiff and, I thought, unsympathetic father, rather than my adventurous uncle, who understood me. With his approval, then, I quit my job. Bappe [dad] asked me what I would do. Out of the clear blue imagination, I blurted out, "I think I would like to be an architect."

Why architecture? I have no idea. I had always had a small gift for drawing and had an innate knack of drawing buildings in proper perspective. My father thought it was a splendid idea.

So, I duly enrolled in the Swiss Federal Institute of Technology in Zurich [ETH Zurich], in the Architektur curriculum [architecture]. Zurich was a long way away -- at least, in my experience at the time -- and I was at the beginning very homesick. I got a room in Zurich but would rush home every weekend.

At first, I was enthusiastic about my new course of study and did well at it. (Maybe it was because I was doing well at it that I was enthusiastic; people seem to enjoy whatever it is they excel at.)

"You have an excellent sense of proportion," my drawing professor wrote on my first exercise. And he was, I learned, not one to lavish praise liberally.

I also did well in Aktzeichnen [nude drawing], the drawing of live models, some of whom appeared before the class naked. As a young and red-blooded boy, this appearance before me of naked ladies was a positive revelation. I had grown up prim and proper like all Swiss and I had never before seen the unclothed female form. It was, I found, a rather heady experience. Thinking back on it, it was amazing, considering my excitement, that I was able to draw a straight line, much less a curvy one. But I did.

I did reasonably well in my other studies, too. However, I found my months studying architecture in Zurich to be lonely ones. Many of the other students were local Zurichers, or from nearby towns, and they had their friends and their families. One or two of them were kind and went out of their way to befriend the poor lost soul from Basel. One youth I remember fondly, primarily because he introduced me to beer. I had never tasted beer in my life until one evening when he took me to an open air restaurant in Zurich and, before I could say a word, he ordered two beers, as a matter of course. I found the taste, at first sip, bitter (which, of course, it is) but eventually came to enjoy it. And, through the years, I have enjoyed quite a few sips of beer.

The Swiss Federal Institute of Technology had one major claim to fame -- the fact that Albert Einstein had not only studied there, but later had been an assistant professor in the Institute's faculty. It was certainly something to be proud of, and I often wondered as I walked the quiet halls whether Einstein had preceded me on that particular walk.

Perhaps if Einstein had still been there, he might have lit a fire in me. But, as it was, the combination of some innate restlessness, plus the unfortunate fact that I never fully got over my homesickness, made me quit after only two semesters.

There was a third factor that contributed to my decision to leave, that was ice skating.

From the time when I was a small boy, slipping and sliding on that makeshift sheet of ice in our back yard, I had never stopped skating. All through my school years, my college years, my brief working years, my period studying architecture, I skated whenever and wherever I could.

It had come easily to me at first. I was always much better at it than any other youngster my age, and, in fact, better than boys considerably older. People would watch me and I enjoyed that attention. I knew I did that one thing well. More and more, then, I skated.

At first, I did the orthodox movements I had seen others do, but since I had never seen any professional or even top level amateur skater, those movements were certainly rudimentary. A few spins, a few leaps, a figure eight that was about the extent of my figure skating repertoire.

More and more, however, in those early years, I discovered something else about my ice skating talents. I could make people laugh with some movements. I think the first thing I did in that vein was an impression of a skater who was trying desperately to stay upright, but kept almost falling. For some reason, this was very funny to the spectators at Margarethenpark, or wherever I did it in those early years. Then I added other funny things -- funny, at least, to those watching me -- such as a "no support" glide and other maneuvers which seemed to defy the laws of gravity and common sense. People roared with laughter when I performed those steps.

When I got to be perhaps ten or eleven, the little next-door boy, Hansruedi Mauch, who had been watching me with his big, idolizing eyes for several years, began to skate, too. He had a natural ability and he got a great kick out of imitating some of my routines.

Gradually, without ever really knowing that we were doing it, or planning it or discussing it in any way, Hansruedi and I started doing some routine together. We would skate around on what was obviously a collision course but, at the last moment, he would zoom left and I would zoom right and we would just barely miss each other. That proved to be another automatic laugh-getter.

We had other little bits we invented and choreographed. He was much smaller than I, so he would slide between my legs while I skated around the ice. We did little pantomime bits and, for the fun of it, we dressed up in funny clothes and painted funny mustaches on our faces which accentuated the humor of what we were doing.

The idea of making money from our funny skating never crossed our minds. There was, as far as we knew, no money to be made. We had never seen or even heard of an ice Show, or anything remotely like that. It was just a way of amusing ourselves, primarily, getting a few laughs from our friends, relatives and neighbors, and being, momentarily, at any rate, the centers of neighborhood attention.

So, I proceeded with my education and my brief forays into the business and architectural world. And Hansruedi's mother pointed him in the direction of a banking career which, in Switzerland, is perhaps the highest calling a young man can aspire to.

Then, when I was around eighteen, the artificial ice rink opened in Margarethenpark. Now Hansruedi and I had a place where we could really skate. There had been no chance to get up any speed in the backyard, but in the rink, we could open up. And, therefore, the routine where we almost collided became even funnier as it became even riskier. (The more risk, the more humor, although I have never understood why this should be so.)

Furthermore, our skating season overnight changed from one of only a few weeks in length -- Basel's climate is probably the mildest in Switzerland -- to one of somewhere around five months. We skated more and more, longer and longer and, as a natural result, we became better and better.

The rink, being the first of its kind in Basel, attracted the finest skaters in the City and in that part of Switzerland. One of those was a man named Armand Perren, an Alpine guide by vocation and a champion amateur skater by avocation. He was the first and only teacher I ever had, even though the relationship we had was hardly that formal. I would watch him and he would give me some advice when I tried to imitate his movements.

Hansruedi and I both benefitted extremely from Perren's tips and suggestions. Soon, we were as good as anybody at the rink, which quickly became a social center in that part of Basel. We were constantly being asked to do our routines and we were happy to oblige. It was fun for us and, although we didn't realize it at the time, it was all marvelous experience and training for what was soon to be our career and our life.

We added more tricks to our "act," although of course we never referred to it as such. We did take-offs of ballet dancers and world class figure skaters. We each had our own pet steps. One day, I realized that I could stay on my feet even though my knees were bent and I was leaning over backwards so far that my back was almost parallel to the ice. Hansruedi thought that was very funny and kept urging me to bend further and further back, so I tried. Gradually, I perfected that step so I could glide around the ice, my back almost flat against the ice -- and going around in circles at a very fast clip (which, later, was clocked at twenty-five miles an hour). That step would become my trademark for more than forty years, a step which would eventually be called "The Frick Cantilever." At the time, however, it was simply "Werner and his impossible backwards glide." At first, I irreverently called it a "Minger," after a Swiss politician and one-time president, Rudolf Minger. He was kidded because he would sit in a peculiar position and my backbend was something of an imitation of that awkward stance. Locally, in Switzerland at that time, that was a very funny joke, calling my backbend a Minger.

I skated everywhere I could, during my early years. It was what has come to be called "compulsive behavior," although to me and I think to most people accused of that sort of thing, it was merely a question of spending as much time as I could do something I enjoyed doing and, perhaps even more important, doing something I knew I was good at.

I even skated while I was in the army. I suppose if there are five things the average non-Swiss knows about Switzerland, it is that Switzerland is the home of cheese with holes in it, good chocolate, the best watches in the world, a lot of numbered bank accounts and, finally, that every Swiss must serve sometime in the army.

That includes every young male unless he is physically unfit. I postponed my service while I was studying architecture, but in 1935 I could postpone it no longer. So, I duly presented myself to the Army authorities and was sent to a basic training camp only ten miles from Basel.

Basic training in the Swiss army is no picnic. Although the Swiss Army has never in modern times had to fight a war perhaps that is because they are always prepared to do so. The soldiers train hard and that training starts immediately. I remember having to shoot at a target on the very first day I reported for duty.

The basic training period was thirteen very tough weeks. After that, it was less severe and we all had some time off. I got myself into Basel on the first pass I had and skated for six solid hours at the Kunsteisbahn [artificial ice rink]. I think if I remember correctly, that I went skating even before I went home to 77 Frobenstrasse to see my family. I suppose, if I must be honestly blunt about it, that I missed ice skating more than I missed my family. I knew my family would still be there, but I wasn't that sure about the ice.

Hansruedi and I had plenty of time as I wound up my year of Army service to work on more bits and pieces of our act. It was starting to feel like a legitimate act by now. What had begun as two neighborhood kids doing some tricks was gradually but surely smoothing into a very skilled performance. More and more, we were attracting attention and a degree of local fame.

We did parodies of famous people. At the time, the Italy of Mussolini had invaded the Ethiopia of Emperor Haile Selassie, so I became Selassie and Hansruedi impersonated Mussolini. During one of our performances, the Italian consul angrily strode out in protest. Rather than risk offending anyone, we never again impersonated political figures.

A Basel theater-critic, Dr. James Koch, who later became an internationally noted ice skating figure, happened to see us do our Mussolini-Selassie routine and wrote a nice article about us in his paper, the Basler Nachrichten [Basle News]. We had known Dr. Koch all our lives. In fact, Hansruedi's aunt used to do his laundry, which Hansruedi would deliver. He remembered Dr. Koch as a very generous tipper.

We played our first genuine engagement in St. Moritz at a place joyfully called The Glitz of St. Moritz. We enjoyed doing it and the audience seemed to enjoy watching us do it. I forget how much we were paid; certainly, it wasn't much, but it was something and I suppose it was then, in the back of my mind, that a seed was planted and I began to think that perhaps this might be my destiny.

But that was still very deep in the back of the remotest part of my mind. In the front, there was still the necessity of getting training for a job and a career I could be happy with for the rest of my life. The insurance business and architecture were not it, obviously. So, when spring came and the ice melted, I enrolled for a ten-week business course in the prestigious Handelsschule [commercial school] Chapalay. I quickly developed a proficiency in such useful skills as typing, shorthand, letter writing, French and English correspondence and book-keeping.

The next winter, Hansruedi and I skated more and more in public. We were, I must say, throwing modesty out the window, the biggest hit at the annual carnival of the Basel Figure Skating Club. Many of our friends and family were watching us, and leading the applause, which certainly helped. But we were good and, of equal importance, we were new and different.

I could and did skate in an orthodox style. In fact, one year I won the Swiss Junior Figure Skating Championship and I suppose I could have gone on to a nice career as a figure skater. But I got bored doing the compulsory school figures that are an integral part of a classic figure skater's routine. I had more fun with my partner, doing crazy things and hearing the comforting sound of audience laughter.

So, we both began to concentrate on our mutual act. After our triumph in Basel, we were called back to St. Moritz at the height of the winter social and skating season. We were the feature attraction at that ritzy, glitzy, St. Moritz Ice Gala.

I had my last fling at figure skating that year at the Gala and I won a silver medal. But I realized that I was a good figure skater, but would probably never be a great one, whereas, with Hansruedi Mauch at my side, I had a chance at being great in the unorthodox field of ice comedy. Besides, the competition in the ice comedy business was virtually non-existent.

St. Moritz at that time was probably the jewel in the social set's crown of resorts. There were practically more millionaires there than snowflakes, and that, remember, was in the era before millionaires became a dollar a dozen.

I was quite impressed, I recall, peeking in the window of the basement of the Palace Hotel, where they had a room that the rich folks used as a bowling alley, and seeing a party of Greek shipping tycoons and their ladies bowling -- using magnums of champagne as their bowling pins.

We were invited, as the stars of the Ice Gala, to some parties ourselves. There was one at Hanselmanns, the famous pastry shop and café, and I gorged myself on all manner of indecent confections piled high with Schlagrahm, or heavy whipped cream. We went to a tea dance at the Hotel Kulm. We gawked at King Farouk of Egypt, the honored guest for the week-long festivities. (He was making his grand entrance at the grand ice show and they had put some boards down for him to walk on, but he got so busy waving at the crowd that he wandered off the boards, slipped on the ice and fell heavily. Since he weighed in at more than two hundred and fifty pounds, when he fell heavily the whole resort trembled for a few shaky moments. It was pretty difficult getting him back on his feet, too.)

Hansruedi and I did our act, with King Farouk laughing and dipping into a box of chocolates one of his flunkies held constantly at the ready.

That year we were dressed in Swiss folk costumes. The feature of that outfit was a short, brown cutaway jacket. The country farmers wear such a jacket on Sundays when they dress up in their best to attend church services. The Swiss call that jacket a Frack.

Both Hansruedi's mother and my parents had only reluctantly given their permission for us to skate in St. Moritz. It was not, in their view, anything to be particularly proud of. It would have been a bit better if we had been doing a graceful, beautiful figure skating performance; that was orthodox and, hence, acceptable. But this silly nonsense we were doing -- our heroic near misses, our Swiss-clock timing as we almost knocked each other over, the way we skated between each other's legs, ours backward bends -- that was certainly nothing to brag about. So, both Frau [Mrs.] Mauch and my parents said we could go, but we were not to use our real names.

We had, therefore, to find names for ourselves. We thought of Frack as one of the names -- it had a funny sound to it, yet it was familiar. But what would go well with it? Then we thought of the town of Frick, which lies on the rail line between Basel and Zurich, and we had both been through it often enough. In fact, when you bought a rail ticket from Basel to Zurich, it read, "Basel-Zurich, via Frick." So, we decided we would be Frick and Frack -- named after a town and a cutaway coat. I don't remember how it was decided which was which, but I became Frick and Hansruedi was Frack.

And it was as Frick and Frack that we skated that day in St. Moritz, with King Farouk leading the cheering and the laughing.

CHAPTER 2

From then on, it was as though we had stepped on a whirlwind. We seemed to have very little control of our destiny. Things happened to us. Things we had not instigated and had not planned or even thought of. We were the passive recipients of the treats fate tossed our way.

We were still in St. Moritz for that initial performance as Frick and Frack, when we were approached by a man we had never met. His name was Dr. Arthur Brandt. He had, he explained, left Germany because of "that terrible man, Herr [Mr.] Hitler," and was practicing his profession in St. Moritz. His profession, he explained, was the law. (Very often, in middle Europe, lawyers and other professional men call themselves "doctor"; they have a right to that title, since they have earned a doctorate in law.) He was also. He went on to say, a great ice skating enthusiast, a fan, in other words.

He stopped us outside of Hanselmanns one snowy evening. We started talking. By the time our conversation was over, we looked like three snowmen standing there on the sidewalk.

"You two young fellows," Dr. Brandt said to us, "ought to go to America. That is where you would really be appreciated, believe you me. Why, in America, they have entire shows of ice skaters and they tour the nation -- a big country, America -- and they do a show for a week in one city and then move on to another city and do a show for a week there, an incredible place, America."

He clapped his hands together, as much to get rid of the accumulation of snow as to applaud what he was saying. But he was applauding himself, in truth.

"You would be a big sensation in America, believe you me. They have never seen anything like you there. If I were you two young fellows, I would buy myself a boat ticket and get over to America as fast as I could go."

And then he added the thought that all of us in Switzerland were thinking in those days -- "There's a war coming, you know, and if you wait too long, it will be too late to go."

Hansruedi was still going to school, so we knew the notion -- attractive though it was -- that was absolutely out of the question. And yet, Dr. Brandt had most definitely given us a thought to mull over, and that thought would one day become an action.

We went back to Basel, exalted by the appreciation for our skating. We had felt and excited about the prospect of, perhaps one day going to America! We went back to the everyday, humdrum world we were part of -- school for Hansruedi, work for me. At the time, I had some unimportant job, just something to do, nothing to give me any real pleasure.

We had only been back a month or so -- it is hard to remember specifics so many years after the fact -- when we got letters containing an offer to skate in England. A man named Claude Langdon had been producing an ice revue called "Patria" in the seaside resort town of Brighton. This was 1937, the year of King George VI's coronation. (He had actually become king a year before, when his brother, Edward VIII, abdicated for the love of Mrs. Wallis Warfield Simpson -- I thought that was all wonderfully romantic! -- But the lavish coronation ceremony itself was in '37.) "Patria" was an ice show in honor of that coronation, although it was really an ice show designed to make money for Claude Langdon.

At any rate, it was for Hansruedi and me, the opening up of the world. I was almost bursting with excitement when I ran next door to the Mauch home to talk to my partner about it.

His excitement, as always, was more controlled than mine. Yes, he liked the idea, but his mother had said flatly, no. I had not yet broached the subject to my parents but I anticipated a similar reaction.

"My mother says I have to finish school," Hansruedi said, with a long face.

"But you are practically finished now."

"I know that. You know that. Now tell Mamme [mom]."

I wasn't about to tangle with Frau [Mrs.] Mauch. I think she had the idea that I was leading her son astray with all this foolishness about skating and clowning on the ice.

I showed Langdon's letter to my father.

"This is very flattering, Werner," he said. "But you must give serious thought to what you will be doing the rest of your life. Do you think doing funny things on the ice is any kind of a decent career for a decent young man? Don't forget, you are a Groebli and a Swiss."

I think what was troubling my father more than my life was his reputation. Fathers love to brag about their sons. He had friends who talked about their sons who were bankers or in the insurance business and one of his best friends at the railroad office had a son who had become a lawyer. He could imagine himself being asked that inevitable question, "And what is your son doing, Herr [Mr.] Groebli?" and having to say, in reply, "Why, my son, Werner, is an ice skating clown!" I think it was his potential humiliation at having to make that answer that colored his reaction to the Langdon offer.

This time it was my mother who came to my aid. She could tell from my eyes or else just from being a mother by trade, how much this opportunity meant to me.

"Oh, come now, Fritz," she said to my father, "it isn't as though Werner was going to be doing this for the rest of his life. It will just be for three months, isn't that what the man said in his letter, Werner?"

"Yes, Mamme [mom], he offered us a three-month contract. It will be like getting a free English course."

"See, Fritz? Three months isn't forever. And he and Hansruedi won't be using their real names, will you?"

"No, Mamme [mom]. We will use those Frick and Frack names."

Next door, I imagine a similar conversation was held. The upshot was that we were finally allowed to go to England. My father examined the contract carefully. He thought the money offered -- six pounds a week, which at that time amounted to about thirty dollars -- was fair. Not great, but acceptable.

"You must save part of that," Bappe [dad] said to me. "I will open a bank account for you. You have to begin to have an appreciation of money, you know. You are a Swiss."

He also wondered if I, as the senior partner of the duo, ought not to get more than the junior partner, Hansruedi, or Frack. It was a sore point with him for as long as he lived, because he felt -- rightly, I supposed -- that the whole thing was really my idea, that I had been the instigator and the driving force, that I had taught Frack most, if not all, of his routines, and so on. But I instinctively knew then, and stuck to that philosophy as long as Frack and I were together, that a partnership must be a fifty-fifty proposition. And so, we split those twelve pounds, actually, six guineas each -- in England in half, and we split everything else we ever made in half down through the years.

And so, it was that, on a chilly early spring day in April of 1937, I left Switzerland for the first time. We took the train across France and the boat-train across the English Channel to our new job in England. We both thought that this was to be merely a temporary thing, and after that three-month engagement, Frack would go back to school and I would go back to searching for my future life's work.

The Channel crossing was rough -- tradition demanded that -- and Frack and I were both heartily seasick en route. But as soon as we disembarked and boarded the Brighton Express, our youthful enthusiasm and our appetites returned simultaneously. I remember enjoying a hearty British tea as we rode down to the Brighton station.

We took a cab to the Sports Stadium. (Incidentally, we had both studied some English in school, enough to get along, and being young and having good ears, we quickly picked up the language.) Claude Langdon met us there and told us about his Show, "Patria," and the roles we were to play in it.

I was still wearing my big overcoat, into which my mother had stuffed lots of things for me to eat along the way "just in case you get hungry." As I took the coat off in Langdon's office, an apple bounced out and rolled along the floor.

"Are you planning to do a William Tell number?" Langdon asked. I am not sure if he was serious or not.

We rehearsed three weeks before the grand opening. It was a pleasant company, made more so by the presence of thirty beautiful chorus girls.

We had been afraid that our meager salary would be gobbled up by the high English rents and the expensive (so we had heard) English food, but we were lucky. The French European pair champions, Andrée and Pierre Brunet, were in the company and we all got along famously, being the outsiders in a company that was otherwise all English. So, we four stuck together and they invited us to join them in what we quickly learned the English called "digs" -- the place where they lived.

They had found a house (in Switzerland or France it would have been called a villa) in the suburbs of Brighton, and we jumped at the chance to join them. Pierre was a marvelous chef, in addition to being a marvelous skater, and dinner every night was a treat. Frack and I each paid a pound a week for the combined rent and food, and considered ourselves extremely fortunate.

Frack and I often invited girls from the Show to join us for dinner at our digs. I had one particular girl I liked, a young lady from a good nearby family, and through her I learned a lot about the English way of life. I learned, too, about ballroom dancing from her, when she introduced me to the Palais de Dance in Brighton, where there was always a good orchestra and plenty of people on the dance floor. I learned that being a skater was a good head start to being a dancer; I used many of the same movements on the dance floor that I used in conventional skating. (No backbends, of course.)

The period we were to spend in England -- originally three months -- began to lengthen. We moved on to another show, this one in Blackpool called "Switzerland." There was another touring ice show in England at the time -- "St. Moritz," it was called -- and when our show got to Manchester we found that St. Moritz was already there. The competition was hard on both shows. They used a kind of composition ice, while we skated on the genuine article. So, I went to our owner and producer, Tom Arnold, and suggested a punning slogan -- "Realize It is Real Ice!" for us. And he liked the idea and began using that slogan on all our billboards in very large letters.

In return he said he would give Frick and Frack bigger billing. That was when I learned the importance of billing and I watched our billing like a hawk from then on.

I felt at home in England almost from the first moment I stepped on English soil. And I quickly became at home speaking the English language, too. I found it had a different sound, softer and kinder and it seemed to me that it lent itself more readily to romance. It was easier for me to whisper soft sentiments to a girl in English than in the guttural language -- German or Swiss, as we called it -- that I had grown up speaking.

I explored London every chance I had. My salary prevented too much extravagance, but I walked over much of that exciting city. No night clubs, but I dated a lot and would take my girl for walks along the banks of the Thames and to an inexpensive restaurant for dinner.

Once I heard of a new ice review playing in Blackpool so I took my date to see that. It was for me something of a busman's holiday; I thought perhaps I could see some new acts and learn a little from them. So, I bought six programs and settled back prepared to make notes of anything that intrigued me.

Midway through the first act an usher came and asked me to leave and he wasn't even polite about it. (No refund, which was the unkindest cut of all.) He confiscated the programs I had been writing on. Apparently, somebody in the show had spotted me and knew who I was and surmised what I was doing there.

At some point during our initial engagement in Brighton, my father came over to see me perform. He had gotten used to the idea of having a son who was a skating clown. I think he was secretly very proud of my ability. As a sometime skater himself, I believe he was also a trifle envious.

He told me that night as we had dinner after the show, that he was proud of me. Coming from him, a man, who was decidedly not the demonstrative sort that was a major admission, his praise was a marvelous tonic for me. He also cautioned me again about saving my money. He thought it should go into a fund in a proper bank to further my future education when I finally decided just what it was that I was going to do with the rest of my life.

As it turned out, there would be nothing left

to go into any such fund for furthering my education or any other purpose. A few days before the Brighton engagement was scheduled to end, I was skating and my skate ran into a hairpin that one of the skaters must have lost. For a skater, there is no hazard as dangerous as the unexpected object on the surface of the ice. (Lost hairpins and bobby pins were so hazardous to a skater's health that eventually the Ice Follies banned their use.) That puny hairpin stopped my skate abruptly. It caused me to twist my ankle and break my fibula. The British Red Cross, always on duty at sporting events, was at my side within thirty seconds and carried me off the ice on a stretcher. It was my first serious skating injury, but hardly my last.

Between medical and hospital costs -- this, of course, was long before there was any such thing as hospitalization -- and the plane fare back to Switzerland, all my savings quickly vanished. Fortunately, I did have some insurance (from the famous Lloyd's of London) which helped. Shortly after my accident, however, there was a spate of ice skating accidents and Lloyd's boosted their premiums so high I never again carried any such policy. I had to cross my fingers (but not legs) and try to be careful from then on.

My bones knitted quickly. They do when you are young and healthy; later on, injuries take longer to heal. Within perhaps a month I was back in the show in England.

We were invited to be part of a Command Performance for the ladies of the royal family. Queen Mother Mary, Princess Elizabeth (later to become queen) and Princess Margaret who was at the time in kindergarten, were to be present. The show was held at the huge Empress Hall, on the southwest side of London. We were taught the protocol, how after we were introduced we were to skate over to the area in front of the royal box and bow to the royal ladies and girls. During the intermission, they were brought backstage and we all lined up and went through a royal receiving line.

We moved on to the "Switzerland" show and then Langdon got in touch with us again. He was putting together a new ice production, "Rhapsody on Ice," and wanted Frack and me to be part of it. We were pleased to agree.

With Langdon's participation, we dreamed up a sensational production number. To the music of Saintsaens' "Danse Macabre," we would skate -- as skeletons. We wore very tight black outfits, and the bones were painted on in luminous paint. Under a certain light -- ultraviolet light -- all that could be seen would be the dancing, prancing bones. This technique has since become commonplace, but it was brand new and very exciting then.

When opening night came, it was a glittering event. The guest of honor was Queen Victoria of Spain, then in exile in London. There was a big symphony orchestra, primarily to give musical body to our bones. There was ice on the rink and plenty of ice -- diamonds -- in the upper crust audience.

One of the skaters making her debut in that show was a beautiful little fourteen-year-old English girl whose entire name was Maria Belita Jepson-Turner. She was known, however, simply as Belita. She was truly an ice ballerina, one of the very first skaters who could make that boast. She was far ahead of her time and later, of course, she would star in many Hollywood productions -- mostly, unfortunately, B pictures -- and in one of them, only four years later, I would be one of her leading men. In fact, we had a very enjoyable kissing scene on a sofa that I still remember with great nostalgia.

"Rhapsody on Ice" was a smash of a show. Another of our stars was the English whiz, Phil Taylor, who did some unusual numbers. One was on stilts dressed up as the Johnnie Walker of the Scotch bottles. (The company kept him supplied with Scotch which was, I believe, one of the chief reasons why he did that number for so many years.) Then we also had Canada's Eric Wait who was, I believe, the funniest man on skates in that era.

But our "Danse Macabre" number brought the house down. It was really something so new and different that we could hear the sound of the audience gasping when they first caught sight of our bones skating onto the ice. The fact that the sink was so dark hid a multitude of sins. One evening for example, I overshot my turn and skidded into the orchestra pit, a drop of some six feet. But I was able to scramble back up to the ice quickly. In fact, my reappearance was so swift, that I think most of the audience, were really entirely unaware of the mishap.

Langdon, the producer, was a strange man. The Show was unquestionably a hit and we all looked forward to a lengthy run. Many of the cast had in fact decorated their dressing rooms and bought furniture to make their backstage life more comfortable, based solely on that prospect. Then one day without warning or notice or, we thought, sufficient cause, Langdon posted a closing notice. "Rhapsody on Ice" would close in a week. He had apparently just gotten bored with the whole thing.

We were all upset and many among the cast talked of dark and dire revenge. My own revenge was a little lighter. I saved up my allowance of free tickets and one evening passed them all out to the hawkers of fruit and vegetables in the nearby Covent Garden vegetable market -- the place made famous later as the area where Julie Andrews worked when Rex Harrison found her in "My Fair Lady." (It was Audrey Hepburn of course in the movie version.)

These hawkers were a colorful crew to say the least. To say the most, they were pretty scruffy, dirty and hardly the type Langdon wanted in the front row seats for his extravaganza. But on that night, there they all were. I had told them all to come in their working clothes, and they did. Langdon was upset but there was nothing he could do about it. They all held legitimate tickets.

To some of our cast on the fringes of unemployment, the closing of "Rhapsody on Ice" was a body blow. To Frack and me who were heading up the ladder, it was only a minor inconvenience. Before we had a chance to work up to a worry we had another offer. A touring ice show called "Wintersport" asked us to join them as they played one- and two-week stands throughout England and Scotland. They carried a portable rink -- only thirty by forty feet -- which they set up generally on movie theater stages. We were necessarily limited by the small size of the rink and could not ever get up to top Speed, but that turned out to be a boon.

In show business, often when you can't do one thing, you are forced to use your imagination to concoct something else. So, it was with us. We had to think up something new and so we came up with pantomime which became a feature of our act for many years. We also added some bits of dialogue and as genuine Swiss we threw in some yodeling for good measure.

We got to see a lot of the British Isles on that tour. I particularly enjoyed playing in a very small theater on the Isle of Man even though it was there that I had a run-in with an English vaudevillian backstage. He was incensed at me for some reason and started to chase me. I wanted to avoid a confrontation so I ran, knowing I was much faster. My natural instinct was to run to my natural habitat -- the ice -- and dashed out on the stage while the show was going on. Fortunately, I was in costume so the audience thought it was part of the show. The performers, however, knew otherwise -- particularly Phil Taylor who was doing his stilt-skating routine at the time. Somehow, he managed to maintain his balance and avoid falling and the audience laughed uproariously, and later the producer tried to prevail on Phil and me to do it every night. But Phil firmly declined; it was only a miracle that he hadn't fallen, and you can't schedule a miracle for every show.

Among the skaters on that "Wintersport" tour was one of the early legends of professional ice skating, a lady who was billed with great modesty as "The Great Charlotte." She also called herself, with additional self-effacement, "The Pavlova of the Ice."

She was a German lady and at the time we shared the Show she was well into her fifties. I realized then as I watched her do her graceful, if not sensational act, that skating was not necessarily only a Sport (or a career) for the very young. It dawned on me then that quite possibly I could make this business my life's work. Until then I think I was still under the impression that I might skate for a few years, have some fun and make some money, but that I still owed it to my Swiss heritage to do something serious and industrious after that. Watching The Great Charlotte, however, made me realize that I could very easily make skating, my life's work.

Charlotte and her husband, Kurt Neumann, did a pair act and Kurt and Phil Taylor discussed international politics often and loudly. We all knew that another war was a distinct possibility and Kurt and Phil argued about it constantly. It brought it home to all of us that awful thought that another World War was imminent.

We were to close our season in Liverpool. On closing night on the men's dressing room mirror in big, bold lipstick red letters was a five-foot long quote from a German poet praising the supremacy of the German race. We, of course, knew that it had to be Kurt Neumann's work, aimed at Phil Taylor primarily, but at all the other non-Germans in the company as well.

Frack and I were Swiss -- Germanic Swiss perhaps, but Swiss first and foremost -- so we tried to maintain the traditional Swiss neutrality in our intra-company League of Nations. Kurt and Phil almost came to blows that night. The "Wintersport" management -- very English gentlemen -- demanded that Neumann erase his handiwork on the mirror. He refused with typical Teutonic stubbornness. They insisted. He walked away. In the end, Charlotte herself came in and carefully wiped all the lipstick off the mirror.

World War II was drawing closer.

Perhaps that is why we jumped at our next offer which was from America. A telegram reached us while we were in Liverpool so the timing could not have been more opportune. There was, the wire said, a new rink being built in Los Angeles and they were assembling a company for "The Tropical Ice Gardens Review" to open when the new rink was completed. The offer they made was fair, barely, but they held out a tempting carrot -- "chance to do movies" the wire said. In those innocent days, Hollywood was the mecca of everybody in the world, and "chance to do movies" were the magic words. We didn't care about the salary for skating -- at least not that desperately -- if there was that "chance" to become movie stars. We quickly wired back that we accepted.

There had been two signatures on the wire. One was from our old friend, Dr. Arthur Brandt, the man who had originally put the idea of going to America into our heads. The other was a man we had not heard of, Harold Steinman, but we found out with some discreet inquiries that he was well-known in America as a fight promoter. He was, it appeared, branching out with this venture and hoping to move from fights to ice extravaganzas.

We sailed to America in October 1938 aboard the huge graceful French liner, the SS Normandie. I was having some second thoughts about the offer and spent most of the passage worrying if we had done the right thing. As usual, Frack had had little or nothing to contribute to our consideration of the offer; he willingly did what I thought was best for both of us. That put a double load on my shoulders, and I wonder whether those four seductive words -- "chance to do movies" -- might not have clouded my judgment. The money we were going to earn was really not very much. I knew that ice shows had folded before; they are expensive to mount and all it takes collapse an entire venture is a few bad breaks, one or two poor houses, an injury to a key performer, a malfunction of the ice-making equipment. If that happened to this show, we would be out in the cold and even in California, being out in the cold can be uncomfortable. We wouldn't have enough money to get back home to Switzerland.

I worried as we sailed across the Atlantic, and I worried as we flew across the United States. But the worrying didn't prevent me from enjoying the trip. Like all new visitors to North America, the vastness of the continent astounded me. We traveled across the United States for 19 hours. There was already some snow on the mountains and that made me experience a small twinge of homesickness.

Those were the days of sleeping berths on cross-country flights, and the hostess tucked me in as we left Chicago bound for Salt Lake City. I woke up to the beauty of the Rockies -- that was when I saw the snow and felt those yearnings to turn around and go back to Switzerland -- but then the excitement began to grab me. We were getting close to California, the Twentieth Century equivalent of the Promised Land, and Hollywood and that "chance to do movies."

We landed in Burbank and Harold Steinman met us -- "Did you guys have a good trip?" -- And he drove us to the Westwood section of Los Angeles where the new rink was located or where it was supposed to be located.

"Where is the rink?" I asked him.

He pointed over to a field where a horse-drawn plow was scratching up the earth.

"Right over there," Steinman said. "Isn't that a great location?"

Fortunately, it wasn't as bad as I first thought.

It was to be an outdoor rink and I could see that most of the grandstand seats were already in place. And actually, the rink was finished and ready to go in only about two weeks from the day we first saw it.

They found us an apartment nearby, just off Wilshire Boulevard. It was a modest little place with a modest rental. Forty years later condominiums in that area would sell for a million dollars or more. But in 1938 it was still a quaint little village, a part of Los Angeles and yet apart from it.

We rehearsed at other rinks and they arranged for us to visit the movie studios. At MGM, we were introduced to Spencer Tracy. We had lunch in the commissary. And we were taken on a tour by a guide who continually walked backwards as he pointed everything out to us. That gave me the idea for a routine I incorporated into our act soon -- skating backwards while the orchestra played the Colonel Bogey March, later made famous in the movie "The Bridge on the River Kwai."

I was the first skater to test the ice when the Tropical Ice Gardens opened [1-2 42-43]. The show was only in the evening. During the day, the rink was to be open for public skating. Ice skating had suddenly become popular in Southern California, an area given to quick fads: That season it was ice skating thanks mainly to the popularity at the time of Sonja Henie and her ice skating movies. So, the Hollywood stars had taken up skating in a big way and the Southern California public always follows the Hollywood stars very closely.

One afternoon as I skated on the rink I saw a pretty girl whose laces on her skating boots had come undone. I quickly volunteered to tie them for her. She introduced herself as Joan Crawford. I said I was Mr. Frick -- I had begun identifying myself in that way and continue to do so even today. I told her I was part of the "St. Moritz Express" which was how the show had come to be called after it opened.

She had just made an ice skating film which was not a bit and she vowed, she said, that if she made another one she would do her own skating. So, she was on the ice every day learning to skate. She was coming along very nicely, too. I taught her a few things in those afternoons over the next few weeks.

We got to know another beautiful star, too -- Betty Grable. Her father was the rink's treasurer. And so, she frequently visited and I skated with her often. She was a dancer, of course, so she had a lot of innate athletic ability and she skated pretty well. She was married to the former child star, Jackie Coogan, at the time. He came to the rink often, too. He was actually a very good skater and the four of us -- Betty, Jackie, Frack and I -- often skated together.

Betty and Jackie invited us to dinner at their home several times while the show was on. It was good to get a home-cooked meal; with typical Swiss frugality, when I was alone I would eat at an inexpensive drug store counter, inexpensive, and not very tasty.

It was Betty Grable's father, a whiz with money and figures, who introduced me to Wall Street. He always had the Wall Street Journal tucked under his arm and whenever he had a spare moment he would pull it out, open it up and start reading. He carried a small notebook with him and made copious notes. I asked him about that and he began explaining to me the workings of the stock and Bond markets, and that began for me a lifelong fascination with the financial world, more on that later.

Money was often on my mind that year. I owed the government of the United Kingdom some money for taxes. I sent them a bit at a time and they were very patient, unlike other tax collectors I would meet in my time. Frack and I were also concerned about how to afford the trip back to Switzerland. The salaries we were being paid by the ice Show were far from munificent. We were living frugally but still, we could save next to nothing and the trip from California to Switzerland was, even then a costly one.

So, Grable's advice and lessons on the stock market came at a timely moment for me. After a while I began buying stocks, using his advice rather than putting my money in the bank or under the mattress.

I felt sorry for Jackie Coogan then, and that seemed to be the consensus of public and private opinion. People would always talk about "Poor Jackie Coogan." They might envy him his wife, because Betty Grable was a gorgeous creature, but Tore and more it was becoming obvious that his best days as an actor and a star were behind him. His wife was far eclipsing him in popularity and money-making capabilities.

He used to talk to me as we skated, and mostly his talk was of the past. His greatest achievement probably was when he was a tiny boy co-starring with Charlie Chaplin in "The Kid." Jackie would tell me stories about Chaplin, how so often Chaplin seemed to run out of ideas and would send the whole cast home early in the afternoon. Sometimes several days would go by with no shooting, as the great comedian/director tried to come up with some new idea. And, of course, he always did.

"You know, Frick," Coogan said to me at least a dozen times during that period, "I was a very big star when I was five years old. Why, all the other kids my age would go out to see Babe Ruth, but Babe Ruth came to see me."

Ruth was then in the twilight of his career, but still a name and a figure to be reckoned with. The whole ice show cast went to see him one day when he was visiting the 20th Century-Fox studio and the studio publicity department invited a lot of people over to take pictures with him. They had an ice rink on one stage and the studio photographer set up a shot of Frick and Frack helping Babe Ruth into a pair of skating boots [4 45]. At the time, I had heard his name, but had no idea exactly what it was he did. I just followed instructions.

I had quickly learned the value of publicity. And throughout my career I have gone out of my way to be nice to reporters and photographers. I know a lot of stars -- on and off the ice -- who think all that is an intrusion, an invasion of their privacy, but I am convinced it helps to sell tickets. And after all, we are businessmen and our business is to sell tickets. The more tickets are sold the better the profit picture of the ice show I am associated with and the better the profit picture the higher the salary they can afford to pay me. So, it makes sense for me -- for any-body in show business -- to do as much positive publicity as he can.

At that time, in the late thirties, the undisputed queen of the ice was Sonja Henie. I still think she was the most exciting woman on ice who ever lived. Some skaters who followed her may have been more talented technically, but Sonja's combination of talent, speed and great looks made her unbeatable.

We were still rehearsing for the opening of the Westwood show when we got a call from a man named Arthur Wirtz, asking us to come to the Polar Palace in Hollywood where Sonja was practicing. She had expressed an interest in meeting us and seeing us perform and would we oblige the Lady? We would, gladly.

Wirtz was Sonja's partner in ice shows and a part-owner of several arenas around the U.S., including Madison Square Garden in New York. He was one of those business geniuses -- Chicagoan. He was heavy into real estate there, in liquor distribution and in warehouses. He was by nature shy and retiring and let his money speak for him. At one point, I read an article about him in the Wall Street Journal in which the claim was made that his fortune was around $400 million. I believe that was an underestimate.

Ice shows to him were a toy, an amusement. And he and Sonja had turned that amusement into another source of revenue for the Wirtz and Henie fortunes.

That day he picked us up in his limousine, complete with chauffeur and bar in the back, and drove us to the Polar Palace. That was a rink that had been built next to the Paramount Pictures studio in Hollywood. He introduced us to Sonja, a tiny thing with a round face dominated by dimples, and those dimples were her passport to fame and riches.

"I saw your skating poses in the pictures in the newspaper," Sonja said to us. "I cannot believe that you can actually skate that way. It defies gravity. I had to see it for myself."

She was, of course, referring to the poses of me doing cantilever where I bent over backwards until my back was parallel to the surface of the ice only a few inches above the ice. So, I did it for her -- a command performance. There was an audience of three -- Sonja, Wirtz and Frack, and Sonja and Wirtz applauded me generously. Frack had seen it before.

We did some more things, and Wirtz asked us if we might like to join the Henie revue next year. We said we would, but we didn't talk money. We knew that that would be a tough hurdle because Sonja had acquired a justifiable reputation for being a tough lady with a checkbook.

And Wirtz had a similar reputation.

There was the story and Wirtz later swore that it was true, testifying to Sonja's skills in the money arena. It was when she was appearing in her first show in Hollywood. Her manager approached her just before the performance one night and said, with great excitement, "Darryl Zanuck is in the lobby! What shall I do?" And Sonja replied, "Why, sell him a ticket, of course."

We found out a few months later exactly what it was like to be in negotiations with Sonja Henie. Even though both she and Wirtz wanted us for their show, when push came to shove and they had asked us to name our price, we were so far apart that we never did join her show. I have always regretted that, because in those days she was the best and it would have been exciting to be working with the best. But the money she offered us was so low as to be almost insulting.

I never failed to visit her whenever our paths crossed. She was always an outstanding performer. She managed to breathe such fire into her ice version of a Hawaiian hula dancer that you would not have been surprised if the ice started to melt. Even though she was a perfect Nordic type -- a blue-eyed blonde with milk white skin -- she made a very believable hip-slinging Hawaiian maiden. I have never seen anyone dance on ice the way Sonja did.

In her later years, she became as passionate about collecting art as she was about skating. The last time we met she was in Zurich on an art-buying expedition and we sat at a sidewalk café and talked of the old days. A few months later as she was being flown in her private plane from Paris to her home in Oslo, she died. I was in Phoenix, Arizona at the time and a reporter from ABC called me to ask for my comments about her passing. I was happy to eulogize her for them and I meant every word of it. I admired her enormously.

The day before our ice show in Westwood opened, I happened to visit the souvenir stand. I saw that they had some postcards for sale with our picture on them. Underneath were the words: "Frick and Frack -- Iced Nuts." or, "Frick and Frack -- Swiss Idiots."

I was very upset at that. We certainly were clowns, but we were not "nuts" nor were we "idiots." The poor fellow running the stand, of course, had had nothing to do with creating those captions, but I took it out on him. I decided the only thing to do was to buy up all of those offensive (to me) postcards and that is exactly what I did. It cost me most of my meager savings and left me with next to nothing, but I felt good after I did it.

For the last few days before the big opening, and before I would start drawing a salary, I literally had no money. I had to rely on the generosity of friends to eat.

It was a good show, with good sets, good costumes (by Academy Award winner Helen Rose), and good music (by the noted band leader Ted Fio Rito). Fio Rito was more than just the leader of the band, he had creative ideas as to how his music could augment our act, and they were very valuable.

One part of our act had Frack and me skating toward each other, backwards. We had done that before, missing each time, so the audience expected we would miss again -- but this time we collided. And Frack, being smaller and lighter, would fly up in the air and then, when he picked himself up, he skated stiff-legged like some mechanical man. Fio Rito suggested he play Irving Berlin's "Cheek To Cheek" during that bit of action and it enhanced the moment tremendously. It was Fio Rito, incidentally, who added a harp to the orchestra, and that instrument had an affinity for ice skating -- it glided as skaters seem to glide -- and ever since, the harp has been a fixture in orchestras for ice shows.

Our show also had a cast of fine skaters, including Orrin Markus, who was only five feet six inches tall and weighed well over two hundred pounds, but with all that weight was still an amazingly graceful skater. Markus and his partner, Irma Thomas, later were part of the Ice Capades show many years, and he was an active skater until he was sixty-five.

The only problems we had were associated with the fickle weather that is part of Southern California's charm. People don't know Southern California think of it as eternally sunny and balmy, but that is hardly the case. We actually had lot of chilly weather, making it uncomfortable for the audience on those outdoor seats. We had a winter storm with that blew down parts of our permanent set. It took two days to repair it.

We had rains and had to cancel half a dozen performances. And we had one of those Southern California forest fires in the nearby hills which sent showers of ashes on us making the rink pitted and unsafe. Later in the run we had the Santanas -- hot winds off the deserts to the east -- that caused the ice surface to melt and again made it hazardous to skate. We even had a sandstorm.

Actually, we welcomed some of those postponements. If they were the work of "an act of God" -- and surely weather was in that category -- our contract provided that we were paid anyhow. So, we had a day off with pay. The chorus girls in the show were very warm and friendly, and happily and proudly showed off their city -- most of them were local girls -- to the strangers from Switzerland. We got to see every part of Los Angeles and for two boys from Basel this was never-never land. Our only problem was money. We never had enough because both Frack and I were determined to save enough so we would have passage money back to Switzerland eventually.

After the Westwood engagement, the show moved north to Oakland. And so, I got to know San Francisco, just across the bay, and fell in love with that exciting city.

There was a curious sidelight to our time in Oakland. While we were there, Walter Brown, then president of the Boston Garden Arena came to see us. He tried to buy the entire show. He had several other arenas set to book the show and for a day or two it looked like a deal had been made. But for reasons I never learned, it fell apart. Only two years later Brown and John Harris and a few others got together, each putting up ten thousand dollars, and formed an ice show which became the Ice Capades. Twenty years later they sold the Ice Capades to Metromedia and Brown, Harris and the others each got around a quarter of a million dollars for their shares. I only wish I had been part of that group.

In Portland, the show had financial troubles, and our costumes were attached by the sheriff. That taught me a valuable lesson. Frack and I rolled up our pants legs, used safety pins to create makeshift "fracks," put on funny old hats -- and the act worked just as well as before. I learned that costumes can help, but essentially it was the two or us and our ability that were important.

We moved on to Vancouver and Seattle then closed in Oakland. The cast scattered as they always do when a show folds -- you are so close, so tight, like a family for the production's duration and then the moment it's over you all go your separate ways and you may never see some of that family group again.

Frack and I then went on tour, arranged by an agent, amateur ice skating carnivals. That kept us busy for six weeks. One of those elaborate carnivals was in Chicago -- the Chicago Figure Skating Club Carnival -- and I met two men who would become lifelong friends while there. Gerald Graham and Thomas Dean were both good amateur skaters and prominent in Chicago business and social set. Later, Graham would become one of the backers of the Ice Follies.

From Chicago -- with a motorcycle escort to the station -- we moved on to Toronto. I was a little fearful about leaving the U.S. to go to Canada because Frack and I had had trouble arranging a visa so we could stay in the U.S. permanently. While we had been in Los Angeles, we realized that our tourist visas would soon be expiring so we began making inquiries about staying. We never consciously sat down and discussed whether or not we should stay or wanted to stay or could stay -- it was just something we somehow automatically assumed that we wanted to do.

It wasn't easy. Somebody said he could fix it for us for two hundred dollars. He had an "in," he said, with officials in Sacramento. We never saw the money or the man again. A lawyer named Morgan Doyle who was a big ice skating enthusiast, tried to help us, but it was a difficult problem apparently. We eventually had to go to New York, to Ellis Island, in March of 1939, and we spent an additional $1000 each and we were told to go back and see a certain Miss Bonaparte. Where was Miss Bonaparte, back in Los Angeles in an office on Hollywood Boulevard? She was an immigration counselor. For a fee, she drove us into Mexico, to Mexicali, where we stayed for three days. While we played tag with the Mexican cockroaches in our flea-bag hotel, Miss Bonaparte played jump rope with the red tape and eventually came back for us. We crossed the border at Mexicali and arrived back in the U.S. as immigrants under the Swiss quota. Between the fees and the cost of the cables back and forth and the hotel bill for us and the cockroaches in Mexicali, it was an expensive procedure. But it was worth every penny.

By the time our immigration status was cleared up we had become members of the fledgling Ice Follies-company. And we stayed with that organization for many years -- Frack stayed with it for the rest of his professional life, and I kept on as an Ice Follies performer many years after Frack left the show and then died. In fact, I stayed with the Ice Follies for more than forty years. By the time, I left that show I was eligible for Social Security.

We quickly became Americanized. It didn't take very long because it really wasn't a culture that was totally alien to our own. The two cultures are really the same basically, with a few surface differences. We had learned enough English in school and during our time skating in England, so we had no problem in expressing ourselves and in understanding and being understood in America. We quickly picked up the idioms. I have never completely lost my accent, but having that slight accent has never inhibited me or caused me any problems. In fact, in some situations having a slight and (they tell me) pleasant accent can be a major help. It lends a certain air of mystery and exoticism to a person, and I can use all of that kind of help I can get.

Perhaps, however, the accent did impede my acting career. That promise that was made to us when we first came to the United States -- "chance to do movies" -- never materialized, really. I brought it up several times with the management of that show.

"When we came here," I said, "you told us there was a chance to do movies. We are still waiting."

"Waiting? Waiting for what?" they would say. "You have a chance to do movies. This is Hollywood, kiddo, and anybody in Hollywood has a chance to do movies. You have more of a chance than most people because the movie scouts and the producers and the agents are here watching the show every night. Keep on skating, kiddo, and they'll discover you yet."

Over the years, I did make a few movie appearances. And a year or so later when we were appearing in San Francisco, I did take some acting lessons. I hoped they might improve my speech and I think they did, but not to the point where I could ever play the American next door. Not unless that person next door had recently arrived from Switzerland.

In April of 1939, Roy Shipstad, Eddie and Oscar Johnson, the powers behind the new Ice Follies, saw us skate and offered us a job with their new show. We quickly accepted but I insisted on a clause in my contract giving me the right to accept a movie role should one come along. That was the dreamer talking and maybe Roy, Eddie and Oscar knew a dreamer when they saw one and recognized the futility of most dreams because they readily agreed and let me have my out-clause.

I did invoke it once or twice during my forty years with the show, so I was glad I insisted on it. Of course, they might have let me out to do those movies even without the clause, but this way I didn't have to ask. I could simply tell them I was going to do the movie and that was that. The two movies Frack and I did were [1943] "Silver Skates" [🎞11-12 📄52-53] and [1944] "Lady, Let's Dance", [🎞13-16 📄54-57] two fairly decent B-movies from the early '40s.

Frack and I never actually sat down and discussed the pros and cons of our mutual future. There never was a moment when I said to myself, "Werner, if you don't leave this ice skating foolishness tomorrow and go back to Switzerland and get an honest job, you will be stuck with an ice skating career for the rest of your life."

It all just happened. We had drifted from the jobs in England to the jobs in America and somehow, without even stopping to consider the implications, we let ourselves be carried along by the dauntless drift. We had a career thrust on us, rather than seeking it out. Before we knew it, we were successful in this career, making good money, having fun, enjoying the fame and the adulation. We never gave it any thought one way or the other. We did one more carnival, then another one and suddenly we had a profession and a career. It just happened.

During all the time, we were with the Ice Follies and even throughout our career before joining that show, our forte was always comedy. I was secure in my own mind with the knowledge that had I wanted to I could have been a straight, orthodox figure skater. In fact, I had my medal -- from my title as Swiss Junior Champion of 1935 -- as evidence of my ability in that direction.

I had nothing to prove because in my heart and soul I knew I could do it. And as so many skating critics have written over the years, you have to be a good serious skater before you can be a good comedic skater.

But Frack had never done any competitive figure skating. I always felt he could have -- he certainly had the necessary skills -- but he hadn't. Consequently, he always had the feeling that people looked down on him in the skating fraternity as "only a comedy skater." He imagined he was classified as a second-class performer because of that. So, from time to time he would suggest to me and to the Shipstad-Johnson team that he be allowed to do some straight skating. He thought that would give him respect among his peers.

When it happened, it only did the opposite.

In 1952, he persuaded them to let us -- he always included me in his pleas, although I was comfortable in my comedy niche -- do some straight skating. They said all right we could skate some character parts in a few of the production numbers. I didn't really want to, but Frack was desperate to do it and I knew he would be more comfortable if I was with him so I went along.

I was given the role of an ambassador in a Viennese ballroom scene in which my big moment was to lead the lovely star of the number on stage, kiss her hand, bow, and gracefully fade into the background.

Frack was assigned the role of "Band Leader." Nothing much for him to do except be on the ice and lead the make-believe band. On the callboard for rehearsals it listed Frack's name among the "specs." A spec in our vernacular was a spectator. So, for all poor Frack's troubles and machinations, he had actually been demoted and was now categorized as a spectator. His ego was bruised.

Backstage can be a cruel environment. Frack had alienated some of the skaters -- that was inevitable in any large group such as an ice Show -- and now his enemies had a Chance to rub it in.

"Good evening, Spec," they would say to him.

"How's the spectator tonight?"

"Keep trying, Spec, and maybe you'll get a solo someday."

I could tell he was becoming increasingly annoyed with that treatment. He probably could have begged off from his role as "Band Leader," but he was too proud to do so. He had asked for that sort of role and he was going to stick it out. But it galled him. And so, one afternoon after a week or so of taking that ribbing, Frack came to me as we were starting our set.

"I quit, Werner," he said.

Just like that, the Frick and Frack team ended. We had had fifteen years of greatness -- to be truthful there was nobody who could touch us in the '40s, and for a few years on either side of that decade. But it ended that abruptly.

There was, of course, more to it than merely that "spec" business. Primarily there was also Frack's declining health. I had long been aware that he was hurting. He had, for one thing, broken a knee cap a year before but it had mended, although he had lost some speed as a result. As it turned out he was also suffering from a degenerative bone disease which would kill him twenty-five years later. I never did find out -- either from his widow or from his doctor or from Frack himself -- whether he knew about that disease on the day he said he was quitting. I have always suspected that he did and wanted to quit while he was on top. He didn't want to wait until it was too late, until he could no longer do the job and somebody (me or the management) would have had to tell him he couldn't cut it any more.

Perhaps Frack and I had kicked away our best chance at movie career soon after we joined the Ice Follies. We were playing in New York and some high-powered agents from MCA -- including the legendary Sonny Werblin -- began to court us. They wanted us to sign with their agency. They wined us and dined us, entertained us, waved contracts under our nose.

I was, to say the least, very intrigued. I wanted to sign. For some reason, however, they antagonized Frack, who was the kind of man who took immediate likes and dislikes to people and seldom changed his mind after that vivid first impression. He disliked these agents from the first moment he met them.

"Get lost," he told them eventually. They could take a hint and walked away without a backward glance.

Perhaps if we had signed with them I might have become the Swiss Charles Boyer. I always fantasized that I could have done those suavely romantic roles. Or maybe Boyer would have become known as the French Frick. Who knows?

It didn't happen. I have often thought that there were two times in my life when I let Frack persuade me to do something I really didn't want to do. The first time was when be persuaded me to let those MCA agents walk away. The other time was when he said he was quitting.

Maybe I should have talked him out of that. I don't know if I could have, but I do know that I didn't try very hard. I let him go. And from then on I either skated by myself, solo, or with a partner I trained from among the Ice Follies show cast.

Even though skating did not prove to be the passport to the movies we had hoped it would be, nevertheless, it was in retrospect a very nice way to spend a life.

For me, skating was always a release. I realize now that my early years had been spent primarily in worrying about my future. What would I do with my life? That was always the question preying on my soul. I think many adults put a heavy burden on children with that constant nagging question: "And what are you going to do when you grow up?"

The poor kids -- and I was in that pitiful band -- begin to think that a choice of career is the most important decision they will ever have to make. I am not denying that it is an important one, but I believe the more important decision is this: "And how do you plan to have a happy life?"

For me, ice skating has led to that happy life we all should enjoy, but which too many of us don't.

Skating first was therapeutic for me. The shy, introverted child I had been totally vanished when I took to the ice. I was no longer afraid of meeting people when I was skating because I knew I was good. I was at home on the ice, I was in my milieu and that gave me the confidence I needed overcome my shyness.

I found furthermore that I could express myself verbal on matters concerning skating and skaters. People listened what I had to say because I was automatically an expert. People listen to experts. It was a pleasant sensation I found to be listened to.

On ice, with our act, I also had the delightful privilege of creating. I was an innovator, a pioneer, a creator. That, too, was a great feeling, the knowledge that was doing some things that had never been done before.

But primarily I think it was the act of skating itself that I enjoyed so much. There is a freedom on the ice, even when one is bound (as we were) by the restrictions of an act. But the process of skating has always felt to me almost like flying. Certainly, it is the only earth-bound activity except perhaps for skiing that gives one the flying sensation.

And, of course, there was also the applause. To anyone has never experienced the sensation of being the object of an audience's love -- and applause is a manifestation of love -- it is difficult to explain. You have done your act and you stand there in the spotlight and the applause begins. There are some nights when it is just average, a nice warm sound and you know your work has been appreciated. But then there are nights when, for some inexplicable reason, the audience absolutely adores you. I don't know why this should be; there seems to be no correlations between the quality of your performance and the degree of adulation you receive. Some nights when I felt our performance was just average, that love engulfed us -- deafening applause, whistles, foot stomping, shouts of "Bravo!" And I would stand there, a silly grin on my face, as the sounds of that love swept down and over us, clasping us in the palpable warmth of the audience's affection and admiration.

There is nothing like that feeling on God's earth.

There are other nights of course, when the opposite occurs -- nothing happens. No matter how great your performance, for some reason you and the audience cannot establish a rapport. So, you go through the motions and your work -- and your work may be the same or better than ever -- is simply unappreciated. Or maybe it is simply that the audience that night is made up of undemonstrative people who may love what you are doing but are just not the sort of people to show it.

It is a natural tendency for performers, confronted with such an audience, to become hostile. You feel there must be something wrong with them, that they are acting rudely or stupidly, and so you begin to hate them. And, of course, that shows in your performance, and so the situation between you and the audience is exacerbated.

I have learned that the best course for a performer -- at least for me -- is to block out the audience totally. I try not to think of them or consider what their reaction to work is, as long as I am performing. I go through every stunt, every bit of action, every routine, exactly the same way no matter what kind of reception I am getting. Oh, perhaps if their reaction is extremely enthusiastic, that penetrates through to me and consequently I respond and put out a bit more effort. But if the reaction is below normal I really don't notice. I just concentrate on my work and block out what is happening in the audience.

With rare exceptions, you cannot see the audience anyhow. The lights prevent that. You are merely conscious of the rustling sound as they turn and fidget and talk and gasp and do all those things an audience does as it watches you perform. But that is merely a background noise. It is like when you go to the movies, you are aware that the others in the theater are there, but it is only a background, and your attention is given to the screen and what is going an up there.

One last advantage of a skating career -- money -- we never realized when we began back in Basel that we would be earning as much money as we did.

Not long ago I ran into an old friend from school. He told me of an incident back at the skating rink in Margarethenpark soon after it had opened. Frack and I were inventing our stunts and we did something this friend remembered and somebody asked us to do it again.

"Only for two dollars will we repeat that," I said, according to this witness. I do not remember the incident and find it hard to believe that I was that crass at that time. I seem to remember Frack and me willingly doing our stunts at that time for free, because we enjoyed doing them and enjoyed getting the reaction we were getting.

But if the story is true, that was our first professional engagement, two dollars for doing a stunt in the park. That income grew by leaps and bounds once we got to America and ultimately, we made a goodly sum. Nothing compared to what today's baseball and basketball and football stars get, of course, but a great deal more than my father made on the railroad in Switzerland.

Over the years our act improved, naturally. We broadened the scope of our act, doing everything from a mock ballet to a take-off on Nazi soldiers and their goose-stepping march. We did funny satires on other skaters -- me lifting Frack by the seat of his pants in an ice dance routine satire -- as well as some of the bits and pieces that we had always done -- the near misses as we skated around the rink. While we knew that the audience came year after year to see our old standbys -- my back-bending cantilever and Frack's rocking chair routine -- we also knew we had to add new things to the act so they wouldn't grow tired of it.

We also knew that part of the appeal of our act was always the risks we took. People still talk to me about my exit, leaving the ice in my back-bent position at twenty-five miles an hour, and barely missing two iron posts as I zipped off the ice. In several instances, Frack and I would come within an inch or two of cracking our heads on walls and props and the audience would first gasp, then laugh with relief. I believe in taking risks, but I also believe in making sure those risks are minimized.

I always insisted that there be a stagehand stationed near every point where we were doing something risky to make sure the ice was clear there. If there was a metal post with sharp edges near where we were going to have a near-miss, I checked to see that it was taped and often a board placed in such a way as to protect our heads if we misjudged.

The one thing there was no way of guarding against was the stray, foreign object on the ice.

All it takes is a little thing -- such as the hairpin I hit in England, or a coin or a nail -- and you can go tumbling. Ruts were another hazard and we all tried to make sure that the ice surface was scraped periodically to keep it smooth and rut-free.

In 1946, I had my first taste of doing a number without Frack. He and his wife had a baby and he wanted to take some time off to be with his new child. So, when the Ice Follies opened that year in San Francisco, I had to go it alone. Not precisely alone, of course -- I had two skaters working with me in a routine I choreographed called "The Admiral and His Aides." Admiral Frick and two sailors -- Ronnie Robert and Frankie Sawyers were both fine young skaters -- were shipwrecked on a desert island. There were chases and falls and lots of comic skating. It was well received and I proved to myself that Frick could go it alone or, at least, without Frack [21 62 | 3 236].

Ronnie, I remember, kept asking for more money, egged on by his wife. They had done an adagio act but it wasn't very good so he was available to me. He did a little solo during the act -- a simple grapevine move to a drum solo -- and the audience liked it. So, he asked me for a one hundred dollar a week raise. I wasn't paying him, a fact I kept telling him, but he kept on with his demands. I don't know why he never went to the proper people to ask for his raise, but he kept asking me. Since I couldn't grant his request, he quit after two months. My other sailor, Frankie, began having delusions of greatness as a result of his time with me, and soon had a big flare-up with the boss, Oscar Johnson, and walked right out of Madison Square Garden, just as we prepared to do the act for 14,000 invited fans of Jack Bailey's nationwide "Que For A Day" radio show. In the nick of time, the act was scratched. I hurriedly rehearsed another skater, and Frick Co. functioned again the following day, proving that nobody indispensable.

While I knew that having Frack with me added greatly the quality of the act, I must admit that that San Francisco engagement was an introduction to the pleasures of being a single act. Over the years, whenever Frack took some time off and later, when he quit, I found skating solo gave me a feeling of relief from the dependency of a partnership. I artistic freedom -- I could do what I wanted to do without having to consult or argue or even discuss. And that was pleasant.

Nevertheless, I still believe that two ice skating comedians make a better act than one. Teamwork is the foundation of funny ice skating. If two people work together, and their timing is right and their conceptions true, then I think the results are four times as funny and varied as when one man skates alone. Further, having two people working together permits the creation and execution of stunts and maneuvers that are totally impossible with one. Frack and I together did things that no one else has ever equaled.

When we worked alone -- even with temporary partners -- we couldn't come close to the deeds we did as a duo. Somehow, the two of us were incomparable -- it sounds immodest to say that, but it is simply the truth.

Late in 1937, I was injured and Frack had to go it alone for a brief time. He came to those same twin conclusions -- first, a feeling of relief and freedom to be by himself, followed quickly by the realization that the act was infinitely superior when there were two of us.

Still, when Frack finally did quit, I was not as upset as I might have been had I not had the experience of skating solo before. I knew I could do it, and I did it, and never took a full permanent partner again.

Picture 1 ✦ Page 33

1938 - Frick and Frack-Ice Comedians
Tropical Ice Gardens, Westwood Village, Los Angeles

1938 - Frick and Frack-Ice Comedians
Tropical Ice Gardens, Westwood Village, Los Angeles
Sally Eilers

Picture 3

1939 - Frick and Frack
Ice Follies

Picture 4 ✧ Page 34

1940 - Frick and Frack
Baseball Legend Babe Ruth
Ice Follies

Picture 5

1940 - Frick and Frack
Ice Follies

Picture 6

1940 - Frick and Frack
Ice Follies

Picture 7

1941 - Frick and Frack
Ice Follies

Picture 8

1941 - Frick and Frack, Jeannie Simms-Backstage
Ice Follies

Picture 9

1942 - Frick and Frack
Ice Follies

Picture 10

1942 - Frick and Frack
Ice Follies

Picture 11 ✤ Pages 37, 133

1943 - Frick and Frack
Silver Skates

Picture 12 ✦ Pages 37, 133

1943 - Frick and Frack
Silver Skates

Picture 13 ✧ Pages 37, 135

1944 - Frick and Frack
Swiss Alps with Matterhorn
Lady, Let's Dance

1944 - Frick and Frack
The Moser Brothers-Swiss Yodeling Band
Lady, Let's Dance

Picture 15 ✦ Pages 37, 133, 135

1944 - Frick and Frack with "Belita"
The British figure skater Gladys Olive Jepson-Turner
Lady, Let's Dance

Picture 16 ✧ Pages 37, 135

1944 - Frick (Instructor) and Frack
Lady, Let's Dance

Chapter 2

-57-

Picture 17

1945 - Frick and Frack
Ice Follies

Picture 18

1945 - Frick and Frack
Ice Follies

Picture 19

1946 - Frick and Frack
"Get in the Driver's Seat"
Ice Follies

1946 - Frick and Frack
Ice Follies

Picture 21 ✦ Page 41

1946 - Mr. Frick, Ronnie Robert and Frankie Sawyers
"The Admiral and His Aides"
Ice Follies

Picture 22

Life Magazine May 20, 1946 **For A Closer Look** at a *Follies* girl, a Swiss comedian named Frick apparently defies gravity. Circling around Rita Peake on skates, Frick is prevented from falling only by centrifugal force.

Picture 23

1947 - Frick and Frack
Ice Follies

1947 - Frick and Frack
Ice Follies

Picture 25

1948 - Frick and Frack
"Sea Foot"
Ice Follies

Picture 26

1948 - Frick and Frack
Ice Follies

Picture 27

1949 - Frick and Frack
Ice Follies

Picture 28

1949 - Frick and Frack
Backstage-Madison Square Garden, New York City
Ice Follies

Picture 29

1950 - Frick and Frack
"In The Bahamas"
Ice Follies

Picture 30

1950 - Frick and Frack
Ice Follies

Picture 31

1951 - Talented and zany Frick and Frack
Ice Follies

Picture 32

1951 - Frick and Frack
Ice Follies

Picture 33

1951 - Frick and Frack
Ice Follies

CHAPTER 3

Being in the public eye automatically makes one an Important Person. Not necessarily a Very Important Person; achieving the "Very" status takes time. But even being just an average run-of-the-mill Important Person carries with it some status. Frack and I were AIPs who ultimately became VIPs, but we enjoyed our AIP status, too.

One morning during an engagement in Boston, there was a knock on my door. I was barely awake, but managed to throw a robe over my pajamas and opened the door. Standing there, smartly dressed in his shiny uniform, standing crisply at attention was a Marine. He saluted me very professionally.

"Mr. Frick?" he asked. I acknowledged that was who I was.

"I have this communication for you, sir," he said, and handed me a small white envelope. I knew that wasn't the procedure the United States government used when they drafted people but other than that, I had no idea what was in the envelope. So, I opened it.

"Admiral Felix Gygax and Mrs. Gygax," it read, "request the pleasure of your company for dinner this evening."

"I am to wait for your answer, sir," the Marine said, and I quickly told him to tell the Admiral and his lady that Mr. Frick accepted with pleasure.

Admiral Gygax, I would later learn, was of Swiss descent, an American Naval officer of high rank and importance in the naval scheme of things. Because of our shared heritage, and his fondness for ice skating we became friends. It was good to have an important naval officer for a friend.

During our years with the Ice Follies, we skated all over the world. We entertained audiences that included the heads, crowned and otherwise, of most of the world's civilized nations. And some of those that were less civilized as well.

We skated under appalling conditions and under the finest of conditions. We skated when we felt like skating and when we didn't. In all the years that we were with the show, and then the years when I was with it by myself, there were only a handful of shows that failed to go on as scheduled.

Once in Baltimore a transformer blew and there was no back-up so we couldn't go on. When President John F. Kennedy was assassinated the show was cancelled -- for one night only. In Denver, a truck that contained vital props got lost and couldn't find the arena until it was too late so we lost a show that night, too. And there was a night in Buffalo when it was so cold that the box cars carrying our equipment froze and they couldn't open the box car doors. Another show cancelled.

One night which I wish I could forget, we were performing in Cleveland, Ohio. Shortly after the second half of the show began -- some ten minutes after the intermission -- I was pushed into the spotlight in a little cart. Just as I reached center ice I noticed the spotlight begin to fade. I was about to curse the spotlight operator when I realized it wasn't his fault -- all the other lights in the auditorium were fading, too. Within seconds they had all faded out and we were in total blackness. If you've never been out in the center of an ice rink with thousands of people waiting for you to do something funny and then the lights go out, you just haven't lived. A few emergency lights flickered on, mostly to illuminate the exits, but we had to cancel the balance of the show.

There are all kinds of hazards in touring with an ice show. In Minneapolis once we had to contend with a bat. The Minneapolis rink had such good acoustics we called it "The Stradivarius of rinks." But it was old and wooden and bats apparently had found a home high in and among the rafters. One night, for reasons known only to the bats, they decided to come down for a closer view of our performance. They began flying just over our heads. Some of the skaters, frightened of the bats, deviated from the performance to chase the animals, and soon the rink was full of skaters wielding brooms and towels and fly swatters and all sorts of makeshift weapons, while the bats soared around them and the audience roared with laughter. Eventually the bats that survived the Great Minneapolis Bat Massacre flew away and the show was able to resume.

I've even had a dog dash out from the audience and bark at me and follow me around the ice.

Once in New Haven, Connecticut, my act was interrupted by a man. I looked up and there was this fellow wearing skates, skating right along with me. He had obviously seen my act often enough so he knew pretty much what was coming next and he was almost like my shadow. Off stage, the security people were preparing to pounce on him if he got close enough, but he was too smart for that. For a few minutes, he kept pace with me and then, apparently tired of the fun, he jumped over the bang boards and disappeared. I have always assumed he was a Yale undergraduate responding to a dare or a bet.

Another hazard was the huge ball of mirrors that was suspended over center ice, revolving and lending a bit of sparkle to the proceedings. We were all afraid that it would fall, and one night it did. Fortunately, it didn't hit anybody but the noise as that ball slammed into the ice was a deafening explosion. Curiously, two days later the mirror ball in our sister show, "Holiday on Ice," also fell, thousands of miles away.

For any artist on or off ice, the biggest engagement of his life is his New York debut. As the line in the song says, if you can make it in New York, you can make it anywhere.

For Frack and me the big night was in 1939. I had never really suffered from the traditional butterflies in the stomach, but they were there that night, only they were so big I thought they must be buzzards not butterflies. It wasn't so much the audience that concerned me -- although the 12,000 people crammed into Madison Square Garden constituted a lot of eyes and voices -- but I was thinking more about the critics. I knew the organization had invited a lot of ranking ice skating authorities and top press to attend our opening and so I was nervous, more nervous than I ever was before or since.

But, like the show biz legend has it, as soon as the lights go on and you get your cue your nervousness vanishes. You concentrate on the job at hand and literally forget the audience, the critics and everything else. Frack and I performed up to our usual standards that night.

And we were rewarded with some incredible, fantastic reviews. The Herald-Tribune's headline on its review of the show read:

Frick and Frack, Swiss Team of Comedy Skaters, Make Garden's Rafters Ring at Ice Follies

I bought one hundred copies of that newspaper and cut out that review [34 89]. I was always conscious of the value of publicity and was beginning to amass a fine scrapbook of our reviews and other stories.

While we were in New York, we were invited by the New York Skating Club to join them in their morning sessions at the famous New York skating landmark, Iceland, atop Madison Square Garden. So, I skated there several mornings and among my partners was Katharine Hepburn. And Arthur Godfrey asked me for some tips. A noted New York politician of the time, Newbold Morris, was another one who was frequently on the Iceland ice when I was there.

The name "Frick" is big in New York. There was at the time a man named Ford Frick who was the commissioner of baseball. And there is the famous Frick Gallery of Art. So, I was constantly being asked if I was related to either Ford Frick or the Frick Gallery of Art family. I would launch into my story of how Frick, in my case, was a town, and then explain that Frack was a gown. (Actually, as I have explained, a "frack" was a Swiss kind of morning coat but over the years it became funnier to say that it was a gown, so we could say, "A frack is a frock and a frick is a hick." It wasn't quite true, but it was close and it was funnier than the precise definitions).

The Ice Follies was San Francisco-based officially, so we felt at home in that city and the people of that city had come to feel a certain pride in our triumphs. Unlike Broadway shows which try out in New Haven or Philadelphia before their Broadway debut, our system was entirely different. We had no way of having an out-of-town tryout before our annual opening night.

We would rehearse at the Winterland rink in San Francisco -- rehearse and rehearse and rehearse, until we had it down pat, or thought we did -- and then we would debut the opening act of the new show. A week later, we would bring on the second half of the show. That way there would be no gap between the old show and the new edition. There would be no dark houses, only full houses, and the new show would slide in smoothly, almost under the audience's noses.

The rehearsal period was important to us because of the reliance I have always placed on music. It is integral to my performance, almost my performing signature. I have used the "Colonel Bogey March" for twenty years and, in fact, once went hundreds of miles out of my way, on a visit to Thailand, to visit the bridge on the River Kwai, because the movie about that bridge featured what I call "my music."

Although we actually started the new show each year in San Francisco, we always had a gala premiere of the new show in Los Angeles at the Pan Pacific Auditorium.

Even though it sounds easy -- the transition from old show to new show -- it wasn't. It was for most of the company a frantic period -- learning new routines, becoming familiar with the new costumes and the new music cues and the new sets, often working with new partners. Frack and I were fortunate in that we did our own act, rehearsed only with ourselves, and really had nobody to please or cater to but ourselves.

The Los Angeles premiere was always a gala, classy evening. Celebrities always attended, by invitation. (The gigantic show business agency, MCA -- the Music Corporation of America -- owned a piece of the Ice Follies so they made sure many of their glamorous clients were included on the invited guest list).

There were flowers in the dressing rooms for everyone. There were telegrams from noted people stuck into our dressing room mirrors. The costumes were fresh and clean (too often in subsequent weeks that detail would be overlooked and you would see girls going out with tears in their costumes, rips in their stockings or tights, and the show, as a result, looked shoddy). Everybody, after the show, dressed in their finest for the annual post-premiere party at the Beverly Hills Hotel.

We always posed, both during the intermission and later on at the party with the movie stars. It was fun hobnobbing with the notables and, I guess it was fun for them, too. Or maybe the smiles they always wore were a permanent fixture, not an indication of inner happiness.

I had always been a big movie fan. Going to the movies was a major source of pleasure for me on our days off wherever we happened to be. So, I looked forward to those Los Angeles premieres. I always managed to get hold of an advance list of the celebrities and where they would be sitting and from a backstage vantage point I would pick up my binoculars and try to find them all. I remember spotting Maurice Chevalier and James Stewart [35-36 90-91] and Joan Crawford and my old pal, Betty Grable. And a young leading man named Ronald Reagan. Reagan always came backstage to visit us, and was very complimentary, and told me how he loved to skate himself. Sonja Henie was always there, of course, until she died. Bob Hope & Lawrence Welk [37 92] were close friends of Eddie Shipstad so they were there as often as their schedules would permit.

That Hollywood opening night was for most of us the festive highlight of the year. During the rest of our season it was pretty much a grind, the job of skating in an ice show. It may have looked glamorous from the outside looking in, but from the inside looking out, it was mostly plain old hard work. And so, we welcomed our one night a year to rub elbows hips and what-have-you with the acknowledged kings and queens of glamour.

One year the management in a burst of unexpected and unexplained generosity decided that immediately following the show itself they were going to convert the rink into a huge party arena. In less than forty-five minutes they had the rink magically transformed into a nightclub setting, with most of the ice covered with carpets and the rest turned into a dance floor. Life devoted two pages covering that party. Another year, they put up a huge tent in a vacant lot opposite the rink and we all had a circus-like post-premiere party.

More and more, Frack and I were becoming stars, too. Certainly, we did not twinkle as brightly as the Hollywood stars, but we were increasingly attracting our coterie of fans and admirers. We found to our pleasure -- mine more than Frack's, because I was always more outgoing than he -- that important people wanted to meet us.

When we appeared in Washington, D.C., we were escorted to the Capitol because the then Vice President, John Nance Garner, wanted to meet us. Even though he was the quintessential Texan, like all Americans he had had ancestors who came from Europe and in his case, they had come from Switzerland. So, he had expressed a desire to meet us and talk about Switzerland. He asked us if we knew the village where his ancestors had come from but, unfortunately, neither Frack nor I knew the place.

I remember something else about playing Washington, too and that something was not as pleasant. The rink there was primitive and the toilet facilities for the cast were a joke. Only it wasn't funny. The john itself was one of those chemical affairs, the kind you use out in the woods. Only this one was right in the middle of the dressing room -- out in the open. Oscar Johnson, a fastidious man, was horrified. He would have raised the roof except there wasn't any roof just a large piece of canvas thrown across the supports.

Our tour gradually lengthened. Eventually, it would last annually for ten months and in that time, we visited an average of thirty cities. For a long time, we did eight shows a week. And then one day, Lew Wasserman, one of the MCA bosses (later, he would become head of Universal Pictures and a great Hollywood power) toured with us for a while because of MCA's financial interest in our show. And he decreed that we should add a Sunday matinee to our schedule. Presto, there went our Sunday afternoons off. Some weeks, depending on the City and the season, we would do ten shows a week.

Every year we had five to seven days off as a pre-Christmas vacation. No vacation pay, of course, that would be too much to expect. They did give each of us a twenty-five dollar bonus as a Christmas gift.

Whenever we played Minneapolis, where Frack's brother-in-law lived, we would have the pleasure of the company of Hubert Humphrey. When we first met him, he was the mayor and then he became senator from Minnesota. Frack's brother-in-law was his body guard when he was mayor. Humphrey, like most people from that part of the United States, knew his way around an ice rink. Nothing particularly fancy, but he skated reasonably well.

I got to know Humphrey on fairly close terms and I admired him as a man. He never pretended to be anything other than what he was. And so, when he told us he was thinking of running for the Senate, I contributed to his campaign chest. In fact, he told me that I was actually his first contributor outside of his immediate family. Sometime later, in New York, after he had been elected to the Senate, he invited me to be his guest at a big political dinner for Americans for Democratic Action at the Waldorf-Astoria.

As pre-arranged, when I reached the hotel I went directly to Humphrey's room. I expected to find everything under control because he was a very controlled, very organized man. This time, however, things were wildly out of control. Humphrey had not yet arrived and his administrative assistant was beside himself. He had laid out the Senator's tuxedo on the bed but there was no Senator there to wear it. Just when it nearly became panic time, Humphrey burst in the door with a tale of misadventures to tell.

"Would you believe," he said, "that the airline would not accept my credit card? Well, believe it, because it happened. They wouldn't take my credit card! I had to get the man who runs the airport to come down and vouch for me. Then, when we finally landed here, there was a monumental traffic jam on the highway. Do I have time for a shower?"

He did, barely. While he showered, I handed him a drink to calm him down.

At that dinner, I met Eleanor Roosevelt -- I was very proud when she recognized me and said he had seen me skate and "I think you are terribly funny" -- and Averell Harriman and many other stalwarts of the Democratic Party. After the dinner, I was asked to be part of a smaller group in his suite.

I had expected, especially at that smaller affair, to be stimulated and excited by the conversation. After all, these were some of the main movers and Shakers of the United States, the greatest power on earth. But the talk was actually dull and uninspiring. In fact, there were often lengthy lulls in the conversation when nothing much was said by anybody at all. The talk backstage at the Ice Follies was much brighter and wittier.

I suggested we all go on to the Stork Club, which was then the most famous of all New York night spots. A few of us -- including Humphrey and Harriman -- taxied to that 52nd Street institution. We were, of course, greeted warmly by the host, Sherman Billingsley, who knew a celebrity (Humphrey and Harriman, not me) when he saw one. He gave us a good table and a bottle of champagne, and he presented the ladies with perfume and the gentlemen with his trademark red suspenders. They were good suspenders and, in fact, I used them in my act for the next several years.

I would have liked Hubert Humphrey to become President of the United States -- he almost did in 1956 -- not because of his political philosophy, but because I knew the man. After all, to be able to say that the President of the United States is a personal friend is a boast that very few people can make. As it is, I believe I can say that the last few presidents have all known who I was, even though we were not personal friends. And furthermore, I think that all of them -- from Franklin Roosevelt through Ronald Reagan -- have applauded me on the ice.

Frack and I were adopted by sports writers from the beginning. That was understandable when you think about their professional problems. Covering an ice show is difficult. Is it a sporting event? Yes, because we are all athletes. Is it entertainment? Certainly, the bottom line is to entertain. Is it news? Not really, no more than a continuing Broadway show is news. But every year in most cities the sports writers were the ones assigned to cover the Ice Follies

What were they to write about? They would search for a new angle, and I became adept at creating those angles for them. I would entice the reporter to join my act (only for a rehearsal picture, of course) and that was always good for a few laughs and a few stories. I would dream up local angles -- in Pittsburgh, as an example, I went to the Stouffers restaurant atop the forty-story U.S. Steel Building and raised a mock fuss about the fact that that Swiss-owned restaurant didn't serve Swiss steak.

I would point out to the Sports writers some of the unusual people we had in the show. There was the Folliette who had come off a midwestern farm where her folks raised pigs. That year, and for several years, we used a piglet in the act and this young lady was our piglet supplier. When the piglet grew into a large pig, too big for the act, she would take it back to the farm and replace it with a new one. There was another girl in the show who had interrupted her medical school studies to skate with us for a year to finance the balance of her schooling.

When all else failed, I went back to some of my old stand-by story ideas. I knew that my breakfast routine was always good for a few paragraphs -- I would eat a grapefruit every morning with a spoonful of bourbon to give it a bit of flavor.

Through the years, the Sports writers learned to come to me for their annual story. I would never disappoint them.

If they were simply reviewing the show, Frick and Frack would always be good for some mention. Figure skaters were not too exciting to write about, but we would always have some new gimmick or stunt. And the reporters who knew anything about ice skating were quick to realize that we were probably the best pure skaters on the ice. As so many people have said to me over the years, "You must have to know how to skate very well before you can skate very funny." And that is true.

So, the Sports writers flocked around us. Even those who didn't know a Figure Eight from a Figure One enjoyed talking to us. I was generally the one who did most of the talking as I was the team extrovert. I quickly realized the value of publicity and took to it like a duck to orange sauce.

Life magazine, at that time the most important publication in America and possibly the world, did a story on our show and most of it was about Frick and Frack [39-41 94-96]. (We felt some resentment about that from others in the cast, particularly the bosses, Shipstad and Johnson, because they were still doing a comedy skating act themselves.)

To make it worse, a short while later Time magazine reviewed our show and wrote this about Frick and Frack:

"...The skaters that brought down the house each night were Frick and Frack, a pair of Swiss comics. Frick and Frack do not depend on costumes, grimaces or falls to get their laughs. With the pantomime of Charlie Chaplin and the rubber legs of Leon Errol, they take the elements of figure skating distort them into crazy positions to create some of the most astonishing feats ever performed on skates..."

Perhaps it all began from that, all the backstage friction and the jealousies. I will talk at greater length about all that in a subsequent chapter, the tragic one leading to my getting fired. But suffice it to say at this point that nothing was quite the same after that Time magazine review. From then on, there was never the same feeling of being part of a family that there had been before.

Oscar Johnson liked the family concept. He saw himself, I believe, as the benevolent daddy of the company. He tried very hard to be one of the team. When we travelled on a train he made sure he had one of the upper berths, not a roomette, as he might have been entitled to. Johnson had started as a chemist for the Koppers Company in St. Paul, Minnesota and had actually begun skating professionally while on a leave of absence from that concern. He liked to tell us that he was still, technically, on leave and that he could always go back to his old job.

He knew his business and he knew skating. Once, only a few weeks after we had begun with the Follies, he said to me, "The secret of a good comedy skating act is to get on and get off." He meant that it was important to have a good beginning, to catch their attention, and a good ending, to leave them feeling that they have been very well entertained. So, I always choreographed the act, both when I was with Frack and later when I was by myself, to have both of those key elements -- a good beginning and a good ending.

Being on the road so much meant, of course, a total lack of what is commonly known as "home life." Home to me for so many years was whatever hotel or motel room I was in, in whatever City the show happened to be playing. My only possessions were my clothing and my skating paraphernalia and the luggage in which all of that was carried around.

I have always enjoyed eating, but for most of my life was forced to compromise on food. Because of my skating schedule, I would eat my main meal no later than three in the afternoon -- lunch or what passed for lunch. Besides the physical benefits of eating nothing heavy before performing, there was a financial benefit to be gained -- at most better restaurants, lunch costs less than dinner and usually is just as satisfying.

After the evening performance, I would eat a very light snack. It was usually something I could fix for myself in my hotel room -- some cheese (kept cold on the window sill, although often in cities such as Seattle the sea gulls would steal my cheese) and that good old nourishing drink, Ovaltine.

I applaud the American custom of the doggie bag. If I ate a big steak at lunch I would save part of it, have the waiter put it in a doggie bag, carry it home in my briefcase, and eat the rest of it after the show. That was particularly beneficial if we were doing two evening performances because I found I needed a little something between those two Shows.

I found that I had inadvertently developed a schedule that was very healthy. I got up early, even after a late show, and walked -- exploring whatever city I was in -- until I had my big meal at lunch. My breakfast and my dinner were light meals, but lunch was hefty. In my last few years of performing I would add an hour or so of resting -- lying down on my bed -- before going on and doing the evening show.

The Ice Follies had some regular, annual stops, and I began looking forward to them. Christmas in New York, for example, was an event that anchored the year. I felt that the huge Christmas tree in Rockefeller Center was my own personal Christmas tree; it was the only one I had. The company, being all strangers in a strange land during the holidays, banded together and formed a family for at least the duration of the Christmas season. And so, it was a pleasant enough time -- not the real thing, of course, but close enough.

I used to love to skate -- another busman's holiday! -- At the Rockefeller Center rink during that time of year. I suppose part of it was the human enough desire to show off a little for the amateurs. I would go down there, put on my Skates, and go out on the ice. I didn't look like a skating star -- I looked, if the truth be known, like a nice young Swiss businessman. So, I skated easily but unspectacularly for a while, and then I would begin to do a few things -- stumbling, recovering, a few fancy turns, whatever occurred to me -- and pretty soon I would have an audience. I didn't like to be a skating rink show-off, but I enjoyed entertaining.

I used the rink so often I left a pair of skates in a locker which the rink's manager kindly let me have. I also had a pair at the Richmond rink in London and later I stashed another pair in Tokyo. (I went for ten years without visiting Tokyo, or those skates, and when I finally did return to that city, the skates were still there, still in amazingly good shape.)

My skates were the primary tools of my trade. I was a compulsive skate buyer. By skates, you understand, I mean boots with blades attached. I learned that the boot portion of the skates wore out generally after approximately two hundred and fifty performances. I needed the boots to fit tightly and snugly for the proper support. (Incidentally, amateurs often talk of having skating problems because of "weak ankles" but there really is no such affliction. It is simply that they do not have skates with the proper support in the boots.)

Breaking in a new pair of boots was agonizing. I used to break them in by soaking them water, but then I learned from a German that the German army broke their leather marching books in with urine. So, I tried that and it worked. Of course, I only did that at home -- and I would discard the first pair of socks I wore.

Still, the new ones would hurt a lot, so I would often switch back and forth during a show -- wear the new ones for a while, but also use the old familiar ones for key movements. I'd wear older ones for the finale, when I didn't have to do anything strenuous, merely skate around and smile prettily.

I would put my old, discarded skates in a warehouse or give them to some of the various ice skating collectors. But lately I've been going back and repossessing the laces because you can't get laces like I had anymore.

I hated to part with my old, broken-in skates. I stashed pairs wherever I thought I might possibly need them. Even after I had given many pairs to those museums, I still had to rent storage space with the Bekins Storage people to keep many others. At one point, I had more than two dozen pairs of skates in storage.

The importance of having good skates and keeping them in good condition was brought home to me when, as I celebrated my eleven thousandth show, I was introduced with a big fanfare during a Madison Square Garden engagement. My partner at the time was a nice young man named Gary Johnson, but he apparently had not taken the proper care of his skates. Soon after the act began that night, he lost a blade. It simply separated from his boots. He had to leave the ice for repairs. That threw the rest of the act off -- the timing was totally destroyed -- and the stagehands were confused about what props to move where and when. I had to improvise most of the act for that performance.

But back to New York and Rockefeller's Center. The rink there was the site of an interview I did with Barbara Walters in 1974. Miss Walters was then doing NBC's "Today" show and was, consequently, a very important lady in the television world. I had contacted the "Today" people myself -- the Ice Follies staff included public relations people, of course, but I always did a lot of my own publicity work -- and so it was something of a coup for me when they called up and asked if I would appear on their show. It was two days before Christmas and they felt a program with an ice skating motif would be appropriate. I was delighted to accept.

It meant cutting short a brief vacation in the Caribbean and it meant that my partner of the moment, Dave Thomas, had to change his plans, too. But we all felt it was worth the effort. They said they wanted a brief routine at the rink, so that took some time to prepare. The Rockefeller Center rink is a nice little rink -- but the operative word there is "little." It was much smaller than our usual rinks and, consequently, we had to curtail our Speed and that meant curtailing some of our best bits.

I won't go into all the details, but putting on that brief act for the NBC cameras was as complicated, perhaps more complicated, than doing my entire act in the Follies. I had to arrange for the music, for the props, for the tools and equipment to utilize those props, for the costumes -- and all for a five-minute act, for virtually no money.

We came into New York a day ahead of time to set up and rehearse. But you can imagine what it was like trying to get space on the Rockefeller Center rink during the Christmas holiday season. We had to push some eight hundred skaters to one side. And then we had the craft unions to contend with -- to set up with union help would have cost thousands of dollars. We did it diplomatically. There were special events going on in and around the rink -- one I remember was a concert involving two hundred and fifty tuba players. Try skating to the sound of two hundred and fifty oom-pa-pas, if you want to have good clean fun.

But it all got done. It always does. And the next morning at five-thirty, right on schedule, we reported for work. We set up our props in the cold, bleak winter morning. A few NBC technicians and cameramen were there drinking coffee and waiting; generally, they were in the warm, comfortable studio, not outside on the cold ice. I went inside into the rink's dressing room to put on some make-up.

"Good morning," I heard a soft female voice say. I stood up and there was Barbara Walters, dressed to kill even at that hour, and somehow managing to look glamorous in those surroundings. "I am so happy to meet you Mr. Frick. Is there anything you would like me to ask you during our interview?"

She was so friendly, so gracious, so pleasant. It takes a noble woman to manage all that before the sun is up.

When I finally did my little act -- it was about eight o'clock by that time -- it was very difficult. There was hardly any audience, and a comedy act relies on laughter for the fuel to propel itself forward. Without laughter, it is like doing an audition -- a very flat, awkward feeling.

After that, came the interview which went well. She asked me how I was able to continue as an athlete at an age -- I was sixty then -- when most athletes are long retired. I told her that I believe in training, in healthy living, in plenty of rest. She asked about my equipment and I pointed to one thing that was different with me -- the steel balls that I had had specially made to go over the points on my skates. Those points are sharp and many skaters have been cut when hit by them. The balls I used might produce a bruise, but a bruise isn't as bad as a cut.

I received the standard "Today" guest fee -- $265 -- but the expenses I personally incurred soared considerably over that sum. Neither NBC nor the Follies expressed any desire to reimburse me for those heavy expenses. So, I learned another lesson -- you can learn lessons even at sixty -- which was to avoid volunteering for anything unless you make sure it won't cost you any money.

Over the years that Frack and I skated together, our joint names had entered the American language. Frick and Frack were names that somehow appealed to the public. We kept hearing about fans of ours who had named their dogs, their cats, even their turtles Frick and Frack. I heard that in Fairbanks, Alaska, the hotel menu featured a Frick and Frack sandwich. In another city -- I forgot which one -- I saw a Frick and Frack store. We tried to stop that, getting the Follies legal firm to institute legal action, but it had no effect. Similarly, we tried to stop an ad agency from calling itself Frick & Frack Advertising, Inc., but for reasons I never fully understood, we couldn't.

It would be presumptuous of me to claim that we were the first comedy skating act the world had ever seen. There had been others; it is a rare thing that can honestly claim to be the absolute first in any field of endeavor. But in all immodesty, I must boast that we took comedy skating to new heights. And we certainly became pre-eminent in our field. Partly, that was due to our names which caught the public fancy. Partly, that was due to our exposure being headlined in one of the largest and best of ice shows, plus our two notion picture appearances and later, considerable work in television. But partly, too, it was because we happened to excel at our unique trade.

As the years rolled along, however, we were continually up against more and more, stiffer and stiffer competition. Our own bosses, Shipstad and Johnson, had a comedy act themselves.

Next followed a group called "The Scarecrows." And "The Kermond Brothers:" a trio of acrobatic comedic skaters from Australia.

There were others, too. That was understandable and forgivable. What was unforgivable, however, was how many of them began blatantly copying Frick and Frack maneuvers, music and even our costumes. So, we had to keep searching for new things to do on the ice and new things to wear on the ice to keep our act fresh and different. Imitation may be the sincerest form of flattery, but it is also the greatest form of annoyance.

When we first started, we wore Swiss costumes, but for long time we didn't. After Frack left I decided to go back my origins and began wearing the Swiss outfit again, and wore it mostly for the balance of my career. I had always been proud of being Swiss and so I enjoyed appearing in the Swiss costume and performing to authentic Swiss music. The audience seemed to like it, too. It became my trademark through my last years as a performer.

"Keep that costume," Eddie Shipstad said to me. So, I did -- for twenty-three years. That original Swiss costume today is worn by a manikin in the Skaters Hall of Fame in Colorado Springs. My figure is next to that of Sonja Henie in that lovely building next to the Broadmoor Hotel there. The only thing my figure lacks is the red cheeks I usually had -- due mostly to the cold, but partly to the judicious application of make-up.

As an aside, you might be interested to learn that at the suggestion of my accountant, I decided to claim that donation of my costume as an income tax deduction. All very legitimate, my accountant had said; I had donated something of my own to a museum. The problem was how much could I deduct? How much is a costume worth? After lengthy deliberations, soul searching, consulting old records for the original purchase price of the various elements that went into assembling the costume, we settled on $270. I thought it could have been more. For one thing, the pants alone cost considerably more than that -- I had them specially made for me by a tailor on the Sunset Strip in Los Angeles. (He was often late delivering my pants because, he said, he was kept busy working and re-working the jackets he made for Liberace.) For another thing, I felt that becoming a fixture in a museum qualifies one for the position of legend, and surely legend is worth more than a $270 deduction.

My on-ice clothes were more important to me when I was travelling with the show, than my off-ice clothes. I often took along just one suit, one shirt, a pair of underwear, one of everything. I knew that in this wash-and-wear era I could wash my shirt and underwear and socks and bang them up to dry on the radiator while I took a nap. When I woke, I would have a clean wardrobe.

Once, however, I had to do with less than that one change of clothing. One night when I was tired and had had a few beers, I put on my pajamas and packed my wardrobe trunk because we were moving on the first thing in the morning. I shoved the two hundred and fifty pound trunk out into the hall so the bell boys could collect it and load it on the truck with the rest of the cast's luggage.

When I woke up, I realized that I had packed everything in the trunk, which was long gone. I had to send to the rink for my practice outfit which fortunately, was still there, and I wore that on to the next City where my trunk was waiting for me.

Life with a touring show is full of such adventures. If you haven't done it, you cannot grasp the extent to which one is a slave to a schedule. You get used to it, of course, as you can get used to anything. But that schedule is constantly in the forefront of your mind, and it severely limits your ability to enjoy the things in life that everybody else takes for granted.

There was usually one day a week -- Monday -- that was free. During the rest of the week my colleagues and I worked while the rest of the world played. It was impossible to attend any social affairs, to go to see a movie or a play, even to have a leisurely dinner in a restaurant. (In New York, I cheated a little. If a play was in a theater not too far from Madison Square Garden, I could time it so I could see the second act. I became an expert on second acts of hit Broadway shows. I remember once literally running ten blocks from the Garden to the theater where the Ballet Russe was performing and managing to catch the last ten or twelve minutes of those magnificent dancers.)

We were stars, at least in the eyes of ice show aficionados and, as such, we were invited to many affairs. I enjoyed them and so tried to attend them as often and for as long as I could. Often, I would go to a cocktail party and have a drink or two and a few hors d'oeuvres and talk and laugh and then, when the clock told me it was time, make my apologies and run to the rink. I felt like Cinderella having to catch the midnight pumpkin. I had special permission from the show to arrive at the arena only thirty minutes before our act went on -- they knew I could be trusted to be ready to go when our act was given its cue. I often cut that very thin, however, but I never once missed my cue.

It was more than just being physically present, however. For me, as an athlete, I had to get myself set physically. That entailed some warm-up exercises as well as getting into my costume, putting on my boots and skates and mentally psyching myself up so I was ready to go. For many seasons, I made my entrance inside a big cheese -- a marvelous prop that glided across the ice on little buttons. I was inside on skis -- my skates were in slots through those skis. I had to bend forward in a ski racing position while two strong skaters pushed this cheese on the ice until we were going about twenty-five miles an hour. Then when I heard my cue, I would pull on a rope handle and the sides of the cheese split open and I would catapult forward. The cheese stopped, of course, and I continued. And when the announcer said my name -- "Ladies and gentlemen: the fabulous Misterrrrr Frick!" -- I would suddenly stop on a dime and immediately freeze in my trademarked position.

I always thought that entrance was so strong that it amounted almost to half my career.

An alternative entering prop was a bed, again propelled by two strong and fast skaters. That one had a trick blanket which would split when my cue came, and there I would be in a nightgown, doing my skating entrance.

Being Swiss, Frack and I were always at the top of any list for any event that involved the Swiss in any way. One year, for example, during our San Francisco engagement, we were invited by the Swiss Society of San Francisco (there are societies for everything, everywhere) to join them in honoring Pilez Golaz, who had recently retired as president of Switzerland and would be visiting San Francisco. There was to be a gala dinner and would we join them for the evening? I could -- but only until about 8:30 because then I would have to rush back for my performance.

I did manage to have a word with Mr. Golaz and invited him to come to the show the following evening. He accepted, but it turned into a near disaster.

He arrived after the performance had begun. Naturally, I had arranged for Mr. and Mrs. Golaz to have rink-side seats. What nobody had told me was that they were given seats which had, until that evening, been "stooge seats" -- seats in which paid stooges sit which had bits to do in the show. In this case, the stooges had to stand up and duck when a skating scrub woman came by and swung her mop "accidentally" in their direction. So there the former president of Switzerland and his lady were, in those risky seats, and along skated the scrubwoman who thought that the people in those seats were stooges. She didn't know that they were instead the former president of Switzerland and his wife. They could have been stooges after all stooges come in all shapes and sizes. So, right on schedule, she swung her mop. Fortunately, Mr. and Mrs. Golaz had good reflexes -- they ducked. The rest of the audience thought it was part of the show. Everybody laughed.

During the intermission, Mr. Golaz was introduced to the audience and everybody who had laughed now gasped. Then they applauded, extra loud. A potential disaster had turned instead into a triumph.

Our show became a mecca for dignitaries. It was a good place to be seen, and since it involved no politics, it was a safe and non-controversial place to be seen, too.

During another engagement in San Francisco, about a half-hour before Showtime, we were suddenly invaded by a swarm of F.B.I. agents. The first thing they did was confiscate all guns in the show -- there weren't many, but we did that year have a cowboys and Indians number and the cowboys carried guns. The F.B.I. men took all the guns -- the fastest U.S.-U.S.S.R. disarmament deal ever made -- and had our property master lock them up. And then they told us that Koslov was coming.

This was 1956, and it is hard to remember now what the situation in Russia was at that time. But Frol Koslov was a rising star in the Soviet hierarchy and as first deputy prime minister he was the heir apparent to Stalin. When Stalin died a year later [1953], however, it was Malenkov and Khruschev who seized power and Koslov was thrust aside and died some years after that, a forgotten man. In 1956, however, when he came to see the Ice Follies in San Francisco, he was a major force in Russian politics and his visit to America was closely guarded by the F.B.I. and the Secret Service.

We watched from our dressing room windows as his cavalcade, with its motorcycle police escort, drove up to the Winterland rink. He was a tall, handsome man and he made a fine appearance as he strode down the aisle. The audience recognized him, of course, but they were not about to cheer a Russian. They gave him a polite round of applause and he turned and bowed formally and then sat down. There were no swinging mops that night. We all had been carefully coached to stay a respectful (and safe) distance away from the box where the Russian dignitary was seated.

That year I had devised a number in our act where I was a toy soldier in a shooting gallery, and other skaters, armed with rifles, tried to hit me as I paraded back and forth. Naturally, the F.B.I. had taken those rifles away, too. So, my assistants had to shoot at me with little toy popguns which the property master had produced and the F.B.I. had examined and approved. It made only a puny pop sound which could not be heard beyond the third row, so a big part of the act's effect was dissipated, but that was a small price to pay for international amity.

After the show, Koslov was escorted backstage where we all stood in a semi-circle and bowed. He made a point of coming up to me and shaking my hand.

"Was very good," he said. The Russians like clowns.

Some years later, when Khrushchev made his famous visit to America, we were playing in Los Angeles. The Russian premier said he wanted to see Disneyland and the Ice Follies, but the authorities said no to both requests. They said they could not guarantee his safety in either place. We remembered back to Koslov's visit and thought that surely Khrushchev would have been protected as well as Koslov was.

San Quentin's distinguished warden, Clinton Duffy, was another notable who enjoyed watching us perform. He was a compassionate man, and one year he felt his prisoners deserved some entertainment so invited a group of us from the show to visit the prison. In the dining hall, some two thousand inmates had been assembled. When Warden Duffy entered, they gave him a big and tremendous, I could tell, heartfelt cheer; it was obvious to me that they liked him and wanted him to know it. Ten of our bounciest Folliettes did a dance -- without skates -- and later Duffy told us they were the first women to appear in San Quentin in many years. We had a film of the Ice Follies in action, and that was projected in the dining hall and they enjoyed that. We were in the first row with the mass of inmates behind us and, I must say, I felt better when the film ended and the lights came back on in that room.

Every year for many years, Warden Duffy and his wife came to see our show on his birthday, which always coincided with our appearance in San Francisco.

Another of the V.I.P.s we met, via our work with the Ice Follies, was the famous founder of the Bank of America, A.P. Giannini. It was his daughter, Claire Hoffman, who first met us and invited us to the lovely home in San Mateo where they lived. He was reputed to have buried gold bars, rescued from the big San Francisco earthquake of 1906, in the garden of that home but as we sat in the garden I could see no place that looked suspiciously like gold was buried there. I became friendly with Claire and several times we went dancing on a free evening. That didn't help at all when I applied for a real estate loan at her father's bank; I received no special treatment and paid the same interest as everyone else.

Over all the years that I performed, first with Frack and later by myself, I must have been seen by most of the important people of our times. And over those years, Frack and I had our ups and downs, personally and emotionally and professionally as well.

During that period, the show had several owners and the backstage politics and in-fighting was often horrendous. I suppose every business and every art form has its moments of politics, its jealousies, its scratching and clawing, but for some reason it seems to me that the ice show business has more than its share.

Once, for example, we rubbed somebody the wrong way and that somebody was at the time in charge of making up the Ice Follies program. So, we found ourselves following a dog act for a time. You have to understand that in the world of show business -- from vaudeville days on -- following the dog act was the lowest spot on the bill. And for good reason -- there were almost always dog droppings on the stage, which didn't make for a pleasant environment.

Now following a dog act may be terrible on stage, but consider what it is like on the ice. Until you have been skating along with your head only inches from the surface of the ice and you find yourself approaching a clump of dog shit at twenty-five miles an hour, you cannot appreciate how it feels. Besides the unpleasantness, it is also very dangerous.

The physical aspects of touring are something that the civilian population cannot grasp. If I tell some of my non-show business friends that touring is a positive drag, that person usually laughs. He or she cannot really appreciate just how large a drag it is. The logistics of clothing and laundry and all that are impossible for anyone to appreciate who has not been there and lived through it.

I toted around from City to city, all manner of things -- books, my tax and other financial records, a fruit-juicer, extra skates, a very nice little travelling bar. After I was married, Yvonne added some other, decidedly feminine touches -- she had a bouquet of travelling flowers that snapped open and became a very full flower arrangement, and transformed a typical Spartan hotel room instantly into a homey place. She also carried a wig in case there was no time to get to the hotel beauty shop.

Frack was more of a dandy. He liked clothes more than I did and consequently, travelled with a wardrobe of ten suits, a few dozen shirts, and thirty-two ties. He enjoyed being called the best-dressed man in the company, and he generally was.

So, he always looked natty. I think that helped us both when we were in Washington one year and were required to show up at the Swiss Embassy to discuss our military obligations. Frack had never done his Swiss Army duty. I had done mine, but only for four months and the typical Swiss are required to do a few weeks every year for twelve years after his initial term. Since we were overseas we were subject to a military tax in lieu of service.

The day we happened to appear at the legation, by coincidence, was the day in which a story on Frack and his wardrobe ran in the Washington paper. There was even a picture of Frack and some of these ties -- the story said he had seventy, but I never counted more than thirty-two.

Many Swiss in America bitterly resented the tax they were required to pay, but I had always paid mine regularly, without any complaint. Still, I felt it was very steep, and that was one of the things that I had hoped to discuss with the consul that day in Washington, that day when Frack's sartorial splendor was splashed all over the newspaper.

So, we showed up at the Swiss embassy in Washington for our appointment with a man with the title of Chancellor, who was to review our tax and military situations.

"Come in, Herr [Mr.] Groebli and Herr [Mr.] Mauch," the Chancellor said. "Please sit down and make yourselves comfortable. Here are some papers you will kindly fill out and sign."

Another declaration of income, we spent an hour or so, on the tedious work of filling out that tedious form. But I have always believed that the fact that Frack was dressed impeccably saved us that time from much worse. He looked like a proper Swiss businessman, not like an entertainer. And so, the Chancellor had empathy for him and we got off easily. No concessions were made, but at least we weren't any worse off than we had been. It helped to have Frack in his $5,000 wardrobe, discussing our $3,000 income problem.

The truth was, of course, that Frack wasn't a businessman, and neither was I. We were entertainers and entertainers of a very special sort. We were athlete/entertainers, and I believe that, outside of ballet dancers, there is nobody in either the world of Sports or the world of show business which has a more rigorous career than professional ice skaters.

To be funny and evoke laughter is a difficult skill, and one that requires a person to be in the finest physical condition possible. My performance lasted on the average, six minutes and yet I had to take care of myself twenty-four hours a day to be ready for that six-minute stint. Many doctors have told me that my six minutes were the equivalent of a full day's work for the average man. I had to get my sleep, eat properly, exercise -- and all on a rigid, unvarying schedule. The great dancer, Nureyev, has told me that he works out twice a day, but that he can skip a day here and there without any problem. I never could. I stuck to my schedule every day for all those grueling years.

And that is why I never argued when John Hall of the Los Angeles Times wrote that he considered me "one of the world's greatest athletes."

New York Herald Tribune, Wednesday, December 6, 1939

Frick and Frack, Swiss Team of Comedy Skaters, Make Garden's Rafters Ring at Ice Follies
Spread Eagle Clowning Act Just a "Natural"
Discovery of Talent Was Accidental; Now They're Never Without Contracts

By Janet Owen

The skating of Frick and Frack, new Swiss comedian team in the Ice Follies at Madison Square Garden, has been called "incredible" in seven languages, but the gaping galleries of two continents haven't known the half of it.

The act as an act, you might say, just happened. It is a success that never was planned for. It is a complete natural.

Neither Frick nor Frack ever intended to become professional skaters. They had a contract shoved under their collective right hand when they were doing what they thought was having a little fun on the free afternoon. They never have looked for an engagement, but always have had one. They have created a new style of comedy without wanting to be comedians. They are internationally pre-eminent after just three seasons.

A year ago, during their first season on this side of the ocean, they skate din the venerable Toronto carnival and set a record for acclaim. The Toronto show makes use of an interesting gadget that scientifically measures the enthusiasm of the crowd. It is a meter that records both volume and duration of applause and other noises of approval. The response to Frick and Frack's act registered greater than the accorded any other in all the six years the meter had been used.

Stunt Just an Accident

New Yorkers remember the pair without the benefit of meter, as the sensation of the New York Skating Club carnival last March. In the Follies tour this season they have been receiving such insistent demands for encores that the number they give have had to be limited arbitrarily in advance to stop their stopping the show.

Frick and Frack are two nice young men from Basle, Switzerland. Frick, whose name is Werner Groebli, was studying architecture and engineering in the University of Zurich in 1936, and Frack Hansruedi Mauch, aged twenty, was taking a full course at the School of Business in Basle. They had lived next door to each other in Frobenstrasse, Basle, all their lives in houses their families had had for forty years. In off hours they skated together.

One Saturday afternoon in 1936, Frick (Groebli), home from the university, was skating on the local rink when a friend of his showed him the classical "first position" of ballet dancing, a matter of bringing the right heel close against the left instep with both toes turned out. Frick, with a burlesquing leer in his eye, imitated the position and then let his feet slide apart into an inner-edge skating position sagged his knees and bent forward. There was an uproar from the crowd of skaters standing around.

Make Spread Eagle Famous

Out of this have come Frick and Frack, skating comedians inimitable. By popular demand, Frick repeated the stunt on the rink and in the course of a few more odd Saturdays had perfected it and worked up some others. The original stunt is the now famous spread eagle that both Frick and Frack, do but no other skaters. In effect, it is a spread eagle with bent knees and body lying out behind, like reclining on the air while spinning around a tremendous circle. Actually it is a combination of having blades and lower legs in an inner-edge position and the body thrown back in the position it takes for an outer-edge spread eagle.

Frack, amusing himself in another corner of the rink, copied the stunt. He also produced his own specialties, a pair of Leon Errol ankles on ice, and a knee that apparently goes out of joint sidewise, which Frick now slaps back into position. The manager of the local rink asked Frick if he and Frack could work up a pair together for the rink's annual series of three amateur shows.

From the Day Frick and Frack appeared in the first of these shows, to this, they have been skating with a seriousness they are still surprised at. Directors of other amateur carnivals saw them in Basle, asked them to skate in St. Moritz, Zurich and Berne. A manager of a professional English show saw them in St. Moritz and offered them a five-month contract. Frick wanted to polish the English he had learned in school. Frack who had chosen Italian instead of English at school wanted to learn it. They signed the contract.

Contracts Forced on Them

"We've never been able to get out of it," they said in the same breath yesterday during an afternoon relaxed hour before the show. One contract-offer followed another, each new one always before the current engagement had ended.

The new treatment of ice comedy this bright young pair has created springs directly from their original stunting. They don't depend on costumes, properties, pantomime grimaces or a buffoon's falls to produce laughs. The laughs they get come straight from their skating movements. They take elements of orthodox skating, put together parts that don't belong, exaggerate them, and arrange them on a timing scheme that keeps the audience in a constant state of surprise. Nothing finishes the way it looks as though it would when it starts, and the crazy positions, rhythms and near-calamities they go through hits a new high in the realm of the ludicrous.

"People think our skating is eccentric," said Frick, the taller, blonder and four-years-older of the two. "Actually it is not. We simply take liberties with standard movements. Any figure skater should be able to do a serious spread eagle asleep. It becomes comedy when you use the ability you have left over beyond this ease of competent execution to let go and do odd things with your body while the spread eagle is going on. We use our brains, our nerve-control and intense concentration."

They also have built their success superb sense of timing, which they have in common, and a pair of senses of humor which work for them all the time. In working out new stunts, they don't think about what the audience will consider funny. They do what strikes them as funny. So far they had not failed in being a good test of their galleries.

Picture 34 ✢ Page 76

Swiss Comedians Here With the Ice Follies
Frick and Frack, who defy the laws of gravity with their back bending spread eagles,
will be seen at opening night benefit tonight at Garden

Picture 35 ✧ Page 77

Mr. Frick & Celebrities
Maurice and Nita Chevalier
Ice Follies

Picture 36 ✧ Page 77

Mr. Frick & Celebrities
James and Gloria Stewart
Ice Follies

Chapter 3 -91-

Mr. Frick & Celebrities
Lawrence Welk
Ice Follies

Picture 38

Mr. Frick & Celebrities
Tony Bennett, Richard Dwyer, Werner Groebli & Fred Astaire
Ice Follies

Frick and Frack from Switzerland
Life Magazine, February 5, 1940

There is poetry in skating. The flashing strides of the racer as he cuts across a frozen lake recall a ballad by Kipling. The graceful tango steps of a beautiful dancer, skating to lilting music and soft lights, are a love poem by Shelley.

The skaters shown here, however, are busy reducing this poetry to buffoonery. Calling themselves Frick and Frack (real names: Werner Groebli and Hansruedi Mauch) they are a pair of Swiss comedians who this winter are making their fortunes by burlesquing everything graceful and beautiful in figure skating. And they are very, very funny. Traveling with Shipstad & Johnson's *Ice Follies*, they have panicked audiences everywhere with incredible positions into which they twist their bodies. Most incredible twist is shown below.

Are Top U.S. Skating Comedians

Gliding in a tremendous circle in top speed, with his body in a cantilever spread-eagle, position, Frick lowers his back until it is horizontal with the ice.

Frick and Frack have been in the U.S. only since last winter, have already become the top skating comedians in the land. They both learned to skate 7, but never took it seriously until one day when they tried imitating buxom ladies attempting spread eagles. Nearby skaters roared with laughter. Soon they were appearing in amateur shows at Basle and St. Moritz, then in a professional show in London. Today, in the U.S., they make $500 a week, like everything about the country except the ice on the indoor rinks. It is frozen too fast and imprisoned air bubbles make it crack and chip easily.

Picture 39 ✦ Page 79

1940 - Life Magazine
Frick does Back-Bend Spread Eagle. His Back is Ten Inches.

Picture 40 ✤ Page 79

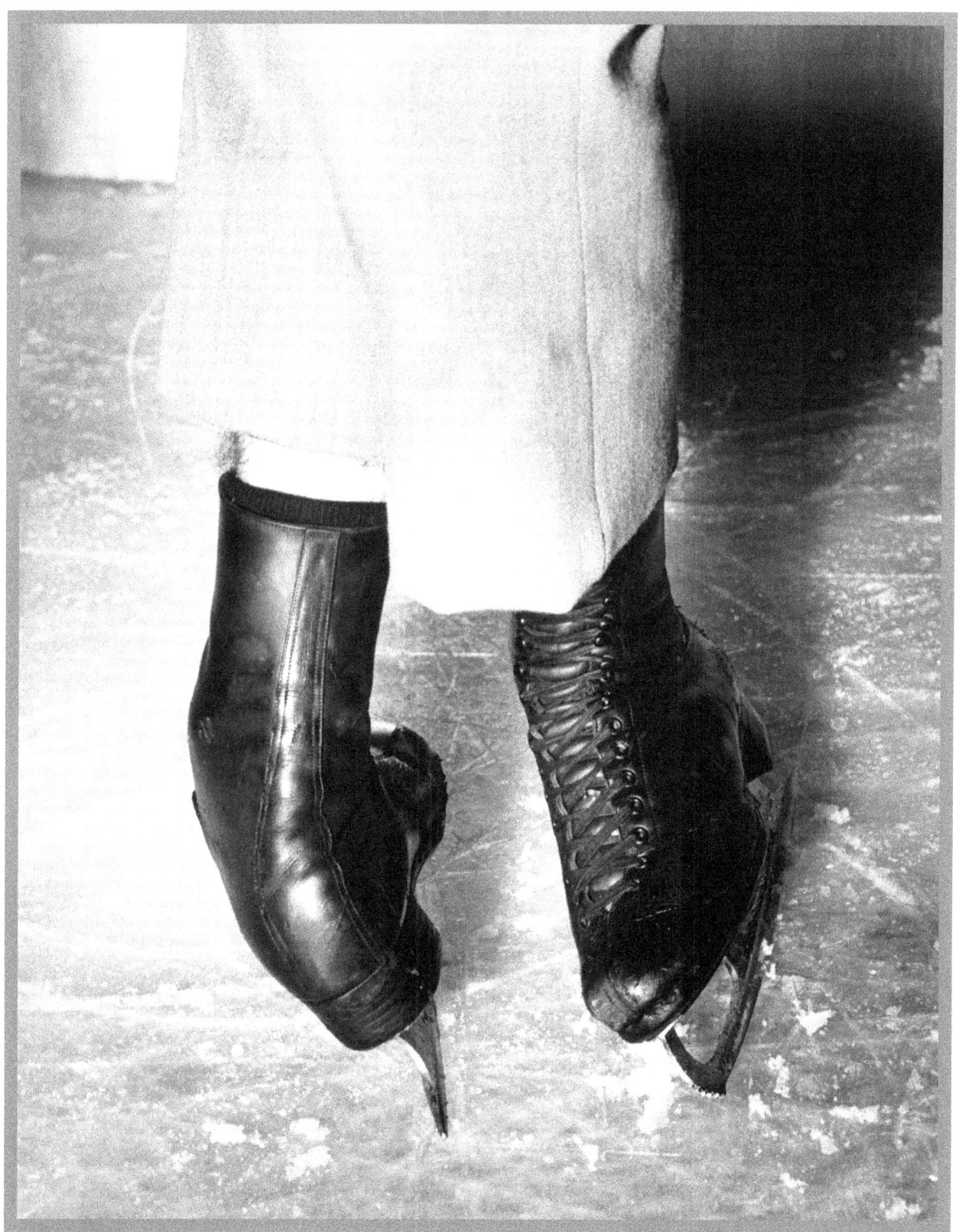

1940 - Life Magazine
One foot skates forward and the other foot goes backward. In every stunt
Frick and Frack do, they use this basic position. It is called a cross-foot spread eagle.

Chapter 3 -95-

Picture 41 ✦ Page 79

1940 - Life Magazine
Frack's Spread Eagle Cantilever Position
Ice Follies

CHAPTER 4

I have mentioned how as a young boy I was shy and lacked self-confidence. That changed in a flash one afternoon when I was, I imagine, fifteen or sixteen. It isn't often that one can pinpoint the moment of a major personality change, but I can. I do not remember the exact date or even the exact year, but I can vividly recall where it happened, what happened and how it all came about.

I had been skating in <u>Margarethenpark</u>. It was winter and so it got dark early. There were a few other skaters and one was a pretty girl. At fifteen or sixteen, a boy begins to notice such things -- which girls are pretty and which are not. I noticed this one. I might never have done anything about it that evening because of my terrible case of terminal shyness. I had been consumed with desire, or whatever it is that a naive teen-age boy feels, and had considered and rejected several approaches to that pretty girl. Then matters were taken out of my hands. She approached me. She asked me for some help with her skating, and I was then on safe, hospitable ground. I was willing and able to talk to her without self-consciousness.

"Make sure your ankles are straight," I said, and then emboldened by her rapt attention, I added, "and later, can I walk you home?"

We walked a bit and then sat on a bench and then -- I will never know where the courage came from -- I kissed her.

If she had objected, it might have condemned me to more years of shyness and fright, but she didn't. She kissed me back. Suddenly I was free. I could feel the shyness fly away as though I had taken off some heavy, burdensome coat. The curse of shyness was gone forever. That was all that happened with that particular pretty girl that particular evening. But the old Werner Groebli had vanished and the new Werner Groebli took his place.

The next morning, I looked at myself in the mirror and I could see the change. I still had the same face -- I knew I was neither God-like nor unpleasant to look at, but somewhere in the middle and perhaps even a bit nearer the plus side than the minus side -- but there was something inside that manifested itself outside. I had lost the cringe. I stood a little straighter, the eyes had a touch more sureness the line of the jaw was a bit stronger and firmer.

I had kissed a girl. And she had kissed back. Unless you have lived through that moment and recognized it as a turning point, you cannot imagine how brave, that made me feel.

Thus, began a lifetime of appreciating the beauty of women. I must confess that one of the pleasures of fame, of being in the limelight, is that it can help in the pursuit of women. The limelight is an allure akin to the flame that attracts moths.

I do not want anyone to get the wrong impression. There was never anything unhealthy or immoderate about my interest in women. It was all very healthy and very moderate. But it was always there. And once I joined my first ice Show in England, I realized that there was a bonus to the job over and above the money to be earned and the enjoyment I received from the act of skating.

The bonus is that ice shows are necessarily full of beautiful girls, all equipped with good legs. Because of the extensive use of make-up and the glare of the spotlight, many are not as attractive as they seem from the balcony, but many of them are. I like the ones who were.

Once I arrived in America and joined the Ice Follies, I had the run of the place. They called the girls Folliettes and, to a young man from Switzerland, those Folliettes were really something! And they liked me -- I think they like my accent, which gave me a touch of the exotic, and they liked my attitude toward them. I had always been taught to respect women and to be a gentleman toward them and they liked that. (Today, of course, women claim to sneer at that and call it foolish and old-fashioned and sexist because of the Impetus of the feminist movement, but I still believe a man who behaves as a gentleman has a head start in the pursuit of women, even today.)

On an average, there were forty-five Folliettes

in each show, and over the years I estimate that there were some eight hundred girls who worked in the show while I was with it.

That is a lot of girls to have to watch, but I managed.

I often did more than just watch. It was a tough job keeping track of all those girls. I never had a little black book, or even a brown one. I kept them all in the computer bank in my mind. It took a great deal of concentration and attention to detail.

Many of them were eliminated automatically because of some failing on their part -- they could be underage (it was not unusual for a girl of seventeen to join the show) or they could be married. And there were some unfortunates who simply were not my type, but those sorry souls were, happily, a small number.

Mostly, the Folliettes were girls from good families who joined the show like other girls become airline stewardesses -- it is considered a fun life for a few youthful years until marriage, hearth, home and children beckoned. We had mostly American girls, but also many came from Canada, and a sprinkling from Europe, especially England, and Australia.

On the road, staying in hotels and being thrust into each other's company, it was a continual party.

It was intriguing to watch the romances flower -- many quickly withered, but a few became permanent. Frack, for example, began going with a lovely young Folliette named Mary Elchlepp from Minneapolis, and that ultimately led to a lasting and happy marriage.

But I was never tempted to go that route. I went with any of the girls, but always stayed out of any entangling alliances.

Still, I had my romances. Nina was one of the original Folliettes (as was Frack's Mary) and we went together, off and on, for years. I remember one night in Minneapolis when I was in bed (alone) in the old Curtis Hotel, and in the middle of the night I was awakened by an energetic pounding on my door. It was Nina.

"Frick!" she called, between knocks on my door. I opened up as quickly as I could. Nina was tall, blonde and beautiful and on this particular occasion, overwrought.

"I was at this party," she said, slamming the door behind her and collapsing into my willing arms, "and this man began chasing me and I had nowhere to come so I came here. You don't mind, do you?"

Why should I mind? I dismissed the thought -- why didn't she go to her own hotel -- and welcomed her into mine? In those days, hotels frowned officially on ladies going into gentlemen's rooms in the middle of the night, and I fully expected the house detective to visit us at any second. It had happened to me before, and the Curtis was unreasonably strict. But he didn't, so I was able to give Nina refuge. I felt good about that.

Then there was Jane, the child of very wealthy parents. She was another who would barge in on me in the middle of the night without bothering to call first. For a time, I thought it was amusing, even though I recognized the fact that Jane was what has come to be known as a flake. She had other features that made up for that.

It was an unconventional society, the Ice Follies. Nobody thought twice about a girl asking a guy, "Are you busy tonight?" and things proceeding from there. If they asked me, as they frequently did, I would say yes or no, depending on (a) if I was busy and (b) if I like the prospect of spending the evening (and possibly the night) with that particular girl. Our time schedule was backwards from most people -- we worked late at night, played later and slept in until noon generally. I needed eight hours of sleep at least for my own physical well-being, so before I could make a commitment for an evening with a girl, I had to consider whether I had any plans for the next morning. And I frequently did have some publicity assignment or business engagement for the morning, which meant I couldn't sleep late, which meant I had to get to bed reasonably early, which meant I would be forced, reluctantly, to turn the Lady down.

The idea of a free and easy society infected everybody connected with the show, even the top stars. The biggest star, the Ice Follies show ever had, had been the sensational Peggy Fleming [Olympic champion 1968 in Grenoble (France); World champion 1966 in Davos (Switzerland), 1967 in Vienna (Austria) and 1968 in Geneva (Switzerland)/ 📷42 📄113]. During one show, as she skated near me to line up for the grand finale, she whispered, "What are you doing tonight?" Fortunately, I had no plans. Furthermore, this happened the night before a free day, so Peggy and I enjoyed a night on the town in New York. All very innocent because Peggy was then as now married to Dr. Craig Jenkins and worked at being Mrs. Jenkins.

Among other features of that night with Peggy was a party she took me to. I remember few details, but one sticks in my memory. The mayor of New York -- Edward Koch -- was one of the guests. It was pleasant to talk to him, particularly since he recognized me and said that he enjoyed watching me perform.

Later, Peggy and I went to Trader Vic's and Peggy, with a wicked gleam in her pretty eyes, suggested that perhaps I should open a restaurant if I ever decided to retire.

"I have the perfect name for your restaurant," she said. "You could call it Trader Frick's."

"Ok," I said, "I'll get rid of my Fleming (the stock) to pay for it."

Our Folliettes, like the chorus girls of Broadway shows in years past, had Stage Door Johnnies waiting for them wherever we played. Men -- usually wealthy ones -- waited inside the stage door with flowers and/or candy at the ready and limousines to take the girl of their choice out to a late supper and who know what else? One of the most popular Folliettes for quite a few years was a beauty named Elsie Bronson. I dated Elsie often myself and, because she knew gentlemen in many cities, I got to know some of them, too. Elsie and her roommate, Ricky Polin, were two of the original swingers. For one exciting season, there was a number in the show in which the girls would each have a carnation and at a certain point, skate up to the edge of the rink and pin their carnation on a gentleman in the first or second row. Elsie and Ricky made a big thing out of that opportunity. They often picked out specific targets and wrote little notes -- "I'll be waiting for you after the show" -- and put them around the stems of their carnations. Elsie eventually married W.R. Stevens, who may have been the biggest Buick dealer of all.

So, I skated through my youth, my prime years, and on almost to the far side of maturity. I had a lovely time, with so many fine specimens of femininity at hand. The idea of marriage had never entered my mind. I suppose I was like the boy whose father owned the candy store. Why should he buy candy? And why should I think of marriage with so many charming, beautiful girls so handy?

Once, in 1950, I slipped on a beer puddle during an after-show party, and broke my elbow. (I used to joke that I had been injured more on the dance floor than on the ice rink.) My arm was in a sling so I couldn't perform. One of the Folliettes accompanied me on a dash to Paris and back during the period I was out of action. That was the way it went; if you felt lonely, you only had to look around you and smile and, presto, your loneliness was remedied. The supply of girls was, it seemed, inexhaustible, ever-changing and, by and large, remarkably willing. So, I continued to indulge myself and the years slipped by.

I was thirty-eight when our train, bound from Syracuse to Milwaukee, stopped in the railroad yards of Chicago for reasons only known to the locomotive conductor and his friends. A few of us jumped off there, knowing we could have the night in Chicago, which was a more promising prospect than a night in Milwaukee. We would have to make our own way to Milwaukee in time for the opening there the next night, but that was no problem. We always enjoyed the surprises that our travelling brought us from time to time, and that extra night in Chicago was in that category.

I remember we learned that our competition, the Ice Capades, was playing at the Chicago Arena, so a few of us went to catch that show. And then Fran Claudet -- she was skating director of our show -- and I went shopping. Roy Shipstad's birthday was coming up and we felt that this was a good chance to buy him a nice gift.

I suggested we go to a shop I remembered from previous visits. It was a Swiss shop in the Bismarck Hotel. In fact, I told Fran I knew the manager of the shop, a lovely Swiss lady named Sylvia. So, Fran and I went to the Swiss Shop, but when we got there, there was no Sylvia. Instead, we were greeted by a pretty blonde girl.

"Where's Sylvia?" I asked her while Fran began looking at the merchandise.

"She left," the blonde said. "I'm the new manager."

I wasn't much help with Fran's selection process. I too busy talking to the new manager. Fran finally settled on a wood carving a top-hatted man leaning against a lamppost whistling, "Show me the way to go home." We both felt that was appropriate, since we had frequently had to show Roy the way to go home in the past. So, the blonde wrapped it up -- cost $80; I remember a lot of details about that day's events -- and I noticed that she wrapped very adroitly and gracefully.

"You go along," I said to Fran. "I think I'll look around here a while longer."

Fran was no dummy. She knew what was up. She left quietly. And then I zeroed in on the blonde and gave her my best Swiss-skating-star smile, it semi-worked. At least she told me her name -- Yvonne -- and gave me a brief history of herself -- she had come over from Switzerland a few months before, had worked at a shop in New York before accepting the Chicago job offer. But she emphatically turned down my offer to take her out to lunch.

"I cannot, "she said, "I have a lunch hour at one o'clock and I cannot go out to lunch prior to that time. We close from one until two and it would be unfair to our customers if I went out before that time."

There was nothing for me to do except wait until one, which I did, impatiently. Then I wanted to show her I was the last of the big spenders and started to lead her to an expensive restaurant for an expensive steak and an expensive bottle of wine.

"I cannot," she said. I soon learned that "I cannot" was a major part of her vocabulary. "All I ever eat for lunch is a sandwich. If I ate a large lunch I would not be able to work very efficiently this afternoon."

There was again nothing I could do except buy her a sandwich. I urged her to sneak an extra half-hour or so; "we could go for a walk or something" I suggested.

"I cannot," she said. "I must be back in the shop no later than two o'clock precisely. The customers expect the shop to be open at two o'clock precisely, and it is my responsibility to see that it is open at that time."

"Precisely," I said.

"Exactly," she said.

But I had seen enough of Yvonne in that one hour and one sandwich to know that I wanted to see more. Our next stop with the show was Milwaukee and, fortunately, that is not a long distance from Chicago. (It might be a long distance in Switzerland, but it is just a hop, skip and skate in America.) So, I invited Yvonne to come up and see the show while we were in Milwaukee. I suggested that the next Saturday would be nice.

"I cannot," she said in that now familiar cadence. "I must work Saturday. However, I do get a day off on Monday, and I will be pleased to come to Milwaukee on next Monday."

"Monday, it is," I said.

I met her at the trolley station in Milwaukee on Monday and came very close to blowing the whole romance the first moment I saw her. She got off the trolley looking lovely, but with a scarf wrapped around her head to protect her hair from the wintery Wisconsin winds.

"You look like a market woman," I said, which, on reflection, I realize was not the most tactful or complimentary thing I could have said. I could see her' withdraw a bit and resolved that from that moment on I would be very careful what I said to her. I was used to the girls in the show who gave back as good as they got in the repartee department. Yvonne, I quickly understood, was a different kettle of woman.

I think, in the excitement of our first date, I had rashly suggested that perhaps she could join the show. Could she skate? Yes, she said, she could skate reasonably well. Do you have skates? Yes, she said, she did own a pair of skates. Bring them along with you when you come to Milwaukee, I had said, with something of the attitude of the spider as he seduced the fly. I said I could arrange an audition for her.

"Then you can join the show," I had said, "and become a Folliette and we can have a lot of fun together."

So, she showed up in Milwaukee, scarf around her head and skates clutched in her hand. However, I decided that she was too nice to become a Folliette -- or, I suppose my reasoning was really that I had discovered this pearl and I wasn't about to cast her before those swine who vied with me for the favors of all the girls. This one I was going to keep to myself.

"Sorry you went to all the trouble of bringing your skates," I said, "but there are no auditions this week. The director of new acquisitions has gone to Poland to look at some Polish girls."

Fortunately for me, Yvonne was not especially keen on joining the ice show; she had only brought her skates along, she later said, to please me.

We had a lovely day, but not a lovely night. I asked her to stay but was not at all surprised to hear her say, "I cannot." She had to be back in Chicago in time to open the store the next morning at nine o'clock.

"Precisely" I asked?

"Exactly," she said.

But I was firmly hooked. We moved on from Milwaukee to Minneapolis and I asked her to come and visit me there. She said she would and she flew to Minneapolis. As luck would have it, she arrived on a Saturday and we had three shows that day so it was impossible for me to meet her at the airport.

"I cannot," I told her over the phone, with a perverse joy at being able to use her own words.

"No matter," she said. "I will therefore take a taxicab to the arena."

I was on the ice when I saw her come in. Blonde hair over an elegant black dress, walking purposefully down the aisle to the seat I had had held for her. I couldn't miss her. I think I knew I was in love at that precise, exact moment.

"Where did Frick find that beauty?" I heard them all whispering. There are no secrets in a show as close-knit as the Ice Follies. Everybody knew I had a new discovery and they had all been waiting to inspect her. I knew immediately that Yvonne had passed with flying colors -- blonde and black.

She came to my hotel room after the show. I hadn't expected that she would, so I had had no chance to hide some of the evidence of my ill-spent years -- notably the beer bottles (some full, more empty) that littered the room. I had gotten into some bad habits of late, primarily the conspicuous consumption of beer. As a result, my weight had exploded, up to a bit over two hundred pounds, about twenty-five pounds too much for my height and the size of my frame. It hadn't affected my performance but I knew I was looking a trifle on the pudgy side.

But the quantity of beer bottles was awesome to Yvonne.

"You shouldn't drink all that beer," she said, picking up an empty bottle with obvious disgust and tossing it into the waste basket where it clunked and rolled around.

"I know," I said.

It was the beginning of the end for me. I suppose every man likes to have somebody take care of him, mother him. And Yvonne seemed perfectly cast in that role. For all those years that I had been touring, nobody had really cared about me. Oh, I know people liked me and certainly Frack cared about me in a professional way, and I know there had been girls who fancied themselves in love with me, but there had been no one person who was always on my side, come what may. That is what a wife is, that is what love is, the feeling that you are no longer alone, but are part of a two-person team.

I was thirty-eight years old [1953] and I didn't realize how much I wanted to become part of such a team until Yvonne came along.

She was fun to be around. Conversation came easy with her, and that is also a part of that magical commodity, love. We sat up late that night in my Minneapolis hotel room, just talking, exchanging confidences, trading dreams.

She told me her trouble with the English language. Like all Swiss, she had studied it in school and spoke it remarkable well, but there were still some words that caused her problems. She told me the story of a date she had had long before with a man in Chicago. She had a room in the Allerton Hotel and her date came for her and called her from the lobby.

"I will be down in a few minutes," Yvonne had told him. "I am just now finishing my douche."

When she got to the lobby, she found her date looking at her very oddly. She asked him what was wrong.

"It's you Swiss girls," he said. "You and I have gone out for dinner a few times and you keep telling me that I cannot come to your room. And now you tell me you are finishing your douche, so obviously, you have been intimate with some other guy."

The trouble, of course, was that word, "douche." In Switzerland that simply means a shower, nothing to do with its American meaning. Poor Yvonne blushed in a pretty pink when she learned what her date had thought she had meant.

It was during that Minneapolis engagement, incidentally, that my American citizenship came through. And on a Saturday matinee, George Hackett, the show's orchestra leader, surprised me by playing the National Anthem and arranged for the spotlight to be on me while it was played. I was very proud of having become an American citizen and I felt a chill down my spine as I stood in that particular spotlight while the audience cheered for me, the newest American in the land.

We had a break after that week in Minneapolis. I had been planning a trip to Switzerland with our stage manager, Bert Lundblad, and his wife, Isabel. But I wanted to see Yvonne again. So, I compromised and managed to push the Switzerland trip back a few days, and squeezed in two glorious days with Yvonne in Chicago. And when I left, I promised her that I would see her again as soon as I got back [43 114].

One of my reasons for going to Switzerland was that I had been invited to speak at a regular meeting of the Swiss Friends of the United States. I had long before joined that group and attended as many meetings as I could. This one was to be in my honor at the Hotel Elite in Zurich. We were having cocktails before the meeting when I saw my name on the bellboy's bulletin board. I was being paged, as it turned out, by Yvonne's sister, Cécile, and her husband, Ernst.

We arranged to meet after the luncheon. I felt as though I had been given the once-over by the girl's family and, in point of fact, that was exactly what was happening. Yvonne had written to Cécile and told her about me and Cécile, representing the entire Baumgartner family, was there on an inspection trip.

Cécile told me something I didn't know. Yvonne had been engaged to marry a respected Zurich attorney. This young man was a good friend of Yvonne's father and, consequently, it was a marriage that had approval in high family places. Now here was this upstart, this ice clown, this rather elderly man of thirty-eight, upsetting the romantic apple cart. Cécile was polite, but cool, and later Yvonne told me that her report had been terse.

She had said that I seemed like a decent sort of person but I was a little on the fat side.

I have never been quite sure what made Yvonne decide on me rather than her finance, the attorney. I like to think it was my scintillating personality, wit, good looks and masculine magnetism. But it also might have been that the prospect of going back to Zurich and spending the rest of her days (and nights) as the wife of a stuffy, plodding attorney did not appeal to her. There is a little bit of the adventurer in most women's souls, and that spark was certainly present in Yvonne's.

At any event, when I got back to the U.S. and rejoined the show in Seattle, I kept calling Yvonne every day. And I found, to my joy, that she was responsive to my romantic overtures. In fact, I convinced her -- and it didn't take too much convincing -- to quit her job in Chicago. I mailed her a train ticket and she boarded a train bound for Seattle.

While she was en route, it suddenly dawned on me that I had acted like a typical Swiss, watching every franc. I had sent her, my intended, a coach ticket. How cheap can a man be? Here I was, trying to woo this fair maiden and I was making her ride the coach halfway across the North American continent.

I tried to make amends. I contacted the railroad people and paid them extra and they made the arrangements so that Yvonne was moved into a Pullman car. The switch, she later told me, was made somewhere in Montana, so she had one good night's sleep in a lower berth. When she arrived in Seattle she looked rested and she was obviously very happy to see me. She said the scenery on the trip had been breath-taking and I felt pleased, as though I personally had landscaped North America just for her personal pleasure.

I got Yvonne a room on the same floor as I was staying at the Olympic Hotel. I remember this was 1954, long before it was deemed proper for unmarried people to share a room. So, I had my room and she had her room, and the proprieties were observed.

It was obvious to me that Yvonne was the

kind of girl who fit in well with the crazy life style of a performer. Some women adjust to that kind of life easily, while others find it difficult and occasionally impossible. But Yvonne liked it, and the people in the show liked her. She has always had the marvelous gift of making friends easily and keeping them for many years.

Bert Lundblad invited Yvonne and me to drive from Seattle to our next stop, San Francisco, with him in his new Cadillac convertible. We accepted with pleasure. Yvonne volunteered to make some sandwiches for our first day on the road, so she bought some cheese and kept it in a plastic container which she carefully placed on the window still so the cheese would stay cool. But she reckoned without the persistence of the Seattle sea gulls. One of them zeroed in on the cheese and with his sharp bill, managed to make a hole in the plastic container and flew away with our cheese. So, we stopped at a restaurant along the way for our lunch that first day. It made a great story, however, and Yvonne told it often over the years when she recounted her problems adjusting to American life.

Our first night on the road was spent at Shasta Springs a beautiful resort. It was during the height of the tourist season and all we could find were two rooms -- and one had to be for Lundblad. I told Yvonne that I had tried to find a separate room for her -- and, truly, I had tried -- but without success. She would have to share mine. It was not too uncomfortable.

We always stayed in San Francisco for quite a while, so we all had acquired places where we felt comfortable and at home. For me, that was the Canterbury Hotel. I always had a certain room there, and this time I got Yvonne a nice, airy, corner room with a lovely view of San Francisco Bay. She immediately set out to look for a job so she could pay her own way. I told her that wasn't necessary. I said she would be very useful to me, and she was.

In the past, Frack and I had always tried out our new material during that San Francisco engagement. Now that I was by myself -- Yvonne never did see Frick and Frack skate together -- I still had to try out new material. Now I found that Yvonne was a marvelous judge of what was good and what wasn't. She had a gift for knowing what the public would like. It was an instinctive thing, and she had it. That first year, for example, coincided with the beginnings of rock-and-roll, a type of music that left me ice cold. But Yvonne felt -- correctly, as it turned out -- that rock-and-roll was here to stay and urged me to do a number to a rock tune. I did -- the first ice act, as far as I know, to do so -- and it became one of my most popular numbers that year.

We had three months in San Francisco together and they were marvelous. One incident marred our time there, however. It involved Yvonne's health and, while it had no real connection to the serious health problems which were to follow, it was a portent of things to come.

Yvonne seemed to radiate good health. She always had the rosy cheeks one associates with physical well-being a happy smile and her blue eyes were clear and bright. We were unaware of the insidious developments which were apparently going on inside her seemingly strong body.

One evening after a performance, we were to join Claire Hoffman for an evening of dancing. We had agreed to meet at the Claremont Hotel, behind Berkeley, and as we waited, we were a bit nervous -- after all, Claire was the daughter of the legendary A.P. Giannini, the founder of the Bank of America, and was herself a director of the bank and also a director of Sears Roebuck -- so we had a couple of martinis for the sake of our frazzled nerves. When Claire and her escort, whom she introduced as "Count Mario," arrived, we had more, followed by dinner and dancing. It was a rich and heady evening for us.

The next day, Yvonne developed severe pains in her abdomen. We saw a doctor who said it was a gall bladder condition and urged surgery. She kept going, however, and we had another month in San Francisco and then we moved on.

We moved on to Los Angeles. I enjoyed showing Yvonne the glories of Southern California, and she particularly liked Beverly Hills. This was long before Rodeo Drive zoomed into retailing prominence, but even then, there were some lovely shops in Beverly Hills. And that year we had our post-premiere party at the Beverly Hills Hotel, with many celebrities on hand, and my Yvonne was wide-eyed as she stared at all those faces she had only previously seen on the screen.

In fact, a couple of the stars asked her to dance -- she bad studied ballet and moved with exceptional grace -- and she was thrilled by all the attention.

Yvonne was accommodating herself to my life, my routine. She was much more flexible and adaptable than I was. Perhaps it was her nature, perhaps it was her youth. I realize now that I was the proverbial old bear who was set in his ways and I demanded -- not in words so much as in my attitude -- that she does the changing and the accommodating, not me. Of course, in my own defense, I did change some, too, but the changes on my part were considerably slower and more gradual. Yvonne, on the other hand, changed virtually overnight and became the perfect companion to a travelling ice skater. There is no way a girl can train for such an assignment; you either adapt or you don't, and Yvonne adapted.

But she also insisted on some changes in my way of life. Gone were the beer bottles all over the room and, to a large extent, gone too was the beer itself. She thought, she said, that it would be good for my appearance as well as my overall health if I lost some weight, and the beer was the chief culprit of my less-than-sylphlike silhouette.

The next change came when one day I went to my closet get out one of my favorite old suits to wear. It wasn't there.

"Oh, Frick," Yvonne said, I threw that old suit out. It didn't flatter you. We'll get you some new ones some suits that make you look younger."

She also began to look after my professional life, too. Soon after we met, she realized I was going through a difficult time because of being on my own following Frack's abrupt departure. I would begin skating with a new partner and then he would leave. Having to adjust to a new partner frequently was hard on me.

I realized that every partner was probably only a temporary partner, but I would still have to train him as though he were permanent. It was a frustrating experience, and I came to rely more and more on Yvonne's sympathetic understanding of the situation. With her urging me, I would do my best to bring out the talents each person possessed adjust my routine to take advantage of that particular talent.

Around 1974, for example, I picked a skater named Dave Thomas to be my new partner. This went against the recommendations of the production staff, because Dave was taller than any partner I had ever had and people said it wouldn't work. But Yvonne liked him and his attitude, and so did I. I knew he had certain important qualities -- he was reliable, he was consistent, he was intelligent. We worked together backstage using even small pieces of dirty, rutty ice, and so when Bob Shipstad saw us rehearsing on the big ice he said, "The guy is terrific!" He was so enthusiastic, in fact, that he jumped over the bang boards and rushed over to both of us and shook our hands. Today, incidentally, Dave Thomas is company manager of the Disney on Ice Show, the direct descendant of the Ice Follies.

Yvonne had become so valuable to me -- and therefore, I thought, to the Show itself -- that when we were about to leave Los Angeles, I went to the company manager and asked him to assign a berth on the train to Yvonne.

"Is she Mrs. Frick?" he asked. I had to say that, no, she was not Mrs. Frick.

"Sorry, then, Company policy. Only wives can ride on the Follies train."

"I'll pay for her."

"Doesn't matter," he said. "No wife, no go."

Since she couldn't go with us, I determined to give her the most pleasant trip I could arrange. I booked her on the Santa Fe and they had a deal whereby some of the sleepers -- hers included -- were shunted off the main line from Flagstaff, Arizona, for a side trip where the passengers could view the Grand Canyon. Then, twenty-four hours later, they would be hooked on to the next eastbound Santa Fe train.

The sky was a brilliant blue. Suddenly I was overwhelmed with romance of it all -- glorious view, clear and crisp and invigorating weather, a girl I loved by my side. I knew then with clarity to match the clear air that I had to marry this girl.

And so, I proposed. Maybe it was the altitude that weakened her -- I know the altitude weakened her voice -- but she whispered a faint but firm, "Yes."

"I love you," I said. "By the way, I forgot to tell you that the cog railway cars are made in

Switzerland -- you know the Swiss Locomotive works in Winterthur? -- and you want to know something else very interesting?"

"Tell me," she said.

"The name of the man in charge of the cog railway for the Broadmoor is Frick. That's his real name."

"How romantic," she said.

We decided to keep our engagement a secret for the moment, but it must have been apparent in our faces. We were having dinner at the Brown Palace Hotel, either that night or the next, and the waiter brought us a note from Thayer Tutt. Tutt is a legend among skaters; not only is he a wealthy man (head of the Broadmoor Company, a hotel conglomerate, and a director of many large corporations), but he is a benefactor of skaters and skating events. He happened to be in the dining room of the Brown Palace that night.

His note said that whenever we decided to "tie the knot," as he put it, he wanted us to be his guest at the hotel for a week.

Our next stop was Chicago. I decided to join Yvonne on the regular train for the Denver-Chicago trip and we had a lovely journey on the Santa Fe Superchief. We were met in Chicago by Gerry Graham, a good friend who was one of the top-seeded stage door Johnnies and a noted Chicago patron of the arts. We told Gerry that we were engaged (so much for that secret) and he promptly invited us to dine with him at his Club, the Tavern. I don't know if he spilled our beans, but suddenly the world seemed to know about us.

In fact, on the bulletin board backstage there was the announcement in bold letters, FRICK IST VERLOBT (Frick is engaged), so now everybody knew our secret.

I ran out and bought a diamond ring -- wholesale of course -- from a jeweler friend. 'I presented it to Yvonne evening and she proudly showed it to everyone in the company.

"When are you getting married?" they all wanted to know, but we could not tell them. We weren't sure first if we wanted to get married in Switzerland with our families present, or if we wanted to get married (as the Ice Follies publicity people urged) in center ice during intermission, or just have a simple wedding somewhere with only a few close friends in attendance. And so, we simply postponed making definite plans.

But the company manager ruled that since we were now engaged and Yvonne would soon be Mrs. Frick, she could travel with me on the Ice Follies train. That solved a lot of problems.

We had fun in Chicago with one of Yvonne's old friends a Swiss named Fred, who was a taxicab driver. She had met soon after she landed in Chicago when, with a couple of other Swiss girls, she had hailed a cab and the three girls had begun talking among themselves in their Swiss language.

(Is there a Swiss national language? Technically, no; the Swiss speak French and Italian and Romansh in certain areas -- Yvonne came from Neuchâtel where the French they speak is as good as Parisian French -- and Swiss German, or Schwyzerdütsch in other areas. But Schwyzerdütsch, while rooted in German, differs from German in many ways. In fact, Swiss who speak it still have to go to school to learn how speak real, or High German. And most Germans cannot follow conversation in Schwyzerdütsch. Curiously, the Dutch spoken in Pennsylvania by the Pennsylvania Dutch is closer to Schwyzerdütsch than it is to the Dutch language itself.)

As the cab drove along, the three girls were having fun talking about the cab driver, criticizing his driving and admiring his good looks, confident that he was not able to understand a word they were saying. But then he suddenly pulled over and stopped.

They were amazed when he said to them in Swiss, "If you don't like the way I am driving, you can get out and walk.

Then he laughed and said, "But I will take you anywhere you want to go, for free, if you sing me a Swiss song."

So, they did, and he did, and Yvonne had made a friend. Fred, the cabbie, became my friend, too, or really our mutual friend. From then on, whenever we were in Chicago, he was our driver. In exchange for a chance to talk Swiss and to talk about the old country, he would shut his meter off and Chauffeur us around wherever we wanted to go. Once he drove us to the race track, where Yvonne won the daily double -- $270. He was, when we got to know him, also a serious student of the stock market. That was a field that had become increasingly important in my life, so we would have long and serious discussions on economics and market tactics, and I learned a lot from Fred. I think he learned from me as well.

The pains inside Yvonne's abdomen had grown increasingly severe and, after consulting several doctors, she realized that surgery was the only answer. She didn't want to be operated on anywhere but Switzerland, however, so she flew back to Zurich from Cincinnati. And she had what would turn out to be the first of many operations back in Zurich. This time, she had her gall bladder removed.

As soon as I could, I joined her in Switzerland. It was a chance for her to meet my family and vice versa. My family had just about given up on me getting married. They had become reconciled to the fact that I was bound to be a lifelong bachelor. I was thirty-nine by now and so they were delight with the news that I was, at last, going to become a husband.

I was due back in Philadelphia to rejoin the show the day after Christmas. We left Zurich on Christmas Eve, flew Paris, and then boarded a TWA Constellation [44 115] -- a propeller driven plane, of course, since this was some years before jets -- on Christmas morning. We were schedule to arrive in New York in plenty of time to take a train to Philadelphia and be there for the opening. But there were terrible headwinds that day and our plane fell further and further behind schedule.

Not many people were flying on Christmas, so I got to talk to the captain and explained my plight. He said he was going to Philadelphia himself, by happy coincidence, and volunteered to drive us from New York right to the arena. He was as good as his word, but travel was much slower then -- no New Jersey Turnpike yet, only conventional roads that led from town to town, from red light to red light -- and besides, there were intermittent storms and snow squalls. But I arrived at the arena a bare five minutes before show time. The pilot took Yvonne on to the hotel while I dashed in and got ready to do my act. Between the jet lag and the fact that I had been travelling well over twenty-four hours straight, I was absolutely exhausted, but I went on and did my show. I doubt it was one of my better performances.

As the New Year approached, I suddenly realized that it was to my advantage, from a tax standpoint, if I got married before January 1 dawned, the Swiss philosophy at work, of course. So, I began thinking about when and where to get married in the few days left in 1954.

I asked Senator Hubert Humphrey to find out for me what state did not require a blood test for a marriage license. Now that Yvonne and I had decided to go ahead and do the dire, drastic deed, time was of the essence. Humphrey's Secretary said Maryland was our best bet. And so, one day we took the train from Philadelphia to Washington, and it was Humphrey's secretary who told us to go to Rockville, Maryland, and get our license. She gave us all the details and we followed her instructions and got that vital document. We went back to Philadelphia then, but two days later we were back and, in a little church in Rockville, Yvonne became Mrs. Groebli -- or, as most people called her, Mrs. Frick -- on December 30, 1954.

Just in time to give me that very important income split.

Curiously, even though economics had been one reason why we picked our wedding date, it never occurred to either of us that we could also achieve an economic advantage by moving into one room in our Philadelphia hotel, probably a little vestigial trace of my bachelor life hanging on. After the wedding, we sent telegrams to our families in Switzerland, informing them of that fateful event. Then we took the train back to Philadelphia. Our wedding dinner was on the train. Our wedding night was spent with me out on the ice and Yvonne watching. And then, for some reason, while we slept together in my room at the hotel, Yvonne kept her room and most of her things were still in that room.

It was the room clerk who suggested that we weren't being too smart. Why pay for two rooms, he wondered, when you are legally married and one room is cheaper than two? That appealed to me, so Yvonne gave up her room and crammed her things -- of which she had a large quantity -- into my closets -- of which I had a distinct scarcity.

I think that if I had any lingering doubts that

Yvonne was the right woman for me, they vanished a few days after we were married. (One always has doubts; the trick is to cause them to vanish as soon as possible.)

I was going over my books in our hotel room and discovered that because of my new status as a married man, I could now take advantage of the tax provision enabling married people to split their incomes. The result would be a considerable savings to me -- to us.

"Yvonne," I said. "We can save enough doing it this way so I can buy you a nice fur coat. How would you like that?"

"Thank you, Frick," she said. "But I'd rather have a few shares of Texas Instruments or IBM."

As things have turned out, her investments in Texas Instruments and IBM, over the years, could have purchased several fur coats for her. IBM's shares, since we began accumulating them, have split as often as my costume pants -- which were made to split.

So, I knew that Yvonne was the wife for me. We have stuck together ever since, through thick and thin, and there have been lots of thin. There has been her health, which has never been what you could call first rate, not since that first gall bladder problem. She has been through Hell and back.

There has also been the thin of my career. The back-biting and jealousies that we have both endured have often been hellish, too. Yvonne has always taken my career as seriously as though it were her own. When I perform, she paces back and forth at the rear of the auditorium, nervously biting her lips. She is a marvelous coach and critic, telling me later where I deviated from my usual performance, where I neglected to project, where I forgot to smile or perhaps smiled too long or too broadly. All this has been of tremendous help to me, and I give her much of the credit for my longevity in the public's good graces.

As soon as my act was over, she would run from the rear of the arena, her pacing station, to the backstage area. Some of those arenas we played in were huge and her run was a lengthy one. She always greeted me, however, as I came off the ice with a kiss and a critique. I welcomed both with equal fervor.

When I finished my act, I was often not very tactful. In the flush of excitement following a performance, I could very harsh on someone who had done something wrong a miss cue or whatever. And Yvonne was always there as a buffer zone between me and the object of my displeasure.

I think I may have picked that up from Sonja Henie. She was a nitpicker of the highest order and she would yell at any offender in no uncertain cusswords. Then, if she was called back for a curtain call, she was able in a twinkling to stop her yelling, put on her best dimpled smile, go out and take her bow. Then, when the Spotlight left her, she would resume her berating of that offender without missing a beat.

I was, I believe, considerably less harsh, but still I could be difficult on someone I felt was being less than perfect, and Yvonne was always there to smooth any ruffled feelings.

But increasingly, she was not there. Beginning less than a year after our marriage, her health problems increased alarmingly. There was a recurring tumor, and over the next fifteen years she had to undergo major surgery five times. Often the prognosis was not good. I was told twice that she was "near death," and she will never forget lying in the recovery room following one of her operations and overhearing a nurse say, "Poor thing -- she isn't going to make it." But she fought valiantly and she clung to life with a tenacity that amazed me and her doctors and everybody who knew about her condition. She has the strength and determination of a dozen women and she fought for life time and time again. And always, she was the victor.

Once an American expert examined her, his advice, which he gave me privately, was that I should let her go home to Switzerland where she could die peacefully.

Another time a Swiss surgeon -- the man who performed most of the operations on her, the noted <u>Professor</u> Ruedi -- told me point blank, "Your wife only has a few more years to live." That was more than twenty years ago.

So, she fought, and I fought beside her. I kept those dire predictions to myself. It was hard on me, keeping those secrets and smiling, but it was harder on her because she hurt and she was the one facing the knife, and she was the one who had to live with the scars and the traumas.

I frequently thought, through those terrible years, that she might be better off and stand a better chance of a full recovery if we lived a less frantic life. I often volunteer to give up my skating -- I knew there were other things I could do, other ways I could earn a living -- so we could have a normal home and she would not be subjected to the constant moving and travelling and the erratic hotel life that was our lot.

She wouldn't hear of it. She knew I loved performing and no matter how much I said I wouldn't miss it, she knew I was lying. So, for my sake, she insisted I stay on with the show. (I also think she came to enjoy life on the road, too and began thinking of the Follies people as her extended family.) The least I could do -- which I did -- was to make sure that we always had the finest hotel accommodations available and that we always ate only the best and healthiest foods. We travelled with our own big vegetable- and fruit-juicer and made healthy juices in our room to augment our hotel dining room diets. We would rearrange the furniture to increase the sitting area -- our attempt to create a suite for ourselves. Today, suites are the in-thing in hotels; we pioneered that.

But wherever we went, it seemed we were in and out of doctors' offices and clinics and hospitals. The Cleveland Clinic, where they could not find the cause of Yvonne's constant pain. The Stanford University Hospital, where they probed deeply and painfully with a needle, then casually dismissed the problem as being nothing serious or important, a Los Angeles hospital, where a noted Beverly Hills specialist removed a tumor from behind Yvonne's ear. He said it was non-malignant, but added that for some reason, he hadn't been able to get all of it. I think if he had done a complete job at that time, she would have been spared other major operations later.

And time and time again, the University Hospital in Zurich, where Professor Ruedi operated on her so frequently and with such kind attention. I was at her bedside as often as possible, until she would urge me to go back to the show, and Ruedi would say that he felt I could safely return to the United States.

As soon as she could, she would fly back to wherever the show was playing and join me, and I would be so relieved to see her familiar figure at the rear of the arena, pacing back and forth as I did my six-minute turn.

Usually, Yvonne liked to go home to Switzerland for a few weeks in the winter. She and her sister, Cécile, and Cécile's husband, Ernst, would spend some time in Gstaad at the Palace Hotel. Ernst died in 1979 and thereafter it would be just the two sisters. I would have loved to join her, but of course, winter was our prime season with the show.

After each operation, we would cross our fingers, hoping that this was the last one she would need she always looked so well, so beautiful, so healthy. But always, the pains would begin again. Once, Professor Ruedi called me at Cécile's villa to tell that this current operation had gone well, but that he had found it necessary to sever the carotid artery -- the blood vessel that supplies blood to half the brain. That left her with some permanent physical damage, but never daunted a fraction of an inch of her magnificent spirit.

One year -- it is difficult to distinguish one year from another, but I believe this was 1956 -- we were in Chicago when the pains began, very severe this time. She underwent four days of testing in a Chicago hospital and the results were sent to Ruedi in Zurich. He confirmed the Chicago specialist's diagnosis that she needed more veins replaced he advised that American hospitals were better equipped for that procedure than were the Swiss hospitals.

We searched out specialists all over. In Cincinnati, encountered a German-born doctor recommended by the Swiss consul. I knew him; he frequented our show, wolfing down hot dogs as he watched. He had treated the deposed German Kaiser in his exile and he had once told me that seeing our show was "like going to church." He also said that if Hitler had ever seen our show and how efficiently American workmen tore down the show after the last performance, he never would have risked war against America. But he wasn't much help to Yvonne.

In Boston, we found a doctor who recommended that Yvonne take aspirin, would that it could have been that simple.

Eventually, we found tumor specialist Dr. Grantley Taylor and cancer specialist Dr. John Raker, who had been a close friend. They could see that Yvonne was very nervous and upset and felt she would be better off in Switzerland because of the confidence she obviously had in her friend and physician, Professor Ruedi. Meanwhile, Ruedi had located a Swiss surgeon, a Dr. Dimza, who was skilled at the kind of vascular surgery she needed.

So, she flew back to Zurich. I was unable to accompany her that time because I simply could not get away from the show. When I finally got away, I immediately flew to Zurich and literally ran to the hospital. Ruedi had performed some exploratory surgery and he and Dimza had determined that the vascular surgery could be postponed. A few days later, however, Yvonne developed an embolism of the lung. That took a few painful weeks to clear up and then there was more surgery and another long and nervous wait for me on the hard wooden benches outside the operating room at University Hospital.

As they had taken her into surgery, I had held her while she lay quietly on the gurney, and she had whispered to me, "Mutz, if I don't open my eyes any more, take care." It was as though she were saying good-bye. And it came very close to being just that.

This time, she was on the operating table for nine hours. The tumor had been found to extend well into her chest region, and another surgeon who specialized in that area had been called in to complete the work. The anesthetist told me that in all his years, he had not seen an operation of that magnitude. But a dozen years later, Yvonne would undergo a worse one.

She was in critical condition for many days, lying there under that grim plastic tent. I could do nothing except be there by her side. And I was there until I was told to leave for the good of myself and Yvonne and the hospital staff.

In a month, she had recovered sufficiently so she urged me to go back to the show.

"Don't feel guilty about leaving me," she said. "Go back to the show and I will join you as soon as I can, and then we will have a marvelous time together and enjoy all those beautiful things in life we used to enjoy."

So, I went back. And year after year, we would go through the same thing, in varying degrees. Year after year, I would suggest that I quit, and year after year, she wouldn't hear of it.

I often put out feelers to certain large corporations, both in America and in Switzerland, and felt that I would have no trouble finding a good job in some minor executive capacity. Besides, my investments were doing well even though medical expenses were constantly depleting them. Nevertheless, I knew we could have survived, but Yvonne always shook her head and said no.

"You belong in the show," she would say, and so I would sign on with the show for another year. But always I signed only for one year at a time. I wanted to keep that option open so I could leave if Yvonne changed her mind, or the condition of her health made my leaving the show an absolute necessity.

In 1969, we spent a pre-Christmas vacation week on the beaches of Barbados in the Caribbean. We both had physical problems at the time -- I had a bad knee, the result of a fall, and Yvonne was having problems with her breathing. She could move only very slowly as a result. We flew back after that difficult vacation, rejoining the show in Philadelphia on Christmas Eve.

We had one of our typical on-the-road Christmases -- we even had a six-foot-tall tree which had been cut by our friends, Walter and Irene Muhlbronner, and their children in the Pennsylvania hills. The ornaments for the tree had been brought by another old friend, Joe Maxwell, a member of Philadelphia's skating elite, and his attractive wife, Zell. They had taken our dog, Lulu, for the duration of our Caribbean holiday so we could relax and have an old-fashioned Christmas. All of us on the show, as usual, exchanged Christmas presents, and most of us had our holiday dinner in the hotel restaurant.

We were used to that kind of Christmas and yet, each year, there would be a slight twinge of nostalgia as we recalled Christmases past, Christmases back home with our families, Christmases of our youth.

That year we strung up our Christmas cards in our two adjoining hotel rooms and Yvonne and I decorated our tree -- in a record twenty minutes -- even though she was having trouble breathing.

But the festive feeling was short lived. Soon we had to take it all down. Yvonne's breathing problems grew increasingly more severe, and I was having difficulty with my knee. For one of the few times in my career, I was forced to cancel my appearance in the show. I was back the next night, feeling guilty for having missed one performance, but it had been impossible for me to go on.

As for Yvonne, we knew that something serious was wrong. We went to Bryn Mawr Hospital for the first step -- X-ray of her chest. We were thrilled when the next morning, the doctor called to say that all was well, the chest X-rays had showed nothing amiss. We laughed and hugged each other. The relief was so vivid we could touch it.

Then the phone rang. It was the doctor again. He was hesitant and I knew he had bad news for us.

"I hate to say this," he said, "but there has been a mix-up with the X-rays. Sorry, but Mrs. Groebli's X-rays clearly show a tumor in the chest area. I strongly recommend surgery. Shall I schedule her for tomorrow?"

"No," I said. "She will be going home to Switzerland for the Operation." I took down the Christmas tree then and all the decorations. They didn't seem appropriate any more. Then I rented a car and we drove to Kennedy Airport in New York in a near-blizzard and went to Swissair and boarded the next flight to Zurich. The Swissair people, as usual, were solicitous and kind; they made three seats available for Yvonne so she could stretch out for the long flight. But she was having a great deal of trouble breathing, and felt more comfortable sitting up.

It was, sad to say, almost like going home when we entered University Hospital. We had been there so often in the past, and Professor Ruedi had already operated on Yvonne five times there. We were very anxious for him to give us a second opinion, but he wasn't there; he was off on a skiing holiday in the Alps. And so was his able associate, Professor Ake Senning.

We waited four days, while the hospital staff tried to make Yvonne as comfortable as possible. Senning was the first of the surgeons to return and he took one look at Yvonne's X-rays and said that there was no time to waste, that surge must be done, and done immediately.

Within a half-hour, Yvonne was in the operating room. There was preliminary surgery one day and the full-scale Operation the next. Senning removed a tumor as large as baby's head from her chest. Senning said if they had waited day or two more, Yvonne might well have suffocated. As it was, he said the prognosis was very dubious.

She was on the critical list for days that time. Once again, I stayed at her side or paced the corridor outside her room. All in all, she stayed at the hospital for five weeks and it was only her fighting spirit and her will to live that pulled her through.

She recuperated in a pleasant room at the Palace Hotel in Gstaad. Her sister, Cécile, and her husband, Ernst, were with us. Gradually, the color returned to her face and the laughter to her eyes, and she began talking about us both going back to the show. I felt she needed more time and I didn't feel much like going back myself. My foot began bothering me; I am not sure if there was anything really wrong with it, or whether it was some sort of psychosomatic ailment my mind cooked up to prevent me from leaving Yvonne and going back to work.

But my Swiss sense of duty prevailed and a week or so later I flew back and rejoined the show in Cleveland. My foot didn't bother me, but my timing was a bit off after all those weeks away from the ice. Before my first show back, I had called Yvonne and she had given me one of her usual pep talks: "Go out there and give them all you've got -- the audience loves you!" I knew I had to do it, for her sake, if not for my own.

Finally, in the early summer, she was able to make the trip and rejoin me. And for a while, her health seemed good. "We crossed our fingers and hoped that the worst was behind us. It wasn't.

A few years later there was another operation. This time she was in the hospital for three months. This time they had to sever a nerve in her face, causing her mouth to be twisted almost sideways for a time. She kept working at controlling her mouth, working at achieving a normal smile, but it was very difficult. My heart went out to her once more as she struggled valiantly to overcome her physical problems.

She took to wearing brightly colored clothing on the theory that if people's eyes were attracted to what she was wearing they wouldn't be looking at her face and her crooked mouth.

She visited a beauty consultant in Los Angeles, hoping to find some hints as to how to minimize the effect of the injury to her face. What she got was more psychological as aesthetic, but still valuable. He told her that if she stared at a man's tie knot, or if he was not wearing a tie, at his Adam's apple, he would become distracted and therefore be unaware of her disability. She has often said it was the advice she ever got, because it invariably works.

The difficulties with her mouth affected her speech, as well. Lesser people would have kept quiet, but Yvonne kept talking and gradually her speech improved.

I will always remember with great love how so many of the Follies people helped her through that period. Girls such as Lesley and Betty Jane and Anna and many more would visit her in our dressing room and chit-chat and gossip and laugh, as though Yvonne was the same Yvonne she had always been. She was, but only her true friends realized it.

I kept saying that maybe now was the time for me to quit and take a job in industry, or go back to Switzerland and run a small hotel or something. She wouldn't hear of it. She knew, she said, and I knew she was right about it, that performing was the great passion of my life.

Every time I started to talk about leaving the show so her life might be more regular and comfortable, she would hold up her hand.

"No, Frick," she would say. "You should always be with the show. If I don't open my eyes some day and der liebe Gott [god] takes me away from you, even then I want you to stay with the show. The show is your family and your friends. This is your life."

There was one thing, however, she said, which would brighten her life and make her pain and discomfort easier to endure. She wanted a dog. Not just any dog, but a poodle. And not just any poodle, but one from a kennel she knew in Switzerland.

I said, of course, anything. But it wasn't that easy. The owner of the kennel was very fussy about who took the dogs she bred, and when she heard that this would-be purchaser planned to take the dog on the road in America, living in hotel rooms, she said absolutely not. None of her dogs, her dear little dogs, was going to be subjected to that kind of life. They were to the manor born -- actually, a lovely villa outside of Zurich -- and she was going to see that they spent the rest of their lives in comfort.

I don't know what finally convinced her to change her find, but I suspect it was the way Lulu, as we called her, ran to Yvonne when they were first introduced. I was not there to witness that, but I heard the story from Yvonne and Cécile and I think from the way Lulu barked at me that she often told me the story, too. When the two sisters went to the kennel originally, Lulu took one look at Yvonne and ran into her arms. That was when Yvonne determined to have that dog and she ultimately got her wish [📖 45 📄 116].

Travelling with a dog added a lot to the difficulties of life on the road, but it was worth it to Yvonne and, I must confess, ultimately to me, too.

I imagine a psychologist could make a case for the proposition that to Yvonne, Lulu was the child she never had. It had been our conscious decision when we married, to have children. I felt in the first place that at thirty-nine I was too old to become a father. (Now I am not so sure about that because as my life has unfolded, I have always been healthy and have always looked much younger than my actual years. Yvonne's reason for deciding to have no children was my profession and its demands for life on the road.)

She knew that she had married a performer and that my career called for me to be travelling constantly. It would have been terribly difficult to raise a child under those conditions, especially after the first few years of the child's life. And she didn't want us to have one of those marriages like a sailor's, where the husband is away for months and the wife stays home with the children and they see each other only for brief periods every year or so. It was a dilemma that, in her eyes, had only one solution -- no children.

Yvonne had been raised in a loving home, complete with the total presence of both parents, and she would have wanted nothing less for her own offspring. It was a decision she reached reluctantly, but with the conviction that it was the right one. And I concurred with that decision.

When I realized that she was firm in her determination never to become a mother, I went to Zurich -- without telling anybody but Yvonne the reason for my trip -- and had a vasectomy performed. Now we would never have to worry about an unexpected, unwanted surprise. I never regretted it, because with all of Yvonne's health problems, I doubt that she could have carried a baby to term. At least, I never added to her physical problems or worries.

Picture 42 ✧ Page 98

1969 - Mr. Frick works as suitcase carrier
Mrs. Peggy Fleming
Ice Follies

Picture 43 ✦ Page 102

1954 - Werner & Yvonne Groebli
The Conrad Hilton | Chicago

Picture 44 ✤ Page 106

1951 - Mr. Frick is boarding a TWA Lockheed Constellation by snow shoes
New York International Airport

Picture 45 ✦ Page 111

1969 - Mr. Frick, wife Yvonne and poodle Lulu

CHAPTER 5

Certainly, the person who played the biggest part in my life, next to my parents and my wife, was Hansruedi Mauch -- my partner, Frack.

When anyone looks back on his life he sees the series of accidents and lucky (good or bad) breaks that brought him to the position he currently occupies. With me, I believe that had I not had the Mauchs as neighbors on Frobenstrasse, I would not be where I am. Quite probably, I would never have become a professional ice skater. I would most likely have spent my days as a minor functionary in some Basel or Zurich office leading a life of predictable dullness. Or maybe I would have built some lovely Swiss chalets.

But Hansruedi served as a catalyst for me, and I for him, and together we were able to forge our mutual career.

Many show business partnerships -- from Gilbert and Sullivan to Martin and Lewis -- are notorious for being full of hate and anger. Ours was not that way at all. We always remained good friends. This is not to say that we never had any disagreements, never felt irritation at one another, because we did. I doubt that any two people thrown together for many years can exist without irritating each other from time to time. It's only human.

I believe our greatest area of disagreement, always, was the different way we approached rehearsing. To me, a rehearsal was the key to perfection, or as close to perfection as any of us ever gets. I believed whole-heartedly in rehearsing and then rehearsing some more. It was only through constant and thorough rehearsing, I believed (and still do) that you can create new routines and polish old ones.

Frack, on the other hand, could take rehearsing or leave it. He preferred to leave it. We had worked together for so many years. He felt that we didn't really need to rehearse more. He also was a great one for ad-libbing. I am sure that ad-libbing is a worthwhile talent, in an improvisational setting, but ours was not an improvisational art form. Our act relied on split-second timing, on calculated near misses, on everything being planned and executed to (as they say in the American south) a gnat's ass.

Frequently, therefore, I would find myself rehearsing myself. Since we were a team, and did our act as a team, solo rehearsal wasn't much help.

When I could persuade him to join me, he was inventive and he worked hard and the tragedy is that it happened so seldom. Together, we had fun on the ice in what might be called a skating jam session and often came up with ideas and movements that we later incorporated into our act. He had potential to be very creative and the pity is that he failed to exploit that creativity.

The maneuvers which the audiences found thrilling were to us, great fun. We never stopped to think of the danger that we could, quite literally, break our necks or other parts of our bodies. We had fun being funny and that was the way it was. I spent a lot of time at the old drawing board, trying to figure out new maneuvers and entire routines, while Frack just went out there and did it -- when he could be convinced that it was something he should do.

That was the main area of disagreement between us, and as far as I can remember, the only point of any serious dispute. And it was never very serious. Nobody shouted or yelled. I would shake my head in wonderment -- "Why does he not see how important this is to us" -- and I imagine he had a few words to say about me under his breath -- "Why does he keep insisting on rehearsing when we already know it all so well?"

But we started out good friends, and we ended up good friends, too.

We were different types, of course, with different personalities. He was more witty and sarcastic and he would greet everybody, "Hi ya Doc." And he had a lot of friends and acquaintances. We both enjoyed kidding around, but he was more exuberant, sharper, more biting in his remarks.

He was very serious about his skating, however, once he was on the ice. He was probably the most daring performer I have ever seen. One year, for example, we had as a prop an igloo that stood perhaps two and a half feet high, with a very small opening. Frack would suddenly squat down and glide into that opening, going some twenty miles an hour. He had less than a few inches clearance all around, but he never hesitated.

During one performance in Boston in 1953, he miscalculated and hit his head. He was taken to Massachusetts General Hospital that time, and suffered from double vision for some weeks afterwards.

While he was recuperating, I did a solo. I had done a solo before, once for a whole year when, from September 1945 on, he took a year off to be with his wife and their new-born son. Again, only a year before Frack's accident involving his head, he had broken a knee cap and had been out of action some time. He had, in the best show-must-go-on-tradition, suggested that he skate on only one leg, but Oscar Johnson took a look at his "one-legged" attempt and said, "The thing is to entertain," and that ended that.

So, I took some time off too, and went to New York. My intention had been to stay a few days, see some shows, ate some good meals, that sort of thing. But the first morning, woke to the sound of an ocean liner's haunting fog horn, and I suddenly got the urge to sail. I looked in the New York Times and saw that the SS United States was sailing at noon.

By now it was close to eleven. I quickly packed, paid my hotel bill, checked out, grabbed a cab and went directly to the pier. They were just pulling up the gang plank when I ran up and was stopped by an officer on the deck.

"Whom do you wish to see off, sir?" he asked.

"Nobody," I said. "I would like to go along."

The officer took it in stride, and consulted his passenger list. He said there was one cabin available. I immediately wrote out a check for my passage, showed him my passport, and as the ship was being nudged away from the pier, I was taken to my cabin.

I think I was also taken in my cabin, too. The purser had told me that this last remaining cabin was in the first-class section of the ship, and I paid first-class fare. But later I learned that it was actually a second-class cabin, at the edge of the dividing line between the classes, and the purser had simply moved the rope which separated first from second class and, presto, I had a first-class cabin -- and paid the much higher first-class rates.

I like such spur-of-the-moment adventures. It was, I remember, a similar event -- stopping off in Chicago -- that led to my meeting Yvonne. And through the years, I have frequently decided on instant vacations with just that sort of spontaneous decision.

But back to Frack's injury to his head in 1953, and my doing a solo as a result, we played in Buffalo when I did it first, and it was well received, so I continued to skate by myself. Frack came back when we reached San Francisco, and we started working on a totally new number -- "Puttin' on the Ritz in St. Moritz." For a new number, of course, he was happy to rehearse.

We had reserved the ice one day for a certain time. We were, by now, in the fourth week of working on the new routine. I was there waiting when Frack came onto the ice and skated slowly over to me and said, "Frick, I have to tell you that I just had a meeting with the bosses, and I handed them my notice."

It was as though somebody had said the sun had decided not to rise any more. Here was my partner for sixteen years, professionally, and for perhaps a dozen years before that, when we were boys and semi-professionals, and, just like that, he was walking away from it all. And it left me on the spot. There was only ten days left before the new opening, and that was all the time I had to convert from a double to a single act, and to break in a new partner -- providing the show wanted me as a single. They did.

I think one of the causes of Frack's retirement was the degradation he felt at playing a bandleader -- a spec -- in that production number. Another cause, as I subsequently found out, was his health. He had, unbeknownst to me, been battling a strange and progressive bone disease. At the time he quit, I don't think it had yet been diagnosed. He had several times consulted doctors, quite a few of them, without any one of them being able to identify his problem. I later found out that a symposium of doctors had convened at Los Angeles' Veterans' Hospital to consider all the evidence in his case, and had been unable to reach a conclusion as to what was causing his difficulties.

It meant that he easily fractured his bones; they were increasingly brittle. That fractured knee-cap a year before was one of the first manifestations of the disease. At the time, I wondered how a seemingly minor fall could have resulted in such major damage.

After he left, when the disease was diagnosed, it improved for a few years. But slowly, over the ensuing years, it grew worse again. And ultimately, he moved slowly and with difficulty. Yvonne and I would visit Mary and Hansruedi, who lived on a cliff overlooking the ocean in Santa Monica, whenever we played Los Angeles.

Frack and Mary had two daughters and a son who were lovely youngsters, and very well brought up. I remember Michael, the son, as a Boy Scout, asking me if he and the other members of his troop could visit the show and see how it worked backstage. I enjoyed guiding them around for a few years, until he outgrew that.

Frack always came to see the show when we were in Los Angeles, and when we visited him he would always critique my act for me. I welcomed his suggestions because they were uniformly good and constructive. (Mostly, he would tell me how my assistants were not up to par, which I suppose was a very normal and human reaction, under the circumstances.) His critique would make me nervous, but it was useful.

People have often asked me why I never tried to find another skater to be my permanent partner, to become another Frack. Honestly, I never even tried. Over the years, I had dozens of assistants -- the act required somebody else to be on the ice with me, to handle the props, to hit me over the head with a plastic baseball bat, that sort of thing -- but never another partner. Frack was one of a kind. He was a master at pantomime -- many critics compared him favorably to Charlie Chaplin -- and his seemingly rubber legs have never been duplicated by any other ice comedian.

My first assistant, immediately after Frack left [1953], was a skater named Ray Armstrong. Being my assistant was a demanding job, involving considerable skating skill, good timing in the handling of props, precision, efficiency, style. Ray was neither the best nor the worst I would have, simply the first. I found I could do the act without Frack, and that was a major realization. From then on, I was billed as Mr. Frick & Co [46 122].

We made our debut in San Francisco, and everybody was pleased. But Armstrong demanded an extra fifty dollars a week. He didn't care who paid it, but felt his added responsibility merited added money. I think I would have felt the same way had I been in his skates. The thing was, however, that the show steadfastly refused to pay him that extra money. They claimed he was already being paid to do whatever they asked him to do, and this was just another skating job, and therefore not deserving of more money. So, it wound up with me paying him that money out of my own salary. You can be sure that, in subsequent seasons, I made certain that didn't happen again.

In the years that followed, I had a succession of assistants. There was Gary Johnson for twelve years and then Dave Thomas and later Ted Barton, who had been a Canadian champion before he joined the show. There was John Hadlich and several brief pinch-hitters -- Richard Dwyer went on with only a 45-minute rehearsal and Jay Humphrey, the show's treasurer who had been a North American champion, jumped in at a moment's notice and did an amazingly competent job considering that.

There was Chuck Davidson, a former Ontario champion and a very reliable assistant. We were in Portland, Oregon, with our next stop San Francisco, and Chuck asked if he could drive my car from Portland down. He and his wife, Jeannie, had never seen that part of the world, so I handed him the keys and told him to have a good trip. I was asleep in my Portland hotel room when I got the word that Chuck had crashed. He and Jeannie were killed. They had taken along a Folliette, Karen, and she was hospitalized with severe injuries. The car was totally destroyed, of course. Eventually, Karen sued me -- her lawyer was an ex-Folliette's husband -- for two hundred thousand dollars. The Claim was that Chuck was "representing" me when I allowed him to drive my car, and he was negligent (he fell asleep at the wheel) and so I was responsible for Karen's injuries. The case was settled, with Karen receiving thousands of dollars.

Chuck, like the others, had been a good assistant to me. They were all clever, talented, willing -- but none of them approached Frack's innate skill and ability. So, I was never even tempted to suggest that any of them become a partner, a second Frack.

There were other skaters in the company who, in an emergency, could jump in and work with me. After all, many of them had seen my act for years and knew it almost as well as I did. So, whenever an assistant was injured or ill, there was always somebody ready, willing and reasonably able to fill in. Even my ultimate nemesis, Richard Dwyer, once, with only one forty-five minute rehearsal, skated with me for a few shows. (Dwyer actually played it too close, and in a near-miss maneuver, he skated too close and cut me; fortunately, he only sliced open my skating boot and missed my foot itself.)

With Frack gone, I realized that I had to do something else. I knew that the majority of ice skating teams -- after a break up -- suffer with neither of the partners doing well -- by himself nor herself. I was determined that would not happen to me.

I worked very hard to turn my act into a solo, but with some assistance from others. Primarily, however, it was Frick, by himself. I had my own new moves (and some old ones) and my own bag of tricks. And when all is said and done, I honestly believe that I got better, that the departure of Frack somehow gave me a certain freedom I had never had before, and that I was able to turn a potential disaster into a triumph.

There were assistants that I recruited from among the Ice Follies personnel to help me, but they could only help me so far. I had to have new twists to my act to compensate for the loss of Frack. So, during the next few years, I added more and more props and mechanical maneuvers -- my famous "sliding barrel" with me sitting on the barrel and gliding around rapidly, and then the barrel slides away (pulled by an almost invisible wire) and I continue gliding around in a sitting position as though the barrel was still there. I also had a similar sliding bench, with me and an assistant sitting on it. I fall asleep and drop off the bench but continue skating around while supposedly asleep. This ingenious prop was designed and built for me by a Swiss -- a Mormon, curiously -- and it was a masterpiece that combined strength with lightness. I had several other gimmicks and gadgets to spice up my new solo act, too.

Every year, after Frack left the show in 1953, he and Mary would visit all of us when we came to Los Angeles. They had front row seats and the cast would make a point of smiling at them. But in 1964, when Frack and Mary got to the arena, they found themselves seated off to the side, and I could see -- I was peeking from behind the curtain -- that he wasn't too happy about it. But it was all part of an elaborate plot.

When the intermission came, the announcer requested all the audience to remain seated. And then a familiar voice came over the loudspeakers. At the time, it was perhaps the most popular and most familiar voice in America, and the words that voice said had become a national catchword.

"Ladies and gentlemen," the voice of Ralph Edwards said: "tonight, Hansruedi Mauch, Mr. Frack -- THIS IS YOUR LIFE!"

That splendid and exciting evening was the culmination of months of work for Edwards' staff and our staff and in particular me. When we were first approached about it, I was recruited to line up as many of Frack's old friends and relatives as I could. Some came from as far away as South Africa and all with total secrecy. We were told that if Frack learned of it, the whole deal was off. But he never did, and before the evening was over, there was his sister -- he hadn't seen her in years -- and teachers and friends and gifts of a car and some bonds and a typewriter and a dinner for everyone.

I must say that I was almost as thrilled as he was, and he was as thrilled as he had ever been.

In 1978, Frack and I were invited to the Sahara Hotel in Las Vegas for a Skating Hall of Fame banquet. Donny and Marie Osmond were headlining the show at the Hilton, which had some ice skating in it -- Donny is a pretty fair skater -- and we had a pleasant time.

I met Frack and Mary at the airport. I could see immediately, that he was having some trouble walking. Otherwise, he seemed fine. We had a nice day around the Pool, reminiscing the enjoying the hotel's hospitality.

At the big banquet, we were both touched

when the Ice Skating Institute, through Merrill Baxter, an ex-skating star who was now an official of the Ice Skating Institute, presented both of us with plaques for our services to ice skating.

There were pictures taken of the two of us, smiling and holding our plaques. Frack left the next day, and I never saw him again. He died the next year.

Picture 46 ✧ Page 119

1953 - Mr. Frick & Ray Armstrong
Ice Follies

CHAPTER 6

It wasn't all hard work and tragedies.

You have to realize that the Ice Follies consisted of (it varied) anywhere from sixty to seventy people. Mostly, they were young people. And, like any group of normal young people on the road away from home, they were looking to have fun. Certainly, it was a job and they were, almost always, conscious of the responsibility of that job, and the job came first and all that, but that still left a lot of time and energy for fun.

I must confess to being one of the leading co-conspirators and instigators of the fun and frolic we had on the show. Even in my later years, when I was the acknowledged dean of the show -- in my sixties, there were few if any rivals for the deanship -- I held my own in the lets-have-fun-department.

Perhaps because I didn't look in the least zany, I was able to get away with much more. Many newspapermen, reviewing the show, would write that I looked more like a small-town banker than a performer, more like a college professor than a comic. Nobody expects a small-town banker or a college professor to do anything wild and crazy, so I always had a comfortable head start.

Many of my comedic adventures involved the area of transportation. When you are on the road as much as we were, the job of getting from Point A to Point B, from one stop to the next, becomes a big, bloody bore. You have to do something to put some fun in it. Besides, I dislike most public transportation companies, from the major international airlines to small local bus services. The majority of them seem to be designed primarily to make the passengers pay as much as possible to be as uncomfortable as they can possibly make them. There are some exceptions, but not many.

So, whenever I can, I get even. I love to outwit those companies, and it really doesn't take too much wit to do it. Since we travelled so frequently by air, we were plagued by those annoying overweight charges, and I would do anything I could to outsmart the airlines in that area. (Those domestic charges have been relaxed somewhat lately -- but too late to do me much good.)

Before I was married, I would stuff my overcoat pockets with the heaviest items I could find, because they never weigh anyone's coat. I would get on a plane barely able to stagger; my coat pockets were bulging with shoes, books, portable lamps, whatever I could force into them. I had extra-large, extra-strong pockets sewn into my coats to accommodate all the stuff I carried therein. It made it difficult for me to walk, but I recovered rapidly when I realized the overweight charges I avoided as a result.

The shopping bag was another marvelous way to circumvent those absurd charges. Before I went to sleep each night, I prayed for the continued joy, whoever it was that invented that glorious contrivance.

I became, I say immodestly, a champion packer. I was able to fit the following into an expandable leather briefcase: two grapefruit, a bottle of whiskey, a pair of ice skates and assorted bits and pieces, plus odds and ends and this and that.

The airlines rarely weighed carry-on luggage and the shopping bag is a seemingly bottomless pit. One can practically live for a month on what I was able to put into my shopping bag. I searched for the largest, sturdiest shopping bags I could find. And then I developed the method of packing them until it became a fine art.

My relationship with shopping bags was so well known that on the occasion of my fiftieth birthday, which I celebrated in Omaha, Nebraska -- my partner at the time -- Gary Johnson gave me a matched set of shopping bags as a present. I could not have received a more useful gift.

Between what was in my suitcases -- never overweight, of course -- and what I carried on board in my shopping bags and in my overcoat, I travelled in style.

If I felt we might be getting too close to the inner limit of overweight, however, I had one last trick up my sleeve. I would pack a heavy suitcase. Then just abandon it in the middle of the airport terminal waiting room. A friend would keep an eye on it for me, to make sure it wasn't picked up by some larcenous stranger. Usually, however, it would be spotted by an airline employee. He would read the tag -- which I would have thoughtfully affixed to it -- and immediately realize it must have been overlooked, so he would rush it to the plane. That way, it was never weighed as part of my allowance and yet travelled on the same plane as I did. (A bonus to that play: that bag would be considered lost luggage and airlines deliver lost luggage freely to the address on it, so that bag would be sent directly to my hotel.)

My skates were obviously a heavy item. They were too big for the overcoat pockets and too bulky for the shopping bags. So they would have to be packed in the suitcases checked through. A few times I experimented and wore a pair of skates on my feet as I travelled. I was used to wearing them, of course, so they were not uncomfortable for me. But the airlines complained, saying that my skate blades were slicing up their carpets. They were wrong -- I was always careful to wear rubber guards over the blades -- but I stopped that practice anyhow.

I also worked out a complicated method of avoiding the overweight charges by buying round-the-world tickets. This is no longer the case, but for a long time passengers on round-the-world flights were allowed an extra weight allowance of twenty-two pounds. That's a lot of socks and shirts. So I would buy a round-the-world ticket even though I was only planning on going say, from Los Angeles to Zurich. Then when we landed at Zurich I would simply disembark, and there I was. Later, I would get a refund for the balance of the round-the-world flight and I would have flown from Los Angeles to Zurich without any of those annoying overweight charges.

Yvonne and I, when her health permitted, loved to take advantage of any break in my schedule to visit places, to take a few days here and there for trips and sight-seeing and spontaneous vacations.

The height of our holiday spontaneity was reached once when we had a week off and were about to fly from New York to Zurich via London. We were on board the TWA Constellation and it had left the gate and was waiting for take-off clearance. Then suddenly the captain announced that the plane would be returning to the gate because of some mechanical problem. The passengers groaned, of course, because that always means a delay of at the least an hour and more likely two or three.

We had a very brief connection scheduled in London to catch our flight to Zurich so we immediately knew that that connection had been blown. Of course, there would be a later London-Zurich flight available, but suddenly I had an idea.

"Why don't we forget Zurich?" I said to Yvonne. "Why don't we just get off now and with the money we'll save by not flying, have ourselves a good time here in New York?"

Since we had been married, we had never really had a holiday in New York. I had always been working or, at the most, we had had a day or two. This would be a whole week, with a chance to enjoy the marvelous restaurants and see a few Broadway shows and let Yvonne explore the glorious shops to her heart's desire and pocketbook's content.

So when we got back to the gate, we left the plane and the TWA people were able to dig out our luggage (it was nice, but we could have gotten along on the carry-on contents) and we took a cab into Manhattan and had our week's holiday in the big City.

We did wonderful things -- like having cocktails at the famous Twenty-One Club on West 52nd Street and then, when I asked Yvonne where she would like to have dinner, she said she always had so much fun at the Automat, so we segued from the Twenty-One Club across the street in our finery and had the best dinner the Automat could provide.

We saw shows and hockey games and went shopping and when it came time to rejoin the show, we didn't have to go far. We saved a lot of money and had no jet lag, either.

My act was also a source of our fun. Had I been an orthodox figure skater, this would not have been the case. But since comedy was at the core of my performance, comedy ruled both my private and my professional lives. The two were in a permanent partnership.

I was constantly on the lookout for new devices and gimmicks which would make the act funnier and more unusual. Once, I was fortunate to meet a fellow Swiss, the remarkable Herman Faenger. I was told -- although I am not certain this is true -- that Faenger had a lot to do with the development of sonar. He told me, too, that he helped Prof. Ernest Orlando Lawrence of the University of California at Berkeley build the first cyclotron.

He once took me to his backyard machine shop in Redwood City, California and showed me the prototype of a new gadget he was working on. It turned out to be the first video (cassette) recorder and Faenger made it for his friend, Alexander M. Poniatoff, whose company (called AMPEX, a name coined from Poniatoff's initials) made the very first VCR.

Faenger was a fan and a friend and he built several props for my act. The one that I had the most fun with was his lightweight -- only forty pounds -- gyroscope. We put it in a suitcase and in the act the suitcase would glide on the ice on one edge, off balance, all the way across the rink. It made a marvelous prop and the audience was always amazed and delighted.

Of course, I used that tricky suitcase off the ice, too. I wasn't about to let a device as marvelous as that go to waste. I would set the mechanism then hand the bag to a porter. That poor soul would be fine as long as he didn't try to change direction, but the moment he wanted to go left or right, he couldn't because the gyroscope forced the suitcase to continue in a straight line. You can imagine the expression on the face of those Red Caps when they couldn't make the suitcase go where they wanted it to go. They would often just drop the bag and run, without even waiting for a tip.

I found that many props, such as that gyroscope, which had been created for the show, were useful for outside pranks. I remember when one of the other comedy acts in the show used a loud air horn to get some laughs. I thought that was a spectacular device for a little innocent fun, so I bought one. I had that horn with me once at a dinner party in Zurich, hidden under a flowing overcoat. Midway through the main course, I doubled over and gasped to the host, "I am terribly sorry, but I feel dreadful, awful pains in my stomach. Could I please have some soda water?"

I continued to moan and groan for a bit and they rushed over with the soda water and everybody clustered around me with great concern. When the worry was at its peak, I touched the button and the air horn let out its incredible blast of noise.

For a prankster, that was a most effective moment. The fact that I was never invited back to that particular home was of small consequence when measured against the joy of that prank.

Occasionally, I was on the receiving end of jokes and a good prankster has to be able to take it as well as dish it out. One of the greatest gags ever pulled on me began just outside the dressing room at Madison Square Garden in New York. I was getting ready for a show when a man approached me. He was well-dressed, had a trace of an English accent and seemed very serious and official.

"Mr. Groebli?" he said. I acknowledged that that was who I was: "Mr. Groebli of Frick and Frack?" Again, yes, that was me.

"I am Oldfield of the Immigration Service," he said. He took my arm. "Please come with me."

"Where are we going?"

"Inside, where it is quieter," he said. "We wouldn't want your friends and co-workers to hear this, would we?" "Hear what?"

He didn't answer, simply led me into the dressing room and sat down on a bench and motioned for me to sit beside him.

"Now, then," he said, and he pulled some very official-looking papers from his inside jacket pocket. "Let's see where we stand, shall we?"

Some of the others who had witnessed the immigration officer lead me out, came out of the dressing room, too, and clustered around us. And then Oscar Johnson, the boss, came along and became very belligerent.

"What's going on here?" he asked. And before I knew what was happening, he hauled the immigration officer up and took a swing at his chin. I thought to myself, dear God, that's a terrible thing -- if I am in some trouble with Immigration, now it's ten or twenty times worse.

"Don't do that, Oscar," I said. I turned pale.

"Don't do this?" he said, and hit the man

again.

Right about then, I began to suspect that something was fishy. Oscar was not that sort of person and the immigration officer was falling too professionally. And then some of the others started giggling so I realized it was all a gag. It turned out the "immigration officer" was actually that marvelous night club stooge/comedian, Frank Libuse. He was at the time working on Broadway in Olsen and Johnson's big hit, "Hellzapoppin," and our Johnson knew their Johnson and had worked it all out for my benefit. Libuse was the performer who often worked at the Latin Quarter pretending he was a waiter and spilling soup and other liquids on unsuspecting patrons. He was an expert at stunts like that.

I was famous, or infamous, among Ice Follies people, for demanding good service when I was paying for it. I often found as I travelled that the airlines and railroads and bus companies advertised one thing, but delivered something far less. I would never let them get away with anything like that. I would write -- generally to the president of the company involved -- and very often I got satisfaction. On the other hand, if the service was particularly outstanding, I would write to commend them. What's fair is fair.

Once I flew from Los Angeles to Denver on Continental Airlines. At the time, they were the cream of the airline crop. One of their boasts was that on every flight there was a "flight director" to see that the passengers' needs were met. I had flown first class on that occasion and there was no such person on board. I had also felt that the hostesses were busier discussing their love lives than they were in serving the passengers. So I wrote to a Continental vice-president in Denver, complaining about all that and ended my letter with these words, "Don't bother to answer, just send me a couple of your flight bags as an apology."

Back came a package by return mail -- with two flight bags and a note that real, "Ok, no answer, just flight bags." I thought that was excellent public relations, to show a good sense of humor.

Knowing my predilection for writing to airline officials, somebody in our show -- and I never did find out who it was -- plotted an elaborate gag which they worked on me.

One day I received a letter from a TWA executive.

"We are sorry, Mr. Groebli," the letter read, "that you did not find our service to your satisfaction on your recent flight. If you will send us your flight vouchers we will endeavor to make it up to you in some way."

But I had no vouchers to send them because I had not made any TWA flight recently, so there was nothing I could send. For an old complainer, that was the height of frustration. And that was the gist of the gag -- whoever made it up knew I would be consumed by frustration, with a possible refund staring me in the face and no way to claim it.

Another quirk of mine was a love of publicity. I rationalized that if I got personal publicity, it helped the show and if it helped the show it helped all of us. And that was certainly true, but also true was the fact that I thoroughly enjoyed seeing my picture and my name in the paper and to hear about myself on the radio and later, television.

In Detroit, I was quite taken by the weatherman on ABC's local affiliated television station. Sonny Elliot was witty and lively and I enjoyed listening to him on the news program before I had to get to the arena. Every day, as a joke, he would mention what the temperature was in some obscure, oddly-named town (so oddly-named that I have forgotten it) in upper Michigan. So I called him one day and told him what the temperature was (or at least might have been) in Frick, Switzerland. And he mentioned that on the air. It became a running gag. Whenever I was in Detroit, I would call him and tell him about the weather in Frick. And he would report that fact (sic) on the air and generally talk a bit after that about me and the show.

During one of our visits to New York, there was a subway strike [1966]. The newspapers were full of the problems the people were having getting around. One of the props in the show that year was a genuine Chinese rickshaw and as that was unloaded I realized it represented a golden opportunity for some good publicity for the show -- and me.

I told them to leave the rickshaw outside for a while. I persuaded the pretty Denton Twins, in their geisha costumes, to sit in the rickshaw. I put on my good old Swiss peasant outfit and I began pulling the rickshaw. It didn't take long for a crowd to gather -- and some reporters and photographers, too. I ran up Eighth Avenue while the crowds cheered and the photographers snapped and the reporters made notes. The stunt made all the papers that evening, which was good for our box office and did me no harm, either [47 131].

When we played Milwaukee, the beer capitol of the world, one year, we had a shorter-than-usual schedule -- only five nights. There are many more than five breweries in Milwaukee. So, when the financial editor of the Milwaukee paper [48 132] interviewed me (I was frequently interviewed by financial editors because of my fame as a Wall Street investor), I told him and he quoted me, "You know, if all the breweries here invite us for an after-show beer party, we are in trouble. We have only five nights and it will be difficult for us to figure out which one of the invitations to accept."

I thought we would be flooded with invitations to after-show beer parties at the breweries as a result of my quote, but not one was forthcoming. But there was a belated happy ending. Our next stop that year was in Omaha and no sooner had I checked into my hotel room there than my phone rang and it was the desk saying that they had a case of beer for me, courtesy of one of those Milwaukee breweries. That was only the beginning, -- in the next few days, I was inundated with cases of beer from many of those Milwaukee breweries. Later, another brewery saw to it that there were cases of beer on the train as we moved on for our next leg, from Omaha to Seattle.

That train ride, as I remember it, was the one during which I invented one of my greatest stunts. (This is said, you understand, with great modesty, but it needs to be said for the sake of posterity.) I got an industrial-strength needle and thread and sewed the drapes of an upper berth shut tight. I forget who my victim was, but whoever it was woke up and could not get out of his or her berth. That turned out to be such a hilarious (to everyone but the victim) gag that it soon became the favorite gag whenever we took a train ride of at least one night. As sure as ice melts in the sun, one person in our group was certain to wake up and find himself or herself a prisoner in the berth.

I also enjoyed what I came to call my department store routine. This was especially effective in the winter when all the customers were bundled up in heavy coats and scarves and hats. I would make a dash from my hotel to a store, without any outer garments -- as an athlete I was hardened enough to do that. And so I would be in the store, just in my business suit. Naturally, I would be mistaken for an employee of the store, most often one of the floor-walkers.

Customers would come up to me and ask for directions to a particular department. I would take a perverse pleasure in sending them off in all different directions. Pretty soon the whole store would be fluttering, as people rushed this way and that way, upstairs and down, and nobody knew what was happening. Then I would casually stroll out of the store and dash back to the warmth of my hotel.

One of my little jokes once landed me on the pages of the Reader's Digest. At the Victoria Hotel in New York, I went down to the front desk in the hotel to ask for some stationery. The concierge (or, since this was in America, the front desk clerk) said, "Are you a guest in this hotel?" And my reply was, "No, I am not a guest. I am paying eight dollars a day for my room." (You can tell from the eight dollars that this was a long time ago.)

Once in Philadelphia, I got back to the hotel late at night after a show and a post-show dinner and I bumped into a man in the lobby who had obviously had considerable to drink. He was wandering around, apparently trying to find his way home, but nobody was paying the poor man the slightest attention.

So I said I would show him the way home. There was a new car on display in the lobby and I led him to the car, opened the door and pushed him into the back seat. He apparently thought he was in a taxi cab and I could hear him giving the driver -- who wasn't there, of course -- an address. Then he settled back and went to sleep. I went over to the desk clerk and explained the situation and then I went up and went to bed. I figured the man in the car was safer there than trying to find his way home in his condition. When I came down the next morning, I looked in the car. It was empty. I have always hoped he got home safely.

I don't like to see cars displayed in lobbies. I think they seem out of place. I took my revenge during an engagement in Minneapolis. We were staying at the Curtis Hotel and there was one of those shiny new cars on display in the lobby. And so one night, I went over and let a little air out of all the tires, the next night, a little more air. I repeated that for ten days and, of course, finally nature took its course and that shiny new car was resting on four flat-as-a-pancake tires. Nobody ever seemed to notice.

My dislike of automobiles extended beyond those stashed in hotel lobbies. I have never been fond of cars wherever they are. I own them and I drive them, but I have never fallen in love with them like the average American car owner.

I do enjoy observing cars and drivers, however. I am particularly fond of Canadian taxi cab drivers. It may have changed there now, but during the '40s, they would signal a left turn by opening their left door and zooming to the left. The centrifugal force of the turn would slam the door shut halfway through the turn. I began using that technique in San Francisco where I did most of my driving in America. It caught on for a while, too.

I had a lot of fun driving those steep, steep hills in San Francisco. When I had a passenger and I was headed up one of those monsters, I would pretend the car was not going to be able to make it all the way to the top. While I surreptitiously gave it enough gas to keep going up, I would slow it down, let it slowly reverse, then open the door and put my left leg out and make believe I was pushing us up with leg power. I let many pale passengers out at the top of those hills.

Besides the airlines and other transportation companies, I was also in a state of constant undeclared war with the telephone company. I long felt that it was an unnecessary expense for me to have to spend all that money just to call Yvonne in Switzerland and let her know that I had arrived safely back in San Francisco or Boston or wherever I had gone. So we devised a system. I would call and ask for some fictitious name and that was our code telling her I was safe and sound and Yvonne would acknowledge she had received the message by saying, "Sorry, no one here by that name." So she knew I was safe and it hadn't cost us a thing. I understand that many others use a similar system.

I also frequently would have myself paged in an airport or restaurant -- "Telephone call for Mr. Frick of San Francisco" -- which would similarly serve as a message to others that I was there. If you are ingenious you can outwit the conglomerates.

Sometimes people in the show pulled jokes on me. Doug Maxon was with the show for several years. He and his sister were a very talented pair-skating team and did the traditional Follies Swing Waltz together. Maxon also was able to mimic me and my Swiss accent perfectly and he had a pixyish sense of humor, so the combination of his mimicry and wit caused me lot of grief. He would often call one of the Folliettes in the middle of the night and, mimicking me, say outrageous things to them. I never found out exactly what he said because the girls would either blushed or be angry and not tell me and, of course, Maxon never would, either.

There were a few jokes I pulled which, looking back on them from my current vantage point of maturity, I regret. At the time, however, when we were all full of verve and youth and on occasion a bit too much beer or wine, they were hilarious. One of the ones that stick in my memory (and conscience) happened in San Francisco when we were all at the Gaylord Hotel. As usual, there was a party after the Show, down in the hotel's unfinished basement where the only furniture was an old piano and some chairs.

Somebody had gotten a huge pot of spaghetti and some paper plates and some red wine, so we were all sitting around eating spaghetti and drinking wine and singing songs while our musical director, Walter Rudolf, played the piano. What happened next is sort of a blur. I protested at the time that I had not done it deliberately and I still believe I am right in that, although some of the witnesses insist I did it all on my own.

But here is my story and I will stick with it (although some of those small conscience twinges still persist). Rudolf had the piano open so the works were visible and I was fascinated watching the little felt hammers jiggle and bounce and hit the strings as the maestro played. I was holding a plate of spaghetti at the time and suddenly my spaghetti sailed out of my hands and into the piano and promptly got tangled up in the piano wires and, of course, the piano squawked to a halt. I honestly believe that somebody else -- I have my suspicions which pushed my arm, causing me to lose control of my plate of spaghetti. Others say, however, that there wasn't a soul anywhere near me, that it was just Frick' weird sense of humor gone berserk.

We all went to work and picked the spaghetti out of the piano, strand by slippery strand. And the piano was soon playing again, although from then on it seemed to prefer Italian songs. I told everybody that the tone seemed to be improved since the great spaghetti drop and that the instrument had been badly out of tune in the first place. Still, there were those in the company who looked askance at me for a while, with a kind of look that said, "That rascal Frick -- he'll do anything for a laugh."

I suppose I would. In some cities, I got a kick out of putting on a red jacket, similar to our usher's uniform, and directing members of the audience to their seats. If they were rude, I would send them to areas of the auditorium far distant from their actual seats.

In Chicago once, where we played at the Chicago Arena, which was relatively small as arenas go, I often played tricks on the manager, Harry Radix. I would call him and imitate Charles Boyer's voice -- my voice and my accent were not too dissimilar from his to begin with -- and order seats to be held in the name of Charles Boyer. He would get very excited and set aside the number of seats Mr. Boyer had requested. Once, I even asked him if he could arrange a little party afterwards with a few of the Folliettes in attendance, and he said he would be glad to. Of course, Mr. Boyer never showed. I still don't understand why poor Harry kept falling for the same gag. I would call him from a booth right outside his office, so I could enjoy watching his reaction.

Our skaters would stash beer bottles on the window sills of their hotel room to keep them cool. In Hershey, Pennsylvania at the Cocoa Inn, there was an inner courtyard and I had a room there, giving me a glorious view of the beer bottles arrayed on window sills across the way. My friend and neighbor, Harris Legg, was giving a party, so had dozens of bottles on his window sill. As the party began, I started pelting his sill with snow balls and many bottles of beer fell softly into the snow on the ground. I could hear Harris saying, "Where the Hell has all my beer got to?"

At the Boston Manger Hotel, one of the girls somehow got a life-size dummy to her room and at the height of the rush hour, threw it out the window. The hotel was the entrance for commuters taking a train home and the dummy fluttered down on them causing great consternation. It also caused the Boston police to come searching for the culprit, but the Manger was so large -- twenty-three stories -- that they quickly gave it up.

Over the years, Frick and Frack, and then Frick by itself, became names the public took to its heart. There was apparently something about those names that made people smile and then laugh and always remember. So Frick and Frack entered the American language.

We would hear, constantly, of children who named dogs and cats Frick and Frack, even turtles. Dr. Tenley Albright who was a brilliant skater, an Olympic gold medalist, before she retired and finished her medical education, told me her secretary named her cats Frick and Frack. (Just as in real life, the cat named Frack ran away.) What made Tenley's secretary's situation difficult was that a man named Frick moved into the apartment across the hall from hers. So she was thereafter unable to go out into the hall and call, "Here Frick, here, Frick."

I heard from skaters who were in the Ice Follies international troop, that when they played Fairbanks, Alaska, they went to the hotel coffee shop and found the menu offered a "Frick and Frack Sandwich." Nobody ordered it, or at least they never did tell me what it contained. I hope it wasn't ham.

The Ice Follies' legal department brought suit that time and on many other occasions, to try and force people to stop using our names frivolously and without our permission. Personally, I didn't mind; after all, I had made the name up, too, so I had no real claim on it. But the lawyers seemed to think I ought to protect the name and they would do it for me. So they would bring suit, but it never seemed to help. People went right ahead naming cats and turtles and sandwiches after us.

They even named an advertising agency after us. We heard, in a letter from the agency itself, that they had opened their doors in some Eastern city. They were, they told us proudly, "The Frick & Frack Advertising Agency." They closed their letter with "Long live Frick and Frack!" Frack didn't live so long, but Frick is still going strong. I have no idea if that ad agency is still going -- strong or weak.

Frick and Frack -- not me and my partner, but our names -- have appeared in movies and television shows, in books and magazine articles. It is a nice feeling to realize that your name -- and I have long felt that it was as much my name as Werner Groebli -- has become a part of the language.

1966 - Gallant Mr. Frick hauls fellow Ice Follies performers Judi Denton, Dorothy Ann Nelson and Vicki Denton (f. l. to r.) to work at Madison Square Garden

Picture 48 ✦ Page 127

Mr. Frick is reading The Wall Street Journal
Ice Follies

CHAPTER 7

Always in the back of our minds during the early years that Frack and I were skating in America, were those four exciting words that had been part of the lure that attracted us in the first place: "Chance to do movies."

I can't speak for Hansruedi, but I was realistic about that potential movie career. I suppose deep down in all of us lurks a movie star. Human nature being what it is and the human ego being the driving force that it is, I imagine we all have that feeling that, given a chance, we too could be a movie star. But I was fairly honest with myself I knew I would never be a serious threat to Spencer Tracy or Humphrey Bogart or Clark Gable. But still, Frack and I thought we had enough fame and talent that we ought to be in pictures.

And we were.

In the '30s and into the '40s, many movies were made with a sporting background -- first there were Sonja Henie's figure skating films, then Esther Williams' swimming films, a few films dealing with skiing, and some others. Ice skating was always big because of its grace. So there were many films made that had an ice skating motif -- even Abbott and Costello made one.

Monogram Studios was to movie-making what McDonald's is to the gourmet food industry. They ground films out in a few weeks, one after another, like so many hamburgers. Inevitably they decided to do a movie with an ice skating background. They had signed lovely Belita, a skater we had known and work with in England, and decided to turn her into a star [📷15 📄56]. Later, the head of Republic Studios, Herbert "Papa" Yates, would fall in love with another figure skater, the Czech star, Věra Hrubá Ralston, and try to make her a movie star, too.)

And so, eventually, our promised "chance to make movies" came to pass. Belita was making a movie for Monogram to be called "Silver Skates," [📷11-12 📄52-53] for producer-director Scotty Dunlap and they signed Frick and Frack for comedy relief.

The day we reported for work I immediately decided that ice shows were safer than movie studios.

Dunlap's notion -- he had obviously never been to Switzerland -- was to build a little rink supposedly on the top of the Matterhorn. I had never climbed an Alp back home, not even a small one, but I knew there were no places to ice skate, no pretty little hidden ponds on top of those rugged mountains. But this, of course, was cinematic license so, okay, we would skate on top of the Matterhorn.

Hollywood movie sets are magic. The Hollywood set designer can take an empty studio and with his skilled workers (and enough money) build anything in it. This time they had built the Alps, or a reasonably accurate facsimile thereof. The Matterhorn itself soared thirty-five feet high and there, at the very top, was the rink -- all five-by-five feet of it, with nothing on any side except a thirty-five foot drop to the concrete studio floor below.

We were given Swiss costumes -- or at least what Hollywood imagined Swiss costumes looked like -- which further restricted our movements.

"Now, in this scene," Dunlap said, "we are going to have yodeling music. And you two, while you skate, have to lip-synch to the yodeling music."

(They played the pre-recorded yodeling for us six or seven times and we got the hang of it. But then, of course, we would have to be doing our lip-synching while skating on that postage-stamp-sized rink in our tight and uncomfortable Swiss costumes and smiling and watching out that we didn't fall off the edge into oblivion. And those movie lights were very hot, too.)

So, all day long, take after take after take, we did our routine up there on the movie Matterhorn. Then, each night, of course, we had to get back on the ice at the arena for our regular act. It made for a very long and very tiring day.

We had other numbers in "Silver Skates [1943]," which turned out to be probably the finest ice skating film ever made.

One morning I reported to the studio and they immediately handed me a cape and a sword and steered me toward a sound stage where they had built a section of a bullfight arena. Happily for my body, there was no live bull, just a fake bull's head mounted on a platform with wheels. Frack and I skated around in that bullfighting sequence, making up steps as we went along and we had fun and the results, even when I see the film now on some extra-late show, are funny.

Before we knew what had happened, we had done an entire sequence.

We had another scene where we supposedly skated down a mountain pass and onto the frozen lake at the bottom -- and the "pass" was just a chute and we really worked up good speed zipping down that chute and then having to break to a quick stop on the rink itself.

We only had a week to do all the things that Dunlap wanted us to do, because our show was moving on to Chicago the next week. So we packed a lot of work -- rehearsals, takes, retakes -- into every day at the Monogram Studio. And I know I decided that maybe movie-making was not the glamorous profession I had always imagined it to be. A lot of it was too much like work.

Still, it was fun to watch ourselves on the screen. "Silver Skates" and the second one we did, also for Monogram and also with Belita, "Lady, Let's Dance [1944]," both did a lot of good for us. In those days, pre-television, the public went to the motion picture theater for its entertainment. There were double feature and those Monogram releases were generally the lower half of a double bill. So we were seen by millions of people and that helped to make our names further known both nationally and internationally.

"Silver Skates" was a particularly good film for its skating. The story and the acting may have been typically Monogramish, but people who know ice skating know that "Silver Skates" had perhaps the best skating routines ever put on film. Belita's big number was done on the deck of an aircraft carrier (a studio replica, of course) which had been turned into a gigantic rink. It was a good routine and she was a fine skater and Dunlap didn't trick it up with gimmickry. Belita was really the first skater who was as much a ballet dancer as she was an athlete. It was pure skating, photographed simply, and if you ever get a chance to see it on some late show, don't miss it.

Monogram didn't have the time or patience to spend much effort or money on post-production. They made them and as quickly as possible, they sent them out and put them to work. So, a few months after we did our scenes, we were in Buffalo and saw in the paper that "Silver Skates" was playing at that city's Century Theater. The ads in the paper played down the movie's real stars -- Belita, Patricia Morison and Kenny Baker -- and played up Frick and Frack because we happened to be in town at the moment.

So, naturally, we all went to the Century as soon as we could to see Frick and Frack in their movie debut. I don't think I have ever been as nervous as I was sitting in that theater waiting to see myself on the legendary silver screen. I was a little disappointed. I had been aware of course, this despite the large number of retakes, the whole thing had been rushed in typical Monogram fashion -- they had no money to strive for perfection and compromise was their watchword. Watching our numbers, I could see how they would have benefitted from more time, more rehearsals and more different shots from different angles, more of everything.

Still, the picture was good for what it was and all the Ice Follies cast and technicians came around to Frack and me, congratulating us and kidding about how we were going to be big Hollywood stars.

And Monogram did rush in and sign us to do the next one, which turned out to be "Lady, Let's Dance." So, for a while we did have a few idle but exciting dreams about someday making a large splash in Hollywood. I saw myself doing those Cary Grant parts and thought seriously for a time about taking acting lessons and trying to lose my accent completely. That was, happily, a phase that passed very soon.

We moved on from Buffalo to Montreal that tour and again our visit coincided with the showing of "Silver Skates." Curiously, there was another movie that opened in Montreal the same day as our "Silver Skates." It was "Casablanca," with Humphrey Bogart and Ingrid Bergman, which is now considered one of the all-time movie classics. It may seem hard to believe at this late date, but when they both premiered a day apart in Montreal, "Silver Skates" got a better review than "Casablanca." The reviewer went on to urge his readers to see Frick and Frack, both in person and on the screen, and so much for Bergman and Bogart. They weren't skating locally.

We did more actual acting in "Lady, Let's Dance" than we had done in "Silver Skates." We had more time for the second one -- we did it on a vacation break, not while we were doing the show, so there was not as much pressure on us. We had a scene with Belita -- she played a Dutch waitress and we were her customers -- and had another scene in which we were supposed to be chefs getting bawled out by the executive chef in a dialogue composed mostly of rhymes like:

"You, Frick and Frack, are making pies that we get back!"

Our big skating number was one in which we defied a "Thin Ice" sign on a pond and began skating. And, of course, eventually we broke through the ice and disappeared below. There was a huge tank underneath the mock ice for us to sink into. The last shot of that scene was our top hats bobbing up to the surface and floating serenely as the scene faded out.

We had one other routine, after a fashion, in [1944] "Lady, Let's Dance [13-16 54-57]." In this one, Dunlap (repeating his role of producer-director) decided to capitalize on our Swiss origins. He built an elaborate Swiss inn set. We played waiters, but of course, extremely inept waiters and after we did some dumb things, the innkeeper fired us. It would be more accurate to say that he booted us out, for that is precisely what happened.

He applied a boot to our bottoms and we sailed out of the inn and onto the surface of the ice. (Doesn't every Swiss inn have an ice rink conveniently located adjacent to it?) The momentum of the innkeeper's kick propelled us across the ice until we banged into the snowbank on the other side, burying our heads into the snow, with a pair of St. Bernard dogs and their portable brandy kegs right above where our heads stuck in the snow. While all this jocularity was going on, a famous Swiss yodeling band, the Moser Brothers, were yodeling their little heads off.

We knew the Moser Brothers, since they had a restaurant, the Switzerland Café, not far from the Los Angeles Coliseum. Later, after Frack quit the act, I used Moser recordings for my own act for many years.

We had no idea of the movie's plot -- if indeed there was such a thing. We did our two big skating sequences, which gave us absolutely no idea of the film's story line. We later found out that at the time we did those two numbers, nobody else had any idea of a story line either. In fact, we learned much later that the Monogram people filmed our numbers and then went to the bank and borrowed enough money on the strength of those numbers, to have a script written and shoot the balance of the movie.

We were in New York when "Lady, Let's Dance" premiered in Hollywood. The film itself was dismissed with a few perfunctory paragraphs by most reviewers, but they universally had nice things to say about our sequences.

"Frick and Frack are terrific," said the reviewer for the Hollywood Reporter.

Monogram turned a nice little profit on the film, giving us two winners, at least financially. Both of our films had long and honorable careers and were mainstays of Late Show programming for many years. Very often, as I relaxed in my hotel room after a show, I would turn on television and see either "Silver Skates" or "Lady, Let's Dance." It was a kind of immortality I suppose.

Much later in my career, I made a third movie appearance. This time, a year or two after my retirement from active skating, I was pleased to be hired on the basis of acting ability alone. In fact, I don't think that to this day the casting director even knew that I had been a professional ice skater.

I happened to be in Lake Tahoe on vacation and heard that they were shooting some scenes for a movie to be called "Jinxed," at Harrah's Casino on the lake. They were holding an open audition for several parts, one of which from the description seemed right for me, at least physically. So I went over to the hotel.

There were six men -- the other five appeared to be some years younger than I -- and we were all told to sit on the couches outside the casting director's office and wait. So sat and we waited and finally the casting director -- a Lady, blonde and attractive -- came out.

"I want each of you to say "shit," she said, "and say it with feeling, as though you really meant it. If you want to, say it several different times, in several different ways."

I have never sworn in mixed company, so that was difficult for me to do, at first. But after the word had been said by some of the other candidates, over and over, it gradually lost its meaning -- as swear words have a tendency to do with steady repetition -- and became nothing more than syllable of unidentifiable sounds.

"Shiiiit!"

"Shhhiiiittt!"

"Shsshshshshit!"

I had my fill of shit that day, because I heard that unattractive word over and over and said it myself over and over.

Finally, the casting lady said, "Thank you," and suggested we go outside and wait downstairs. I went to the casino and had a drink and in about fifteen minutes the blonde came over to me.

"I'll take you," she said. I never found out if it was the fact that I was the oldest of the group or the passionate way I had read my line that got me the job.

The next day I reported for work as directed at 7:30 A.M. and was made up in the make-up trailer. We got to the set and I found out, to my consternation, that the scene was at the blackjack tables and I was supposed to be one of the players. I had to confess to the director, Don Siegel, that I was not a card player and had never played cards and didn't know a jack of hearts from an ace of spades. No problem, he said. They called over the casino supervisor, a nice young lady, and she gave me a crash course in playing blackjack in an enjoyable hour.

I did my scene the next day with Bette Midler, who was a delight throughout the long day's work.

There were hundreds of extras needed that day and so Yvonne got a job, and a paycheck, too. We all ate -- food brought in from a catering firm from Los Angeles, and movie set food is usually very good and this was -- and we had fun. So much fun in fact that even though my part was over (you have to keep a sharp eye open to see me, but I'm there) Yvonne and I both signed on to be extras for another week.

Through the years, I have done countless radio and television shows. Many of them were arranged by the publicity people for the Ice Follies, but many of them I arranged myself. I believe strongly in the value of good publicity and I think every performer owes it not only to himself, but to his show, to do as much as he can.

Most of the shows I did were simple one-on-one interviews, generally in a studio. Occasionally, the show would send a crew to the arena where we were playing and tape or film a sequence with me doing a little skating. Many of the interviewers liked to get into the act and would skate with me a little while. I even devised a small routine I could haul out for such occasions with a simple little role for the interviewer to do with me on the ice.

A few of the interview shows -- such as once I had with Mike Douglas in his heyday -- were more elaborate. For Douglas, I did a full three minutes and he even had his orchestra there to accompany me. James Stewart was Mike's co-host that show and I had known his wife, Gloria, quite well before she became Mrs. Stewart and I had hoped that a dialogue with him might prove to be entertaining, but it was all very quick, simple, polite and rather dull.

I enjoyed talking. I fancied myself as something of a comedian -- even without skates on my feet -- and a few people had suggested that I could have had a career as a stand-up comedian rather than a fall-down ice skater. So whenever possible, I took those shots on talk shows and tried to be funny and sometimes I think I succeeded. But I never had people knocking on my door asking me to take over when Jack Benny decided to retire, even though each time I did a talk show I fantasized that that was what was going to happen.

I also was Dinah Shore's guest when her talk show was among the more popular daytime shows. It took me almost an entire day to do that show -- to rehearse the skating I was going to do and then to do that act for the cameras and then to talk to Dinah for ten minutes or so.

For a while, late in my career, there was a strong promotional tie-in between the Ice Follies and the Baskin-Robbins ice cream people. We would frequently get to a City and be asked to join in with one of those promotions -- people who had bought ice cream were given coupons, good for free or reduced admission to the show and also we gave special performances at small portable rinks made of some kind of artificial ice. To achieve a gliding effect, we had to push across the surface of this mock ice with five times the normal effort. It dulled our blades and made them sizzling hot from the friction. It was tiresome and unpleasant, but I think it helped sell a lot of ice cream and tickets.

We did one of those performances in downtown Denver in the middle of a severe Colorado winter. I had to dress for my act in a bank that was across the street from the little pseudo-rink where we were to give our little pseudo-show. It was very windy and the mock-up ice cream cones which the Baskin-Robbins people had erected to decorate the sidewalk, all blew over immediately. The winds swirled with what meteorologists have come to call a "Monroe effect" -- after that famous shot of Marilyn Monroe standing over a grating in the sidewalk with her skirts blowing up around her head -- which causes the winds to eddy and do tricks such as blowing a lady's skirt up over her head.

That particular day the Monroe effect could have been classified as Force Ten. One of the Folliettes walking away after our little performance was carrying her costume on a hanger and got caught in one of those rip-snorting gusts and was blown back into a three-foot deep fountain. She nearly froze and we had to rush her into the warmth of the bank or she might have suffered serious frostbite or other injuries.

I did my share of Spots on TV variety shows, too. For a while, I had an agent in Hollywood -- Mary Markham -- who booked me on quite a few shows. I made guest appearances with Donny and Marie Osmond when they had their own show. The Osmonds had a particular fondness for ice skaters in general and me in particular and we had a good relationship. The Osmonds even had a skating director on their payroll, a talented man named Bob Paul. So the skating numbers on their show were always professionally planned and rehearsed and the results showed it.

Over the years, I have often wondered if I might not have been wise to make an attempt at a full-scaled Hollywood career. I took the path of least resistance and stayed with the ice show because I knew that in that arena I was at the absolute top, or beyond, of my profession. Hollywood acting was something else; I believe I could have done some character roles and believe that I could have had a good, solid, steady career. But most of us are frightened of the unknown, of taking chances. In the ice show I knew where I was, who I was, what I could and couldn't do; there were no surprises. I knew the income was there, sure and definite, while Hollywood represented a totally unknown quantity. I had learned from my Wall Street investing not to gamble -- only invest in sure things, whether with a few shares of stock or whether with your life.

Yet in retrospect, perhaps I should have taken that risk. Perhaps I should have hung up my skates say after "Lady, Let's Dance" brought me good personal notices. Perhaps I should have gambled.

Perhaps, but I didn't.

Picture 49

Mr. Frick's Cantilever Spread Eagle
Amazed Kids
Ice Follies

CHAPTER 8

To different people, travelling with an ice show reminded them of different things.

One skater who had spent several years in military service said that travelling with the Ice Follies was like being back in the Army -- "only this time with a bunch of beautiful girls."

Another skater said that it was like being back at summer camp, except that now he was old enough to enjoy it.

And one veteran stagehand always referred to it as "like a Cook's tour."

To me, though, it was like one long, non-stop party.

There were a couple of dozen healthy, sturdy, fun-loving boys and girls and generally they were attractive and distinctly heterosexual. When we worked, we were all business. But when we were off -- and particularly when we were travelling as a group -- we were all play.

In recent years, the friends that Yvonne and I have made outside of the ice show would have wondered how I could have remained a bachelor as long as I did, considering the numbers of beautiful women I worked with every day. I think that it was simply those numbers -- so many of them, so few of me -- that protected my bachelorhood. With all those girls, it would have been undiplomatic to zero in on just one. I know many of the other male skaters did manage to do a bit of zeroing in, but I never did. I played the field for many pleasant years.

Yvonne likes to joke -- at least I think she is joking -- that I was waiting for her. And, in a sense, I think she is right. I didn't know it at the time, of course, but whenever I felt the urge to get particularly close to a particular girl, something made me pull back. Still, I managed to have a good time, a wall-to-wall, non-stop, year-around good time.

Please don't get the idea that the Ice Follies was nothing but a travelling orgy, far from it. The girls were almost always from good families (I don't mean to imply that girls from good families never participate in orgies, but they are statistically less likely to) and the Ice Follies management felt an almost paternal responsibility toward them. They were guarded, chaperoned, watched. If any of the girls were thought to be too promiscuous or too anything, she was called into the office and lectured on propriety and the proper behavior for a Folliette.

One of the cardinal sins for any skater, but particularly for the showgirls, was to be caught putting on weight. They were all weighed every week and if they were found to be adding too much poundage, they were warned. The nurse who travelled with us kept exact records. Three warnings and they were out. They could come back, but only if they proved that they had lost all that weight they had put on.

In my era with the show, drugs were totally unknown. Liquor was the daring thing to use and there were always a few skaters -- both male and female -- who overdid the booze. I have always hated to see women drunk (which may either be a sign of my Swiss morality or male chauvinism or a bit of both). A few of the girls in the show were known to be big drinkers, but they rarely stayed with the show very long.

Many of the girls with the chorus had won skating titles -- some had won major competitions or had been runners-up in major events. We had quite a few gold medal winners who were just part of the skating chorus line. They joined the show for any of several reasons: the fun of it, the money of it; the chance to meet a fellow, the chance to graduate out of the chorus line and win a solo spot.

So they worked hard, especially the ambitious among them. There were generally periods of skating instruction between and after shows. Some of the veteran skaters, for a fee, would give lessons to anyone who wanted them. I frequently took those lessons myself -- especially in ice dancing, as I had never done that -- for the fun of it and also because the better conventional skater I was, the better comic skater I could be.

I usually had six girls working with me in my act. Once I counted up and among the six at that time, there were four gold medalists who had won a total of seven gold medals among them.

One had been a runner-up in the U.S. championship. They were all hoping for a shot at a solo number, but only two of that particular group ever achieved that goal.

The competition was very though, obviously. For a girl with skating ability there were, for many years, only two ice shows worth mentioning -- ours was by itself for a long time and then the Ice Capades came along. Later, Ice Vogues started; that was the forerunner of Holiday on Ice. Eventually, there were two units of Holiday on Ice and two units of the Ice Follies, plus Ice Capades, so there were five shows. That, however, was much later. We had the pick of the ice-skating crop for many years and even girls with several gold medals to their credit were hard-pressed to get a job, much less a starring solo.

Even though the odds against stardom were steep, the girls kept coming to the show. It was for them a good life. What else could they do? They had grown up skating. Probably prodded by their mothers or fathers, they had begun as children, wasting their childhood while they practiced four or five hours every day of their lives. Many parents of these girls had spent easily $100,000 on furthering their daughter' ice skating careers -- skating lessons, skating camps, skates rental of rinks for practice sessions.

On the average, those girls have had three or four years of competing for amateur titles, won a few medals, had their pictures in the local papers and their brief moments in the sun. After that, what were their options? Get married. Work in the local five-and-dime store -- they had no career training, so few jobs were open to them. Maybe they could be an airline stewardess. Maybe they could give ice skating lessons. Or they could join the ice show. It is really no wonder that so many of them tried to join us.

There were girls from all over -- big city, small city and farm. One I remember had been going to medical school ran out of money, skated with our show for three years until she had saved up enough to go back and finish her medical education. But she was the exception. Most of them simply joined the Ice Follies because it was the path of least resistance and for a few years it was a cheerful and painless existence.

If they never did achieve their goal of a solo spot, they would probably get married -- either to one of the male skaters, or to one of the Stage Door Johnnies who constantly pursued them, or possibly to one of the musicians in the orchestra. And they would quit the show and retire to East Suspender, Ohio, and do a little teaching and raise a few kids of their own. Sometimes -- too frequently -- they would come back the next year, back to the show. They found life in East Suspender, after the excitement of touring with the show, just too bland. No small town could possibly compete with the fun they had had travelling with the show.

And it certainly was fun. Because of the fact that so many people tried out for so few (relatively) jobs, the pay scale was low. It was a job that paid out in fun and excitement and a bit of glamour, but certainly not in monetary terms. Nobody (except for a Peggy Fleming or a few other headliners) got rich skating with an ice show. Making the financial position of the skaters even more precarious was the fact that they had to provide their own skates -- which can be rather costly -- and make-up and hotel rooms and meals. (To their credit, the Ice Follies management tried hard to get special rates at hotels for the cast members and generally succeeded.)

To save restaurant costs, some of the skaters tried to eat in their hotel rooms. They carried portable hot plates with them, even though such appliances were almost always banned by the hotels and would surreptitiously cook their dinners in their rooms. They would keep their groceries-on the window ledges outside their rooms because we almost always travelled during the colder months, so there was natural refrigeration outside. One skater, Bob Leduc, even managed to cook an entire Thanksgiving dinner, turkey and all, in his room and then had the audacity to invite the hotel manager to join his guests. And the manager did, too.

We had some free meals. If we did three shows on a Saturday, for example, we were entitled to free meals between both the first and second and the second and third shows. If on a Sunday, we were required to do two shows with less than two hours between them, management had to provide a free meal during that break. A few of the boys and girls would stuff rolls and whatever else they could, into their pockets or purses and try to cadge enough at those free meals to tide them over for a day or two.

The quality of those free meals varied widely. In Cleveland, we were served excellent food in an excellent setting -- complete with waiters in tails and white gloves. In Toronto, there was almost always steak at the meal, whether it was a lunch or a dinner. But in other cities, the "meal" was often nothing more than platters of bread and cheese.

For some reason, known only to the Internal Revenue Service, the skaters of the Ice Follies were their particular target for many years. They continually tried, and frequently succeeded, to disallow deductions we claimed for hotel and meal expenses while on tour. The test was always the words, "away from home." Technically, if an expense was incurred "away from home," it was legitimate. But the I.R.S. claimed that in our case "home" was where we happened to be working -- our hotel room was to them our "home" -- so that we could not claim expenses for being "away from home."

The tax people battled us over every penny we claimed as a deduction and I got more than my share of I.R.S. problems. I was meticulous in claiming deductions I felt were justified -- such as the tips I gave to the spotlight operators in every city, who deserved those tips for keeping me in the center of their light -- but the I.R.S. annually balked and fought and brought me in for audit after audit. The others in the show had their share of I.R.S. strife, too.

Some of their nit-picking was absurd. Can you imagine any expense more legitimate than an ice skater deducting the cost of his skates? Eventually, they accepted our $145 blades as a fair deduction, but they always wondered about the money I claimed for "special balls." (Those were the protective steel balls -- $15 a pair -- which I placed over my blade points for safety.)

One Folliette, fed up with the I.R.S. and their penny-pinching, told her story to a reporter for the Wall Street Journal. They then published a long story about the girl and her tax court decision on the front page. Even that positive publicity didn't help much, because we still had to scratch and claw for every deduction we claimed. It still makes me angry to think about it.

The Ice Follies show concealed many stories. Being with the show had differing effects on people. For some, it was the great adventure of their lives. For others, it was a sad and disappointing time.

There was, as a good example, lovely Karen Kresge [50-51 149-150]. She auditioned for the show one year in San Francisco. They accepted her immediately, but she wanted to finish school first, so they agreed that she could join the show the following year. She did, and skated in the chorus for all of two weeks. The bosses -- the Shipstads and Oscar Johnson -- knew they had a good thing there and quickly asked her to take over for a featured skater who had had to leave the show suddenly. (The lucky ones get all the breaks, don't they?) So Karen Kresge became a star after only two weeks in the chorus line.

She steadily and spectacularly improved and a year later she was one of the top acts in the show. She had never won a medal or a championship of any kind; she just was the type of performer the show liked. She stayed with us as one of the top stars for ten years. Then she left and today she produces the ice shows for Charles Schulz, the creator of "Peanuts," who is a big skating and hockey fan and has his own rink, one of the best in the world, in his home town, Santa Rosa, California.

As Exhibit B, consider an equally lovely girl, Uschi Kessler. She came to the Follies with impeccable credentials -- she had been a champion in Germany and had been signed in Germany and promised the moon. They told her she would be the number one star of the show, and all that.

The problem was her hair. Uschi may have been a brunette or a blonde originally -- I am not privy to that information -- but she was a practicing blonde when she joined the show. She skated like a dream, with that blonde hair flowing free behind her as she glided gracefully about the ice. At the same time, however, the show's male star was Richard Dwyer, a man who took his stardom seriously. Dwyer had a partner who was also a blonde. This young lady saw her position as ranking blonde in the show jeopardized by the coming of Uschi Kessler and told her partner and Dwyer decided to exercise his stardom and complained.

He said that he wanted Uschi Kessler to be-

Chapter 8

come a brunette so his partner's blondness would not be challenged.

Uschi was suffering from homesickness in the first place -- she often talked to Yvonne and me, because we could talk to her in German and that made her feel better. She really didn't understand this foolishness of being asked to change the color of her hair -- what had that to do with ice skating? And between homesickness and blonde-sickness, she became very despondent. She cried often and was a very sad little girl.

But she dutifully changed from blonde to brunette and skated on. Yet there was no question that the verve had gone out of her performance. She was a pro, of course, and always skated well, yet her enthusiasm was gone. And then she suddenly told Yvonne and me that she was going to marry a man who was a long-standing Stage Door Johnny. Everybody knew this fellow and Yvonne and I cautioned Uschi about such a quick, rash decision. But she insisted and Yvonne went shopping with her for her trousseau and saw to it that she had a fine wedding.

Dick Dwyer, who was never one of my favorite people, had won again. Uschi Kessler left the show after less than a year and Dwyer and his partner had the blonde title back -- undisputed now. I considered it a very rotten thing they had done to a poor, lonely girl who only wanted to do her best.

Of course, it's a cold, cruel world out there and maybe the fact that we worked on ice made it even colder and crueler. But there were many stories of heartbreak like Uschi's. Another one who also found life in America difficult to understand was Aja Zanova [Alena Vrzáňová].

You probably remember that name. She had been the skating champion of Czechoslovakia and then of the world in 1950. There were front page stories when she defected and again when it was announced that the Ice Follies had signed her. It was quite a feather in the Ice Follie's collective cap when they got her because she had become something of cause célèbre and there's nothing like a cause célèbre to give the box office a boost.

She joined the show in Seattle. She was tall and powerfully built, beautiful and aggressive, and a truly marvelous performer. We could speak together -- her English was rudimentary at first, so she welcomed the chance to speak German, which she had spoken fluently and quickly latched on to me as a kind of father figure. She asked me to stay with her through her first rehearsals with the show.

"What did you think?" she asked me.

"You are wonderful," I said, "but I think your music (she was using some Hungarian gypsy tune) is too fast."

I was overruled on that by the show's production team, who liked fast music and fast skating.

Aja took a while adjusting to show business -- skating in a production-oriented show like ours is considerably different than skating in competition -- and really wasn't ready when the powers-that-were decided it was time for her to make her debut.

Without any advance warning, they told her she was going on the next night, during our San Francisco run. She had to make her entrance in the dark, a movement that was totally unrehearsed. And as she tried to find her way from the backstage area to the rink, she got confused (understandably) and bumped into several props and ran into skaters from the previous number as they were exiting. So by the time she got onto the ice, her music had already started and she was rather confused and the whole thing degenerated into one large mess.

Undaunted, she did her act, finally getting together with her music, but was disappointed with her performance. She felt that as a champion, she deserved better treatment than she had received. After that near-disastrous first show, I took her to the Papagayo Room at the Fairmont Hotel. She ordered a triple brandy and drank it down in one long, thirsty swallow. It didn't affect her in the least.

That first year for Aja was a year of struggle. The show was patient -- their philosophy always was that no skater is ever a hit in his or her first season with the Follies. The second year they put her in a Japanese number as a geisha girl. Aja was five feet ten inches tall and broad shouldered. Our perception of geisha girls is that they are dainty, birdlike little creatures. Aja looked as much like a geisha girl as she looked like a pygmy.

Most of us were appalled by that casting. One

of those who was appalled was Fran Claudet, an important person in the Ice Follies hierarchy -- but not important enough to prevent Aja's role as a geisha girl. Fran was one of the show's planners, the travelling coach and director of the show. She was a former Canadian champion and an Olympic skater and was a semi-official mother to many of the people in the show for twenty-five years.

She fought against having Aja in that ridiculous geisha number. The next year she again fought when the bosses stuck Aja in a pair of unflattering slacks for her main number. Fran said Aja could slim and trim and become very attractive, the brass at the time felt her legs were too heavy and masked them in slacks. That further destroyed her self-confidence. She skated perfunctorily -- still technically sound, but the spark was gone. At the end of that third season, her contract was not renewed.

She asked me to make a contract for her with John Harris, who headed up our arch-rival, the Ice Capades. I did contact Harris and while there was no immediate opening for her, she joined that show a year later. By that time, she had taken my advice and slimmed and trimmed down and she shone with the Ice Capades. After a decade of outstanding skating, she quit and did public relations work for that show. Then she became a New York restaurateur with several restaurants, including The Duck Joint and the famous Czech Pavilion.

While Aja Zanova ultimately found happiness in America, her first three years here, those years when she was with our show, were unhappy for her. Perhaps it takes any immigrant that long to adjust, but I think the pressures on her to live up to her championship reputation and to be the star that she was expected to be made her adjustment much more difficult than most.

In her era, skaters did not have managers and very few of them even had agents. Later, skaters -- like all athletes -- did have managers who looked out for their interest. Skaters such as Peggy Fleming never had to dicker about money or complain about conditions or discuss such mundane matters as contracts or clauses; their managers did all that grubby work for them. I believe that if Aja Zanova had had a manager her adjustment to life in America would have been quicker, smoother and happier.

Her life with us was not total endless gloom, however. She had fun like we all had fun and I will always treasure the memory of her taking a dare somewhere and pouring a glass of brandy into a fish tank. I suppose animal lovers may think that was cruel and heartless behavior, but those particular fish did not seem to mind in the least.

On the road, thrown together like college kids or Army buddies or camp bunkmates, the Follies crowd turned inward in the search for amusement. We were forced to provide our own fun and games.

Each City we visited had its own particular stamp, its own source of our memories.

Montreal -- I think of that always as a festive City. We usually stayed at the Windsor Hotel, which was old, but regal. Mostly, I remember the weather in Montreal, looking out of our hotel room window the day an ice storm had coated the sidewalks with a thin veneer of glare ice. People were trying to get out of their cabs, but the combination of the blowing wind and the ice made walking on impossibility. I saw one poor businessman go ass over tea kettle and his attached case flew up in the wind, soared two stories high, then came crashing down on the sidewalk where it burst open and all the poor man's papers scattered in the wind.

In Montreal, we played in the same arena where the Montreal Canadians played hockey. What made that nice for us was that the hockey team and the arena were both owned by a local brewery and there was always plenty of cold beer around after our performance.

One morning, faced with the prospect of a long day of inactivity, I left my hotel for a walk on Mont Royal, a hill that stretched perhaps a mile long, not very steep and certainly well within my powers. I had climbed it often enough before. But this time, as I was about halfway up, I felt a chill. I headed for a chalet I knew was there, but for some reason it was closed that day. I had to go on and made it to a high-rise apartment building another half-mile or so along. There, I was able to get a cab back to the Ritz.

The doctor I called said there was nothing wrong. He said it might be something in my stomach and prescribed some medicine. But the next day I was worse and went to the doctor's office. He immediately said it was peritonitis. He said I had to have an appendectomy immediately. I said I would rather go to Switzerland for the Operation and told him there was a plane for Zurich in three hours.

"You may be able to make the plane," the doctor said, "but you will never survive the trip."

So I was operated on. The surgeon later told me that my stomach muscles were unusually tough, necessitating a larger-than-normal incision. I recuperated luxuriously with visits from the Swiss consul and many of the old friends I had made on my several visits to Montreal.

Tulsa -- It was in Tulsa that the Ice Follies had begun back in 1936. And it was in Tulsa where Oscar Johnson peeked through the curtain one evening just before the overture and said, "Kids, we've got them outnumbered!"

We didn't play Tulsa very often after that night.

Buffalo -- Another cold, cold City. The wind would blow in from Lake Erie and they were so powerful that when it snowed there would be little snow drifts on the window sill -- inside my window.

Cleveland -- If the wind was right, the smell from the refineries was strong enough to wake me up in my room at the Statler. But if the winds changed, I would walk along the Lake Erie shore and it was lovely. I would sometimes use the old Basel housewifery trick -- opening the window and leaning on a pillow -- and absorb some nice Ohio sun, using my handy-dandy reflector. That's how I kept my tan, and would astound people in the east in mid-winter with that tan.

Detroit -- One memorable part of our performances in Detroit was the end. The only way back from the ice to the dressing rooms was a walkway which was also used by the patrons exiting after the finale. So there was no choice -- we had to mix with the public as we made our way back to the dressing rooms. They would stare at us sometimes try to strike up conversations, sometimes they smiled. They often merely elbow us out of their way in their haste to get to the parking lot.

Pittsburgh -- Wherever we played, there were always ticket requests from friends to be filled but, for some reason, there were always more in Pittsburgh. Once, I was asked to find a way to get some one hundred members of the Pittsburgh Skating Club to visit us backstage. I managed somehow. Another Pittsburgh memory is the time we were invited by Fran Claudet, who had left the Show when she married a wealthy Pittsburgh man, Worthington Johnson, to join them at dinner at the Duquesne Club. There were six of us who received the invitation and we went to the Club -- so exclusive there wasn't even a name on the door -- and we sat in the foyer and waited, and waited. Eventually, the major domo came with a message. The Johnsons would be delayed, he said, and we should start the dinner without them. They were in Indianapolis because their plane was forced to bypass Pittsburgh because of bad weather. That was a genuine no-host dinner.

Often, the night after we were scheduled to play our last performance at Maple Leaf Gardens, that city's hockey team, the Maple Leafs, would be scheduled for a game on that same ice. The refrigeration engineer would be so anxious to begin his preparations for the hockey game he couldn't wait until our show was over. He would prematurely let the ice melt and then apply a fresh layer of water. The second half of our final show would be played on that sloshy ice with a layer of water over it. I remember our costumes would still be wet when we unpacked them at our next stop, generally Montreal.

We had a little joke among us and whenever we confronted bad ice such as that final Toronto show, we would say, "Better ice they got in Moscow." (Later, when our hockey team played in Moscow, my friend, Tom Naylor, who accompanied them, reported back to me that they actually did have better ice in Moscow.)

Toronto changed dramatically in the years I visited it. It had been, originally, a dull city. Even the natives would go to Buffalo for fun. But it turned around drastically and became a great city with a European flavor. The Toronto Skating Club Carnival helped to contribute to that flavor, especially at the ball, the concluding feature. I never saw so many Scotch bagpipers as they had every year at the Royal York Hotel for that ball.

San Francisco -- That was always one of the great stops for us, almost like going home. We were part of the fabric of the City and they liked us as much as we liked them.

I was an honorary member of the Swiss Club of San Francisco. One year, that group's president, the energetic and glamorous Brigitte Amann, decided it was time to honor me -- a Mr. Frick Night. They held it during the intermission at the Ice Follies and the problem was that they wanted a long tribute with Swiss music and many speeches and gifts to me (that part was fine with me), but the Ice Follies management insisted that they keep it short, that the intermission was timed carefully and could not be extended very long.

There was a party for me after the show that night and the whole evening was one I will always remember with great fondness.

Wherever we played, the last day of an engagement was a frenzied time. The longer the engagement had been, the greater the frenzy. We usually spent six weeks in Los Angeles at the Pan Pacific Auditorium and then usually left for a three-day, three-night train trip en route to our next stop, generally Chicago.

As soon as the Auditorium went dark, after that final L.A. show, there was a tremendous cheer. Then we would all run off the ice and the frenzy would begin -- packing, saying goodbye to family and friends, making all the last minute arrangements that had to be made. In my case, I occasionally kept a car in Los Angeles and had to arrange for the Auto Club to get the key after I drove it to Union Station. And I had many more props than the rest of the cast, so I had to supervise the crating and shipping of all those props.

The Ice Follies special left Union Station as a rule, five hours after the show was over. Those were five of the most hectic, frantic hours you can imagine. The performers raced around, mostly aimlessly, as they tried to say their goodbyes and do their packing and pay their rent and do all those little things that had to be done.

We had six Pullman sleeping cars. We were all assigned to our own berths or bedrooms, not that it mattered very much where you were assigned. It was all one big berth, a sort of wide open society, six Pullman sleeping cars of parties, laughter, drinking and love-making. We could (and did) easily remove the partitions between berths.

I always tipped the porter as I got on and had him make up my bedroom berth to my very special specifications. I had him bring me an extra mattress. Then, between the two mattresses, I put my own inflated air mattress. I had learned early in my travels that railroad roadbeds were usually very bumpy and my little system provided me with my private floating ride.

As soon as the train began moving, we all let out another grand cheer and everybody would get into pajamas or nightgowns and begin opening up bottles of liquor and bags of pretzels and potato chips. Let the partying begin! It was a wonderful spot for a man because the Folliettes had us clearly outnumbered -- about three or four to one. Frequently, there were stowaway boyfriends for a while, but they would be booted off in San Bernardino or Cucamonga, whichever came first.

On one of those Los Angeles-Chicago runs, I was assigned a bedroom next to that occupied by a young lady named Jane. She wasn't a skater. She was part of the quartet that sang the songs during the Show. Jane and I went to the train's club car and had cocktails, toasting a mutually pleasant journey. Then we moved into the dining car. In those glory days of American railroading, the dining cars were havens for the hungry -- impeccable service, marvelous food, a lovely, leisurely time. After dinner, Jane and I strolled through the length of the six cars observing, snooping and making mental notes of where the best parties seemed to be starting up. We literally had our choice of party types -- wild ones, calm ones, parties where they were playing games or parties where they were discussing the world situation, parties that had too many girls or parties that had too few.

Two of the six cars were for women only, although nobody really abided by those rules, but they existed nonetheless. Many of the girls had boarded the train, immediately jumped into pajamas and didn't change again until we reached the outskirts of Chicago. They might not have slept in them, but they wore them.

Frequently, the Santa Fe railroad had hooked an empty baggage car to our train so that we would have a place to dance. That made the parties spread out even more. We had record players and records, but there was a lot of dancing even without music. We had six baggage cars as part of our sixteen-car special train -- to carry our equipment and sometimes a few animals, horses, cows, even the occasional pig -- and splinter groups from our parties would find refuge in those cars occasionally.

I remember one night waking up when something stopped our train and I looked out the window to see if I could see anything. There was a railroad crossing with its barrier down and its light flashing and behind it, a car had stopped. The man and woman in the car were looking at our train with their eyes wide open and their jaws down to their knees. I had no idea precisely what they were watching that had shocked them so vividly, but it must have been juicy. Nobody ever bothered to pull their shades down on the train -- what was the point? So I suspect that that rural Kansas couple was an eyewitness to some genuine Ice Follies romance. (It is also possible that I was the object of their shock. I never wore any pajamas, on the theory that a nude person would be the first one rescued in the event of a train wreck. Perhaps they caught sight of me in my anti-train wreck nude attire.)

Often, I would go to the rear of the train where there was a small platform and sit there and read. I liked to find some solitude occasionally; I can only take partying for so long. If the weather was good -- and through Arizona and New Mexico it usually was -- I would freshen up my suntan during those periods of respite from the revelry.

After one of those occasions -- this time, an hour or so before breakfast -- I headed back to the dining car for breakfast and I sat at a table with an old friend. Clyde had been with the Show forever, give or take a year, as our top stagehand. We ordered breakfast -- the railroad served the biggest prunes for breakfast I have ever seen anywhere -- and I could see that Clyde seemed uncomfortable.

"What's the matter?" I asked him.

"Don't rightly know," he said, "having problems chewing this morning. My teeth don't seem to fit right somehow."

After a few more awkward chews, he left his seat. I figured he was going to the men's room to adjust his teeth. He came back about five minutes later, smiling broadly.

"Must have picked up the wrong teeth this morning," he said. And he explained that when he had retired the previous night, he had taken his teeth out and stuffed them under the pillow. In the morning, he had reached in and pulled out what he thought were his teeth, but they weren't. The ones he grabbed must have fallen into his berth from the one above. When he realized that he wasn't chewing with his ordinary gusto, he had gone back to the berth and found his rightful teeth under another pillow and made the quick exchange. Then he proceeded to finish his breakfast, chewing merrily.

Usually, the train arrived in Chicago a day before the show opened. So we had a day to come down from the high generated by the train trip and to get settled in our new quarters before we opened. But there usually was a party there too, so all it meant was that we went from a moving party to a stationary one.

In Chicago, and in many of the other cities we visited, I developed special procedures for achieving a home-like atmosphere in my hotel room. That isn't easy to do because generally hotel rooms are about as home-like as a Russian gulag.

It begins, of course, with finding the best room the place has to offer. One of our regular stops was Hershey, Pennsylvania. I had found, through trial and error, that I liked Room 428 at the Hershey Inn best of all. So I would go to almost any lengths to get that room for my own. I would reserve it in advance, of course, but that wasn't enough. There was another stratagem I employed to make sure I got the room of my choice.

I first employed my devious scheme the year after one of my colleagues literally stole Room 428 from me. A rascal named Bill Jack, who was in a group called The Scarecrows, had seen my room the previous year and admired it. So he arranged to arrive at the check-in desk of the hotel before me and asked for Room 428. They told him it was reserved for Mr. Frick.

"Yes, I know," said Bill, "but Mr. Frick is not coming this year."

And he got the room. When I arrived, I had my choice of a room on the street -- noisy -- or a room in the back -- sunless. I determined that that would never happen to me again. So I devised my stratagem.

Our train to Hershey stopped earlier in Harrisburg to change locomotives. I had poured over maps and realized that Harrisburg was barely twelve miles from Hershey. So I simply hopped off the train in Harrisburg, took a cab to Hershey and was at the hotel probably before the train left the Harrisburg station. The only drawback was the topography around the Harrisburg station -- it was set into a kind of depression and to reach the cab station, there was a steep stairway. But I was good at steep stairways. I raced up them, just in case Bill Jack or some other ne'er-do-well had designs on my room.

The Hershey Inn was located at the intersection of Chocolate and Cocoa Avenues. I always thought that was a very tasty location. The first thing I would do when I checked in was call for the hotel's carpenter. After the first few times I had summoned him, he would know what I wanted before I asked.

I liked quiet. The Hershey Inn had very thin, plywood doors between the connecting rooms. So the carpenter and I had devised a system of soundproofing. He got a sheet of plywood, covered it with carpet, and stuck it up to cover the door.

Actually, as I told the dubious carpenter the first time I instructed him in the fine art of soundproofing a room, tactics like that are common in Europe. In fact, in many hotels -- such as the famous Palace in Gstaad [Switzerland] -- there are double doors between rooms, one on each side, with a gap between them. It is a common practice to put a mattress between those two doors so that no sound comes in -- or, sometimes more important, no sound goes out, either.

For years, Pennsylvania had its Blue Law, so that we could not perform on Sundays. That meant we always had Sundays off when we played Hershey and other Pennsylvania cities, too. But I particularly remember Sundays in Hershey because then I would rent a car and drive out into the lovely Pennsylvania Dutch countryside out near Lancaster. There, I would often call on Dudley Armstrong, of the Armstrong flooring Armstrongs, and he would show me his factory, of which he was justifiably proud.

I also had managed, with difficulty, to get to know an Amish family. They are notoriously shy with strangers, but perhaps because of my Swiss heritage, they accepted me. And so did one of their daughters, a very lovely girl. One memorable Sunday she borrowed the family's only means of transportation -- a horse and buggy -- and trotted down to Lancaster where we rendezvoused. I then rented a car and we had a lovely afternoon together. Despite the Amish folks' well-known shyness and antipathy to strangers, they did allow their daughters -- from sixteen until twenty-one -- to rumspring. That lovely word simply means to get around, to date to have a good time. At twenty-one, however, things changed and the girls had to buckle down and find a husband and that was the end of their rumspringing. As part of the rumspring freedom, the girls were given use of the "courting buggy" and I had my share of afternoons in that pleasant mode of transportation.

My date for the day would proudly show off the little town called Intercourse -- she knew that all "outsiders" got a kick out of being in Intercourse -- and I would mail some postcards from there. (I had long made a practice, incidentally, of having my Christmas cards mailed from Frick, Switzerland, but that year, I had them all sent from Intercourse. It had a certain ring to it.)

Some years later, the Hershey Inn was torn down and I was saddened by that news. That had been one of my favorite homes away from home.

Another was the Broadmoor Hotel near Colorado Springs, Colorado. Yvonne and I had a sentimental attachment to the Broadmoor; it was our honeymoon hotel. Besides, it was supervised by a friend, Thayer Tutt, who was a big fan of skating and skaters as well as a major business figure. He had married a skater, Yvonne McGowan who, despite that Irish-sounding name, was a Swiss. I had dated Yvonne years before. Tutt had given land and money to the Skating Hall of Fame, which is located near the Broadmoor.

I remember fondly many lovely days in and around the old Broadmoor -- bicycling around the nearby lake on an Indian summer day, with the trees yellowed by autumn; the regular Friday brunches the hotel gave for all the Follies personnel, followed by an afternoon of using any or all of the many facilities; the links where I had my first golf lesson, beginning a late-blooming relationship with that curious, maddening game; a hot midsummer day when I was asked to participate in a skating show on mock ice, for underprivileged children and did my act outdoors with the thermometer registering 104 degrees [40°C].

Or was that hot house skiing in Phoenix? Yes, it was Phoenix. Sometimes, it is hard to remember what happened where. But Phoenix was another regular stop for us and I do remember the Monday night barbecues at Pinnacle Peak where the biggest steak in the place cost $4.50 and then they gave you some to take home.

I learned, through trial, error and the experiences of other hotel habitudes, how to exist as comfortably as possible in hotel rooms. One secret: if possible, get a corner room. I am a fanatic about fresh air in my room. For years, I always travelled with tools so I could open stuck windows. (Once, in fact, I was invited to speak to a hotel convention and the title of my little talk was "Thirty Years of Hotel Living, With Hammer and Chisel.") The need for fresh air was particularly important to us when Yvonne was having her worst physical problems. She often was required to stay in her room as much as twenty hours a day and fresh air was absolutely essential under those conditions.

I learned some facts about air and windows. For some reason known only to physicists and hotel architects, air has a tendency to push into the room from halls and lobbies, forcing air out of the windows. Air from the outside thus has a difficult time making its way into the room. That's why most air in hotel rooms is usually stale and dirty.

Corner rooms give you the best chance of luring fresh air into your room. I also took to putting tape along the door frame to keep the air in the hall from forcing its way in. I would also tape the cracks on any connecting door because if the man next door was smoking, his smoke would seep into my room. Tape also keeps out deadly fumes, in case of fire. Another fire tip: if a fire breaks out, turn on the shower because that produces oxygen which could be a life-saving asset. I learned, too, as I studied hotel room air, that the higher the floor, the greater the inside pressure, keeping air from entering the room. So I would usually ask for a room on one of the lower floors.

Once we were staying at the Sheraton-Cadillac in Detroit. This hotel was very sturdily built and the window frames were metal and very strong. They supplied a special lever with which guests could -- if they were built like Hercules -- lift the window. One afternoon, I opened the window and then left for a matinee performance, leaving Yvonne in the room. A storm came up and she wanted to close the window, but was physically unable to do so. I had, fortunately, anticipated that possibility and had left a supply of towels near the window and she simply stuffed towels in the gap. She was snug and comfortable when I returned.

I took advantage of many hotel services as I travelled, including that marvelous option, the wake-up call. I would much rather have a telephone call to tell me it was time to get up than a jarring and impersonal clang of an alarm clock.

Through the friendly wake-up call system, I got to know hotel night telephone operators on a first-name basis. In Seattle at the Olympic Hotel, the Operator and I would have a pleasant chat every evening when I called with my wake-up instructions. She was a bit on the mischievous side and to amuse me, would hook me up so that I could eavesdrop on other phones in the hotel. On evening, she rang me up and told me she had a great call for me to listen to and hooked me up so I was listening to a husband and wife discussing their divorce settlement.

Each City we visited had its own personality. Toronto was the fun city. New York was the excitement capitol of the world. San Francisco was the closest thing we had to a home. Los Angeles was glamorous. I doubt if anybody gets as much of an insight into a city as a performer with a travelling show. And since I travelled with that same show for so many years, my education might be called post-graduate.

Picture 50 ✧ Page 141

1972 - Mr. Frick & Karen Kresge
Ice Follies

1973 - Mr. Frick & Karen Kresge
The fabulous Mr. Frick assists captivating Karen Kresge
Ice Follies

CHAPTER 9

When the Second World War broke out I was, like everyone else in the civilized world, concerned. My homeland, Switzerland, maintained its traditional neutrality. Yet my emotional response, perhaps because I was living in the United States, was very pro-Allies. Anyhow, I hated Hitler and the Nazis with a growing passion.

I was exempted from the U.S. Army draft because of being still technically a Swiss. Furthermore, there was at the time a treaty between the U.S. and Switzerland which exempted any Swiss from serving in the United States Army.

However, my feelings were so strong that I wanted to do something. So I applied for service in the U.S. Navy. I never doubted that I would be accepted; after all, I was probably in better physical shape than ninety-five percent of the young men the Navy physicians examined. And with my command of a few languages -- German and French -- I might be useful as a translator, if nothing else.

But they turned me down. I failed to pass that physical exam, a fact which stunned and then saddened me. I still don't understand it because I had always kept myself in the best of condition. People have theorized that they rejected me for other than the stated reasons and I suppose that is a possibility.

Actually, sometime later a government official told me that they felt I was making a very valuable contribution to the war effort through entertaining on the home front. I have no way of knowing if the Navy turned me down so that I could continue to entertain or not, but many friends of mine believe that was the case.

The Ice Follies carried on through the duration of the war and I guess we did our part to keep up the national morale. It wasn't easy because we lost a lot of our young male skaters to the draft. Quite a few of our young fellows joined the Army's mountain troops based and trained in Colorado, since they felt at home in that sort of environment. We had to scrounge around to get replacements for them, and some of our male skaters -- if you looked closely -- were not youngsters. A lot of them were ex-Follies personnel brought back out of retirement to do their duty with us.

The show's people -- especially the headliners such as regards me -- were in constant demand to sell war bonds. Every City we played seemed to be staging a war bond rally to coincide with our arrival and we had to get out there and help sell those bonds. Mostly, those rallies were in some major downtown location and we were all called on to give little speeches. I worked up a brief comedy routine I could do on dry land and that seemed to work pretty well. I was very pleased one day in Seattle when some wealthy local man came up and said he was buying a $10,000 bond primarily in response to my sales pitch. I figured I was responsible for manufacturing a Jeep or two, or a barrel of bullets, that day.

(I don't know how I found out but I did, that that wealthy man actually had made his gesture purely for publicity purposes. He cashed his $10,000 bond in only a month later.)

Frequently during the war, the proceeds from our opening night performance in a City were turned over to some national cause such as Armed Forces Relief. And furthermore, the show instituted a policy of giving servicemen admission at greatly reduced prices. So the show's profits were cut somewhat during the war years, but nobody complained about that.

In San Francisco, we had done our show for years at an arena called Winterland, which had been located in a section of the city inhabited primarily by Japanese. The area was always clean and neat and safe and we had enjoyed strolling around between shows, looking at the quaint little shops and admiring the very attractive little people.

With the coming of World War II, all that changed overnight. There was all that anti-Japanese hysteria immediately following the dastardly attack on Pearl Harbor. Americans failed to distinguish between the actions of the Japanese government, who had planned and executed that attack, and the behavior of the Japanese-

Americans living in the U.S. who were as loyal to the American cause and the American way of life as anybody could be. So more than one hundred thousand Japanese-Americans were rounded up and sent off to internment camps.

Their homes in the area around Winterland -- called, naturally, Little Tokyo or less politely, Japan-town -- were taken away from them. At the time, with war material plants desperate for workers, thousands of people migrated to San Francisco from the south and took over the area where the Japanese-Americans had been living.

The next time our show came to San Francisco as that transition was taking place, we hardly recognized the area. The neat, clean and safe section had been transformed virtually overnight into one that was sloppy, dirty and exceedingly dangerous. No more walking around.

After the war was over, the Japanese-Americans came back, but they were never able to reclaim their homes or recover their property. It was a shameful happening.

A few years after the war, the show rented the hall of large church not far from Winterland, for rehearsals. You may not realize it, but many ice show rehearsals take place on a regular surface -- the skaters know how to skate so they rehearse their movements and practice their ballet steps without skates on. We actually shared that church hall with another group. It was a religious group headed by a charismatic minister named Jim Jones. I often listened to him talk and found him an exciting speaker. Later, of course, I learned, in common with the rest of the world, that he was a dangerous and psychopathic nut. That was the Jim Jones who led his followers to British Guiana and ultimately persuaded some eight hundred of them to commit suicide with him.

When the war ended in Europe, there were still thousands of American GIs on that battered continent. And now that the Nazis had been defeated, many of those GIs took advantage of their position and did as much sight-seeing as their passes would allow. Many of them went to Switzerland.

I learned from my father that the American Army maintained small detachments in several Swiss cities to assist those touring soldiers. There were several hundred in my home City, Basel. My father wrote me that he was at the railroad station one day -- he was, as I have written, a retired railroad man -- and heard an American sergeant welcoming some of those GI tourists to Basel.

"Welcome to Basel, men," he said. "This is the home town of Frick and Frack."

My father couldn't contain himself. He stepped up to that sergeant and said, "Good morning! I am the father of Frick."

Everybody wanted to shake his hand. He was very proud that day. Actually, the sergeant introduced himself to my father and said he was going home in a few weeks and he hoped to get to see the Ice Follies and Frick and Frack very soon.

When we played Boston some weeks later, a man came up to me and said he was Milton Hoff, a former U.S. Army sergeant and told me that he had met my father at the Basel railroad station.

Another story from my father was about an old friend of his from the railroad. This venerable gentleman, who had been a conductor on Swiss trains for almost fifty years, was amazed one day when he saw a black American soldier on his train. He had seen a few black soldiers before, but what was amazing was that this one was speaking German with a perfect Swiss dialect. It turned out that that soldier was from Wisconsin and had been raised on a farm that was owned by some Swiss immigrants.

The show went on throughout the war, on days when the news was bad and on days when the news was good. In fact, during my many years with the Ice Follies, the only performance that was ever cancelled was on the night when President Kennedy was assassinated. So we kept performing, even though sometimes our hearts weren't in it.

As you can imagine, travel during wartime was difficult. Our trains were invariably late -- shunted off on a siding while a train carrying war supplies was, naturally, given priority -- and we frequently worried about making it to our next destination in time for our performance. I don't think we were ever late.

The service on the trains declined, too, which was understandable. Personnel were needed for more serious business than seeing that the Ice

Follies people got their steaks done to a turn and the exact number of ice cubes in their drinks. So the dining cars were often missing and we began bringing our own food with us and making dinners out of sandwiches we made ourselves, or dashing off at stops and seeing what we could find in the area in and around the station.

Still, I don't think anybody complained. Many of the skaters had come originally from Europe and had relatives back there and so felt themselves fortunate to be in America where there were no bombs falling.

So we skated our way through World War II and were, like the rest of the world, thrilled and relieved when it all came to a happy ending.

Picture 52 ✦ Page 223

1974 - Mr. Frick and Swiss school children
Arosa (Switzerland)

CHAPTER 10

I mentioned briefly the acquisition of Lulu, our poodle. I failed to mention, however, that while Lulu was theoretically Yvonne's dog, I fell madly in love with her very quickly. We had Lulu with us for fourteen years and I never had a dog before and I doubt that Yvonne and I will ever have another one.

In Switzerland, when I was growing up, I don't remember many dogs as pets. There were the famous St. Bernard's heroes of so many true tales of Alpine rescues, but there were not many pets kept in the houses on Frobenstrasse, a few cats, yes, but very few, and no dogs that I recall.

Still, there must have been some, for our Lulu came from a kennel in Zurich and as I wrote earlier, the lady who ran the kennel was aghast at the thought that one of her products would leave the country. And, even worse, be touring and not have a proper home.

People have often said, or hinted that Lulu was the substitute for the child we never had and I suppose there could be some truth to that. We often talked over the years about whether we had made the right choice when we elected to have no children. I think we did. Even though I remained physically youthful, I would still have been thirty-nine at the youngest when our first child would have been born and I honestly feel that would have been too old to be a first-rate father. Then too, Yvonne's health would have made the fact that she had a child or children to care for an insurmountable burden.

So, as I have said, I had the vasectomy which allowed us to enjoy our relationship without worrying about Yvonne conceiving a child. And we did have a healthy and exciting relationship. I think it was obvious to everyone in the show that Yvonne and I enjoyed each other's company around the clock. The others in the show would often kid me on matinee days when I would come back to the rink after our break, glowing all over.

"Ah ha, Frick," they would say, "you had yourself an extra matinee, I see," or innuendos to that effect. And they were often correct in their assessment of the situation. Yvonne and I -- because of my operation -- made love frequently and joyously and without any worry about whether or not she was going to become pregnant.

Still, there was always the fact that we were not a complete family. Both of us had grown up in a family with parents and children and we knew firsthand the pleasure and security of such an arrangement. There was something missing in our lives and I am sure Yvonne felt that even more strongly than I did -- the maternal instinct is a strong one and one that every woman is equipped with.

So Lulu came into our lives. And don't say to me:" Yes, but Lulu was only a dog." Lulu was much more than "only a dog" to us.

I must confess, however, that when Yvonne called me from Switzerland to tell me, breathlessly, that she had a surprise for me -- a dog! -- I was less than thrilled. Life on the road is difficult enough for unencumbered human beings. How could a dog cope with all the changes and moving's and hotel rooms and differences in food and water? From what I knew about dogs, they liked things the same, they enjoyed a life of stability and familiarity. Besides, wouldn't having a dog along make our already complicated life on the road even more so?

A few days later, Yvonne called again. She was staying with her sister, Cécile, and I knew Cécile -- a woman of outstanding and strict cleanliness. Her home, full of lush beige carpets, was fastidious. Yvonne called to say they had brought the little white poodle puppy to Cécile's house -- and I was all prepared to hear stories of the disasters of what the puppy had done to her carpets. But what I heard was exactly the opposite. The puppy had sensibly waited until she was taken outside into the garden before relieving herself.

"Cécile says this is the smartest dog she has ever seen," Yvonne reported to me with almost maternal pride.

Ok, I thought, that's good. But it would be a lot different once the poodle has joined the show. We already had a dog act -- twelve dogs --

and with them yapping and racing around it might teach our dog bad habits. Dogs are like humans; if they get in with the wrong crowd, they can go wrong.

Yvonne's trip across from Zurich to San Francisco with Lulu was nerve-wracking. As it turned out, it needn't have been because Lulu turned out to be a remarkable traveler. But Yvonne didn't know that at the time she boarded the Swissair plane in Zurich.

Cécile and Ernst saw them off, with Yvonne carrying Lulu in a little bag. This was in the days -- long gone, unfortunately -- when Swissair had berths on their international flights. So Yvonne and Lulu began to retire to their upper berth, but the lady in the lower berth was enchanted with Lulu and insisted that they switch. She said she was a very sound sleeper and was not planning on getting off the plane when it made its stops in Shannon in Ireland, or in Gander in Newfoundland. So Yvonne could have the lower berth and get off to give Lulu a chance to walk around a bit.

As it turned out, the flight attendant turned out to be another dog lover and she happily took Lulu for a walk in Shannon. Lulu was so excited by the adventure of it all that she piddled a few drops on the bed and Yvonne was terribly embarrassed and offered to pay for laundering the linens or whatever. The flight attendant laughed and said, "Don't worry -- if all my passengers were as nice as you and Lulu, my life would be <u>wunderbar</u> [wonderful]!" She told a shocked Yvonne that children very often made water and even defecated in the berths. And that she had even had adults who did that, too -- "Too lazy to get up and go to the restrooms, I suppose."

Yvonne and Lulu passed through customs in New York quickly and without incident because the Zurich kennel owner had been scrupulous about giving her pup all the right shots and had the documentation to prove it. They stayed with friends in New York for one night. Then flew on to San Francisco where I met them.

Yvonne formally introduced us. Lulu wagged her tail and I picked her up and gave her a welcoming kiss.

"Here is your daddy, Lulu," Yvonne said. I wasn't exactly overjoyed at that, but I didn't protest. I took them to the hotel and had a surprise in our room -- a talented Follies star, Lesley Goodwin, had-built a dog-house at my direction, which even had a little balcony with geraniums and a red roof and a large sign which read, "Welcome Lulu and Yvonne."

Lulu loved her little home from the start and she was obviously exhausted from the trip and walked in, sniffed around, curled up and went to sleep. The next morning, Yvonne was up early to take Lulu for what became a daily event, her morning walk.

"I want you to rest," I said to Yvonne. "I will take the dog out for its walk. We have to get to know one another."

So we went out and by the time I got back my heart had been totally stolen. For the next thirteen years, nine months and four days, I was Lulu's happy slave.

I venture to say that Lulu could be classified as the world's most spoiled dog. She ate only the finest food. She had the most careful medical attention. She travelled in style, as I will describe shortly. And whenever Yvonne and I went someplace where we could not take her, she had a baby sitter. We were as careful about who we hired to stay with Lulu as genuine parents are when they hire a baby sitter for their children. We would often call a baby sitter agency recommended by whatever hotel we were staying at, and say we needed a sitter for our dog. They would be wary "How big is the dog?" "Is it housebroken?" "Is it vicious?" and sometimes would flatly say no. The magic words were that we were with the Ice Follies; somehow, that made them feel as though everything would be all right.

(Also, the fact that we were very willing to pay the sitter the same amount as if she were sitting with a baby helped.)

I realized very soon after Lulu's arrival, that she had to be one of the family members. We had to devise some way of transporting her so she could be with us most of the time. And so Yvonne found a marvelous old leather craftsman and had him make a bag for Lulu, which she had designed. It had hidden screens to allow air in and it was very soft. It was constructed so that when it was placed on the ground it spread out to give Lulu a little room to stretch. With all that, it looked innocent -- like a woman's oversized purse -- and Yvonne could carry it over her arm and nobody would ever suspect that it was a dog's travelling quarters.

We took Lulu in her bag with us to the theater and into the finest restaurants and nobody ever knew. Lulu loved her bag; in fact, there were times when she would jump into it even though we weren't going anywhere. It was her private refuge. We would merely say, "Hoppi!" and into the bag she would hop. And once she was inside, she never made a sound.

When we went to the theater in New York, Lulu would fall asleep in the bag which I usually placed under my seat. During intermissions, I would carry her outside, put the bag down, let her jump out, stretch her legs and do her business, then she would get back inside and we would return to our seats and see the balance of the play.

I don't think she was a particularly devoted theater-goer, however. Her usual procedure was to fall soundly asleep during the Show, waking up only when we picked the bag up to take her home. The only exceptions that I can remember were a few musicals ("The Sound of Music" was one) which had dogs in them and the barking of the on-stage dogs excited her. Once or twice, she barked back which was for us, momentarily embarrassing. But only momentarily because a quick command for her to "hush" and she hushed.

Lulu was always, technically, Yvonne's pet. And there is no doubt but what those two were the best of friends and that Lulu's mere existence helped Yvonne over some of her darkest moments, physically.

But because of Yvonne's enforced absence on so many occasions for operations and recuperations, I was with Lulu very often: Just the two of us together. Before the coming of Lulu, I would have thought such a thing impossible. I would have said, "Nonsense, I am not going to play nursemaid to a dog," which is what I had to do very often. But that tiny little creature so ingratiated herself with me that I never once resented the time and trouble she caused. And it is certainly true that travelling with a dog and living with a dog in a hotel is troublesome and time-consuming. Yet I enjoyed her company when Yvonne had to be out shopping or on other brief errands.

It was on such an occasion that the worst thing that could happen did happen. Lulu was lost.

This time, Yvonne was absent for what should have been a happy time -- she was going to California for the wedding of a business associate of mine, Tom Thompson to Judy Denton, one of the skating Denton twins. I couldn't go, of course, because of doing the Show in Chicago, so Yvonne would represent both Frick's. Usually, I would keep Lulu with me, but this time we decided that it would be good for both Lulu and me to have a little time alone.

Besides, in Chicago we knew a marvelous place for Lulu to stay. We had a friend, Heidi, a Swiss girl who used to be a Folliette. She had retired and begun breeding German shepherds in a wonderful kennel she established about fifty miles outside of Chicago. She kept dogs in a garden setting, with a dog-proof fence all around it. So on Friday, I took Yvonne to the airport and then taped a television interview for station WMAQ-TV.

On Saturday, Yvonne called and gave me an ecstatic account of the wedding and told me how much she missed me and how much she missed Lulu, too.

At nine o'clock Sunday morning, Heidi called to tell me she could barely get out the words, because Lulu was missing. She must have found a hole in the fence which wasn't supposed to have any holes and got out.

I quickly called some Chicago friends for help. A man I knew was high up in the Boy Scout movement and he mobilized Scouts in Heidi's area to begin a search.

A radio station owner I had done some favors for began broadcasting hourly reports about the missing dog.

The TV interviewer at WMAQ-TV added the news about our missing dog to that interview plus my offer of $500 reward for any information leading to the dog's recovery.

I began getting calls from people who had seen or thought that they had seen a dog resembling Lulu. Even when I went to the arena to do my show, I would get more calls backstage. I had the promising leads traced, but they all proved to be the wrong dog.

My problem was Yvonne: should I call her and tell her or not? I knew she would be distraught and yet, if I didn't tell her she would be perhaps even more distraught. So finally I decided I had to call her. It was the most difficult phone call I ever made in my life.

She immediately left the post-wedding festivities and dashed to the airport and got the first flight to Chicago.

She was still in the air when, after I left the ice following the second show, I got a call from Heidi's husband that the dog had been returned to them.

I got word to the airline Yvonne was travelling on and when she stepped off the plane an airline representative met her to tell her the good news. Her dog had been found. Yvonne collapsed with joy and was brought to our hotel. It didn't take her long to recuperate.

As soon as we had the time, we ran out to Heidi's place and had our joyful reunion with Lulu. It was, I must say, like getting a child back.

The story we got from Heidi eventually, was that, when Lulu slithered through or under the fence, she made her way, apparently, to the highway. She might have gotten killed but some kindly people scooped her up and took her with them. They were headed for -- coincidence! -- A wedding in Wisconsin. And so both Yvonne and Lulu attended weddings at roughly the same time. When these good people started back to Chicago, they heard one of the announcements on the radio and contacted the phone number given -- which was Heidi's – and that is how we got our beloved pup back.

Lulu was a dog of distinction. She made up her own mind about whom she liked and who she didn't like. One of her dislikes was our boss, Oscar Johnson. This was particularly embarrassing, not merely because he was the boss, but also because he fancied himself as a great dog lover. So he assumed that since he loved dogs they would love him back. He always had a dog act with the Show -- for a long time that act featured poodles, a dozen of them -- and often built lavish production numbers around dogs. One year, for example, there was a gigantic hen with a nest full of eggs and when the hen cackled, or whatever hens do, the eggs opened up and a poodle bounced out of each one. The audience loved it.

At first, Lulu seemed to like -- or at least tolerate -- Johnson. Then one day for no apparent reason, her attitude changed. Yvonne has always suspected that Lulu had overheard an argument I had with Johnson -- something about arranging train transportation for Yvonne (the management was always trying to skimp on wives and/or husbands travelling with the show) -- and decided that if I was angry, she would be angry, too. After all, I was her main man, as they say these days. From then on, the dog avoided Oscar Johnson whenever possible. She never growled or did anything unladylike because she was far too refined for that, but she simply gave the object of her dislike the cold shoulder.

Generally we took Lulu with us on all of our vacations. A few times, however, we left her with friends and there were always plenty of volunteers for such an assignment. However, we missed her so, if at all possible, we took her with us.

One year we went to the Canary Islands. The hotel said "no pets" (as hotels usually do), but with the bag that was Lulu's home and refuge, we were able to smuggle her in and out easily. We were continuing on from the Canary's to Switzerland and the tricky part of that trip was going through Spanish customs with a dog in a bag.

Yvonne was as usual carrying Lulu and her bag. She casually put the bag on the counter -- as if it were her purse -- while the customs inspector examined our other luggage and with his conventional piece of chalk, marked each bag. And then he put his mark on the Lulu bag. We could tell that he was actually marking the spot where Lulu's back bulged out and we noticed that Lulu shifted a bit to get away from that pressure. The bag shuddered from her movement. But the Spanish customs inspector had been moving down the counter so quickly, marking and chalking, that he never noticed that the blonde lady's large purse seemed to have a life of its own.

Lulu inevitably grew old and died. From time to time we have thought of trying to replace her, but then we quickly realized that that was impossibility.

There was, after all, only one Lulu.

CHAPTER 11

Opera singers talk about the temperament and jealousies on the grand opera stage. Television performers frequently tell stories of the bickering and back-biting that goes on TV sets. Tales of fights in baseball dugouts are legendary.

So, I suppose it is true that all performers -- whether they be baseball pitchers or operatic tenors -- are universally subject to jealousy and intramural squabbles to maintain their positions. But I cannot imagine any group of performers more prone to all that in-fighting than ice skaters. I know, because I saw it first hand for more than four decades.

I think perhaps one reason for that is that ice skaters generally have grown up as competitors. Far and away the majority of professional ice skaters have been, at one time in their careers, competitive skaters. They have grown up skating for one reason -- to win -- and you cannot tell them that now that they are with the Ice Follies or the Ice Capades that their performances are no longer being scored by judges. When they are introduced and glide out into center ice, they forget that they are professional skaters and entertainers being paid for what they do and just grit their teeth and compete for those high marks from those non-existent judges.

Through all my years with the Ice Follies, I was always conscious of the fact that every night was a competition. Nobody ever spoke about it, but everybody went out there to show the audience -- and his fellow skaters -- that he was the best.

And so consciously or unconsciously there arose feuds and jealousies and spats and bickering's -- all the ordinary signs of competition between people.

In my own case, I had a private competition. Frack shared that battle as long as he was active. The Shipstads and Oscar Johnson had been and continued to be, a noted comedy skating team through many years while Frack and I were also trying to be funny on ice. And, of course, the Shipstads and Johnson were also our bosses.

We quickly achieved the reputation of being the outstanding comedy ice skating team in the world. The Shipstads and Johnson were thus placed on the ice skates of a dilemma -- it was good box office-to promote us because of our reputation and yet they were still skating and they hated to promote a rival act. For us, we always tried to do our best, but yet we didn't want to show up Eddie, Roy and Oscar -- after all, they signed our paychecks. It behooved us to keep them happy.

It was like playing golf with your boss. For your own pride, you must do your best. And yet if you beat the boss too soundly, you could be endangering your job.

So, for many years, we walked the narrow and delicate path between doing too well -- and thus embarrassing our employers -- and not doing as well as we knew we could do. It was something that was always in the back of our minds and it weighed heavily on the front of our minds, too.

I always had a natural flair for publicity. Reporters liked me and sought me out -- I seemed to be able to give them good quotes for their stories. I was as they say in the journalism trade, "a good interview." Whenever the show landed in a new City, I was the one the reporters wrote about and the photographers shot. That, too, did not sit well with others in the cast.

When the Ice Follies signed the biggest star in the ice skating world Peggy Fleming, this changed. She was, because of her ability, her titles, her personality and her beauty, an automatic star and an automatic headliner. Still, I held my own with Peggy. By then, I had acquired a great deal of personal fame and so the reporters still sought me out and the photographers still loved to shoot pictures of me skating around in my famous -- and photogenic -- backbend.

Ice show contracts spelled out in patient detail, many things which might seem silly to non-skaters. But to us, always conscious of our position relative to the others in the show, those details were important. For example, when Peggy Fleming joined the show, I had a clause inserted in my next contract that whenever the show's publicity mentioned any three other skaters, my name had to be mentioned as well. Of course, the show had no control over reporters' stories -- they could mention anybody they cared to mention -- but my clause guaranteed me a mention in the publicity the show generated itself.

It was self-protection. I always was very careful to monitor the commercials on radio and television to make sure that the show lived up to its part of the arrangement.

In retrospect, I think perhaps I would have been wiser to fight for more money rather than more publicity recognition. In all those years, every contract represented what I now believe was a gross lack of sufficient salary. I would get paltry raises and I would sign reluctantly, knowing I deserved more -- much more -- because I was a valuable box office draw for the show. But they would plead poverty or something and I would settle for that puny raise. And to make me feel better, they would give me a clause like that one I just mentioned.

You can't eat clauses.

Nevertheless, it all helped because the ego needs to be fed as well as the body, and publicity is the best nourishment for a hungry ego. For some years, I was fortunate because my partner at the time -- Gary Johnson -- was also the show's official photographer, so he was always careful to take good shots of me and our joint act and during those years, I therefore was well represented on the show's program cover and on the inside pages, too.

Contract negotiations -- an annual affair I dreaded -- were long and difficult. I would marshal my weapons -- articles showing how good I was and quotes from people about how much I meant to the show -- and the boss (generally represented by Oscar Johnson, the proverbial tough Swede) would marshal his arguments about why I was already being paid enough.

His pet argument year after year was this:

"You have no act. You're always on two feet."

By that, he meant to deprecate my ability and suggest that I could only skate when I had both my feet on the ice. He was saying that I couldn't jump or leap or pirouette on one foot like the figure skaters.

Then I would take my case to Roy Shipstad. He was much more understanding and I'd wheedle an extra fifty dollars a week or so from him and perhaps also a concession like letting Yvonne travel with the company and them paying the costs.

At that, I did a lot better than Johnson's bête noire, the adagio pairs.

"They're a dime a dozen," he would say, and if they gave him an argument, he'd sack them then and there and hire another pair. Maybe they weren't exactly a dime a dozen, but there were enough of them around so he could always find another one.

One year while Frack and I were still, together, we decided we would engage the services of an agent to do our contract negotiating for us. George Good, of the prestigious William Morris office in New York was our choice. We had met some of his other clients and they all seemed well fed and happy, so we figured he was our best bet. He said he would be able to get us three hundred dollars a week more, and that was a lot of money at the time.

He and his office started out by placing some items in the Broadway columns -- items saying we were dickering with another show. Not true, but theoretically helpful to our cause. I remember one Broadway columnist ran an item to the effect that we were going to sign to co-star with Milton Berle in his next musical, "Brazil." Again, false, but everybody around our show started talking about it.

George Good went to Minneapolis to negotiate with Oscar Johnson after that bombardment. It turned out to be the immovable force crashing into the unstoppable agent, a head-on collision. We got a two hundred and fifty dollar raise, which we thought was pretty good, but fifty dollars less than the Morris office had promised. Johnson was tough.

Good and the Morris office actually wanted us to branch out and go into a Broadway show or do some other things. Perhaps we should have, but we didn't. We stayed with the Ice Follies -- the rink of least resistance. There is no way now of telling if that was a wise decision or not. But at the time, it was what we wanted to do.

There were several changes of ownership of the Ice Follies, and each one brought with it new people and, hence, new problems of adjustment. Some of them were more sympathetic toward comedy skating and during those regimes, I was featured more than under others, who were more inclined to favor traditional figure skating. In the pro-comedy areas, I would find my picture on the cover or back cover of the show program. In the anti-comedy eras, I would be lucky to have a tiny snapshot buried somewhere in the middle of that publication.

But through it all, the thick and thin ice of it, I skated day in and day out night in and night out.

It is hard to pinpoint the beginnings of trouble. Trouble usually starts quietly; if it was obvious, you could probably step on it immediately and that would be an end to it. But that doesn't happen. Instead, there is some deep underground source of trouble and before you are aware that it has even started, it has surfaced in all its gruesome glory.

I think in my case it began with the fact that I was continuing to be successful for so many years. As Yvonne has often said, "Your popularity was your downfall [📖 53-98 📄 169-214]."

The truth was that I had become a legend. To me, one test of an act's popularity was if the vendors at the hot dog stand would run out to watch the act. They always ran out to watch mine. Audiences everywhere seemed to love me more and more every season. While the management liked that -- it certainly was a help at the box office -- they didn't like it when any one cast member became so overwhelmingly popular. I was becoming the show's primary attraction; the tail was wagging the dog.

So, in the '76-'77 season, the trouble that had been simmering underneath the surface (unknown to me) for months and perhaps years, began to make itself known. They had agreed to a raise for me and yet that extra money was not forthcoming. Then they withheld a definite contract. Then they moved me to a terrible place on the program.

Once or twice in the past I had begun a tour without having signed on that famous dotted line as we haggled over salary terms, but it had never dragged on like it did in '76. The production staff at the time made no bones about the fact that they favored traditional figure skating. Their fair-haired boy was my old nemesis, Richard Dwyer [📖 86 📄 202 | 🎞 4 📄 233].

Dwyer had begun skating with the show when he was only fourteen. He was a fine skater and a fine young man. He had been a California champion and something of a phenomenon. Oscar Johnson, who had no children, saw something very admirable in young Dwyer, who quickly became Oscar's protégé and, to some extent, my protégé, too, at first. He would visit me in my little room everybody called it "The Frick and Frack Shack" -- and I would help him with his schoolwork because he was still technically a schoolboy. I later introduced him to the stock market and to real estate deals and he was a quick learner. But it took him sixteen years to graduate from college -- not because he was unintelligent, but he could only attend university (of San Francisco) during our annual two-month stay.

He mimicked me. When I bought property, he had his mother, who managed his affairs, buy the same sort of property for him. When I bought stock, he bought stock in the same company. It might only be two or three shares, but he bought it. He had to compete with me.

He gradually took over Roy Shipstad's act because he was the same sort of skater. Shipstad had pioneered the debonair skating routine, in top hat and tails, with lovely girls in evening gowns. It was always "Shipstad Stepping Out," and as he began to step out literally, Richard Dwyer stepped in.

He and I became the two leading lights in the show. We were entirely different, of course, in the type of act we did. Yet, apparently to Dwyer I became the enemy. He tried to polarize the show into Dwyerites and Frickites. With his mother guiding him, he began to woo the press. He would give up three hours of sleep (which he needed) in the morning to have breakfast with a reporter. Even when we were off, he continued his campaign to get publicity and as a result many reviewers adored him (and, consequently, had little good to say about me). But there were others who were in my camp.

Dwyer had informants among the cast who tipped him off as to what I was doing and who I was seeing and what I was planning for my act.

Then he was named company manager and

vice-president. So, in effect, he became my boss, an awkward position for me.

The problems between us magnified. Off the ice and away from the show, he was a charmer. We still had a good relationship. He had a sweet, almost angelic face, and it was impossible not to like him. But then I would learn of some other deed he had done behind my back and what he had said about me (always negative) to reporters and so I would have to say that ours was at best a love/hate relationship.

I am sure that he was partly responsible for the things that began happening to me in the show in that momentous summer of 1976. The failure of the show was to pay me not the agreed on raise and the refusal to negotiate openly for a new contract. Also, they were placing my act deep in the second half of the program.

I disliked the Spot not only because it put me in a less favorable position but more importantly, for technical reasons. For my act to work at its best (and safest) I needed smooth ice. Ruts and holes in the ice meant I might be thrown off balance. At the least, it would cost me speed and therefore make the act less exciting. At the worst, it could make me lose my balance and fall. I pleaded with the Maxons, who were running the show for Hunter, to move me to a better and safer slot on the program, but they refused. I detected the fine hand of Richard Dwyer in that refusal.

Things dragged on like that for several months. Then Hunter talked to me about my new contract and he had a small raise of salary included. Just before Yvonne and I left for a Christmas vacation in Aruba, I signed the contract, but I added a clause: "Subject to regaining my old spot on the program."

Hunter called me on the phone and said in gruff tones, "If that's the way you feel about it, why don't you just quit."

It was handwriting on the wall, without the wall.

I didn't get all the money due me from the earlier raises until my attorney, Fred Leuenberger, got tough with them. Even then, it wasn't until the following May that the money actually reached my eager hands.

I felt more and more uncomfortable as that spring tour got underway. And Yvonne, as always very sensitive to my moods, realized I was uncomfortable and she determined to do something about it. In the middle of May, she cornered Bob Shipstad in the stands in San Diego. She said she wondered what was going on, why they were treating me like they were. Why they had not given me back my old spot, why the new photographs of me were buried, why nobody had yet spoken to me about next season.

"What's going on, Bob?" she asked point blank.

"Nothing's going on," Bob Shipstad had answered. "We love Frick. After all, he is our most valuable asset."

It sounded reassuring, but still all those problems Yvonne had mentioned persisted. Making matters worse, I was approached by the Maxons who suggest that next year I join the Holiday on Ice outfit. I felt that was definitely a demotion, which it was a show that was not up to my usual standards and I said no.

"That would be like being sent to Siberia," I said.

That's where things were -- stalled and unpleasant -- when we arrived in Oakland for the last stop on that year's tour.

When we got to the arena in Oakland, Yvonne and I were greeted by the area manager who shook my hand and said, "I hear you are leaving the show, Mr. Frick."

"What?" I was so stunned I couldn't think straight. "I don't know anything about me leaving the show."

We were walking backstage, still shocked and confused, when we met Richard Dwyer in his office.

"I hear you finally got your wish fulfilled, Richard," Yvonne said with an understandable touch of bitterness.

He didn't say, "What are you talking about?" or "I don't know what you mean."

What he did say was, "I didn't have anything to do with it," which to me was proof positive that he did.

But I skated through the balance of the Oakland engagement, giving each performance my all, as I always had. The last show of the season had always been something special. People in the show enjoyed kidding around and so, as usual, there was a big message chalked on the backstage blackboard: NO FOOLING AROUND. It didn't do any good at all.

There were the normal abnormalities -- male skaters in female roles and vice versa, surprise people popping up in the wrong number to try and make somebody break up with laughter. I was doing my act when suddenly I realized Yvonne was on the ice, dressed as one of the Swiss Misses in that season's finale. So, we had fun that last show in Oakland, which segued into the post-show party with champagne and tears. For us -- no champagne, just tears.

I had an immediate engagement in Toronto for "Stars On Ice," a TV special. Later, I made a guest appearance with the Osmonds and I did a few other brief jobs in that summer. But basically, that early summer of '77 was the low point of my life. I felled into a deep depression.

I knew, intellectually, that I had nothing to fear. Economically, I was in a sound position. And I was confident that I could still skate and that there would be continuing demands for my ice-skating services. And yet, emotionally, it was difficult being idle, even temporarily. I realize looking back on it now, that one reason for that blow being taken so to heart was that really, I had had so few blows in my life. I was unaccustomed to bad things happening to me. My defenses were down.

I would go to bed feeling so low on several nights that I would say to Yvonne, "If I don't wake up in the morning, it will be a good thing."

I had what I have subsequently learned were the classic symptoms of severe depression -- not only the mental ones, but physical ones, too. I suffered from chills and a constant drowsiness. Sometimes when Yvonne and I went for a drive, a pastime I ordinarily enjoyed, I would have to be persuaded to get out of the car. I just wanted to sit there alone and lonely and not have to face reality any more.

What got me out of it was a call from my lawyer, Fred Leuenberger, saying they had offered me a spot in New York. It was with the Holiday on Ice unit, but it was Madison Square Garden, it was New York, it was the big time again. I had to accept. There was a further inducement -- after New York, they would be going on a tour to several cities in South America. That was virgin territory to us and it sounded marvelous and that accelerated my acceptance.

This was the old Madison Square Garden, you understand, that glorious old building. Somebody told me, as opening night approached, that they had checked and discovered that I had played the old Madison Square Garden more than any other person, with the possible exception of the famous Ringling Brothers clown, Emmett Kelly.

It was exciting to be back in New York, even though I had never before played it in August. I was unprepared for the New York humidity. I stayed either in my room at the hotel or in my dressing room at the Garden to escape that crushing humidity and terrible air quality.

But it was wonderful to hear my introduction again -- "Ladies and gentlemen, the fabulous Mister Frick!" -- And to bask in the comforting glow of the warm audience reception.

That week was a triumph for me. Good reviews. Good and enthusiastic crowds. Friendly faces backstage.

On August 26, 1976, I did the first of the three scheduled shows. And there were seven standing ovations.

The climax was, of course, my cantilever -- that backbend, with my back parallel to the ice, my head a scant few inches from the surface of the ice, my whole body gliding around the ice, in and out of some columns, at twenty-five miles an hour.

Then off to thunderous -- yes, it did sound like thunder when you were on the receiving end -- applause. And then back for my curtain call, as twelve brilliant arc lights focused on me and the audience stood to applaud and cheer. It had happened like that for many years and it never failed to thrill me. I would bow for twenty-five seconds.

When I walked off, a couple of the stagehands -- as they always did -- shook my hand and said that I had done it again, and other cheering sentiments. Then I spotted the company manager, who was not usually in that backstage area, so his appearance surprised me.

"This is for you, Frick," he said, and handed me an envelope. At least he had waited until I caught my breath. His expression was serious, so right away I knew whatever was inside that envelope was serious. It was.

It was a note telling me that I was fired.

It also included the one-way airfare from New York to Switzerland.

For many years, I had spent half my time in the United States, half my time in Switzerland. I loved both countries, equally. One was my native land, one was my adopted land. I knew I could never give up either, and the idea that someone was telling me that I was no longer wanted in this country infuriated me.

I was also furious about being fired from the show. I was sixty-two years old, but I knew that I was skating as well, perhaps better, than ever. An athlete is the best judge of his own ability and I knew that my performances were still up to par. Why was I getting the sack?

That was my first reaction. Then there was an almost simultaneous feeling of relief. It was done. A fait accompli.

My third reaction -- and they overlapped they happened so fast -- was that I must tell Yvonne. At the time I was fired, she was in Switzerland. More health problems -- a nervous breakdown this time. (I attributed that to her reaction to all the political in-fighting that was going on and how Dwyer's jealousy and the management's poor treatment of me had upset her.) So, I called her from New York to tell her the news. I had been afraid of how she would take it.

By a happy coincidence, at the time of my call she was entertaining a couple of former Folliettes. They are all over the world, a global sorority. Yvonne had been planning on leaving the next day to join me as we were about to make our way to South America. So, she had little to entertain with and, actually, the girls were dining sumptuously on some tinned sardines and crackers. They all broke down and fell tearfully into each other's arms when my call came.

"How could they do that to Mr. Frick?" the girls had said to Yvonne. "He is such a fabulous performer and everyone loves him so much."

They cried over their sardines, but they must have realized that the evidence proved them wrong; not everyone loved me.

"Don't worry, Mutz," she told me between tears and sardines. Mutz, which is what the Swiss call a bear, was her pet name for me. She told me to be strong, to carry on, to go out and do the rest of my shows the best I could. And that is precisely what I did.

While I was concerned for my future, I was not really worried. I knew that I could always get a job with another show, and there were many other ways for me to earn a living. But I was terribly troubled by the fact of my dismissal and kept trying to understand the reasons behind it.

The note the company manager gave me that day had said something about how I had not been acting in good faith in my current efforts to renegotiate my contract. The show had been planning on going to South America -- Sao Paulo and Rio de Janeiro -- and I knew that living costs were very high in those cities, so I had asked for an additional seventy-five dollars a week to compensate for what I knew would be astronomical hotel bills during our stay there. Surely that was not excessive and could not possibly have been the motive for my dismissal; that had to be the excuse that was masking the real reason.

I never did find out beyond a reasonable doubt, what that real reason was. I have a strong hunch, however, that it was simply jealousy on the part of management and production staff. Mine was considered a classic act and classic acts, by definition, seldom change. They strive for perfection.

Fortunately for me, as soon as the news of my being fired reached the outside world -- the world of the other skating shows -- there were the offers I felt sure would be forthcoming. This kept my spirits up, even though my income was down. I took some of those offers -- a TV show with Donny and Marie Osmond, another TV special for Charles Schulz and the "Peanuts" group, a few carnivals, an ice skating Symposium back in Switzerland -- and they kept me busy and relatively contented through the winter of '77-'78.

A few words about that symposium. There had never been anything like it before. It was sponsored by a company called Gloria International, really a glorified ad agency. They are the ones who put the ads on all the bang boards at European ice shows and carnivals. They invited top skaters from all over the world, and I was pleased and happy to be included in that august group. There were meetings, demonstrations, a banquet at which I was seated, by accident, next to a former lady friend I had almost married thirty years before. Now, by another happy accident, she was the wife of the chief Sports editor of the prestigious newspaper, Neue Zürcher Zeitung, and she persuaded him to interview me. You should know that the NZZ rarely uses interviews of any kind because it is a fairly staid newspaper, printing only hard news. It was quite a feather in my Swiss cap.

I also did a few TV shows for European television, and they were enjoyable and added to the excitement of that season my first away from the Ice Follies.

I was so busy that I did not this time sink into as deep a depression as I had before. The last week in New York -- from the moment I was fired to the closing of the engagement there -- was a tough period. But Yvonne, who quickly flew to be by my side, bolstered my spirits.

My last performance, that final show in New York, is something I will never forget. The word had gotten out, of course -- there is no such thing as a secret in an ice show -- and even the audience appeared to know. There were several standing ovations after my act and then all of the members of the company cast, crew, even office personnel -- gathered backstage as I skated off to surround me and shake my hand and wish me well.

I sent my larger props into storage. The smaller ones were sent to my hotel -- the Essex House -- and my room began to look like a warehouse. I didn't know definitely if I would perform again, but I couldn't part with some of my things. There was, for example, the barrel I had used in my act for more than ten thousand performances. You just don't have an old friend like that onto the rubbish pile.

The show did go on to South America, but without me. Some people said it was because I wasn't there -- comedy is such a universal thing -- that the South American trip turned into a total fiasco. It folded up after playing only a few dates. I was sorry for all my friends who were still with the show, but I must confess to a few twinges of pleasure -- revenge can be sweet.

As the summer and winter passed, I was able to take stock of myself and my prospects. I knew for one thing, that I was in good physical condition. Most doctors say that the key to conditioning is exercise. My act had given me that exercise automatically. Curiously, my excellent physical shape was another source of irritation between Dwyer and me. He was many years my junior, but he had chronic back problems which plagued him. I never had any difficulties going on, but he did, and that obviously gnawed at him.

I had also watched my weight carefully from the time I married Yvonne who immediately began supervising my caloric intake. She got me into the habit of a late lunch. This served two useful functions. We would eat heartily at that late lunch, because we found that restaurant prices for lunch (no matter how late) are generally considerably lower than the price for the same food served at the dinner hour. So, we would eat our main meal at that time and have a snack later for our dinner. Then, too, that was healthier for me as a performer. It gave me time to digest my meal before I went on the ice.

If my luncheon plate contained a large quantity of starches -- potatoes or pasta -- Yvonne would distract me and while I was looking away, scoop a lot of it onto her own plate. She was (and is) a slim, trim woman and weight has never been one of her problems. She also saw to it, that I put only a very small quantity of dressing on my salads, and so with that schedule, I whittled away thirty pounds soon after we married, in a totally painless (and beer less) fashion. I felt much better after I had lost the weight. And I have managed to maintain my weight at a comfortable and presentable 177 pounds [80.3 kg] since then.

My only real temptation is beer. I am really not a beer-alcoholic, but I have a lot of friends who own or operate breweries. They would, as a matter of course and a gesture of friendliness and good will, send over a case or two of beer whenever I checked into a hotel in their cities. As soon as the papers print the fact that I have arrived, the beer shows up. I certainly cannot waste it. What to do? It is a major problem for a weight-conscious Swiss gentleman.

So, I was in good condition in those dreary months and I felt that I was skating as well as I ever had. As one gets older, one learns how to compensate in some areas -- I looked just as fast, but it was through economy of motion and having become a more skillful showman. All in all, I felt my act was still eminently satisfactory, at the least. And the media and the audiences appeared to agree with me.

I had just completely gotten over the shock of being fired when I had another surprise -- the Ice Follies wanted me back! Yvonne and I were taking a brief vacation in Las Vegas when my lawyer, Fred Leuenberger called me from his office in San Francisco with that startling bit of intelligence. After I had left the show with what to me were hard feelings, I hardly expected them to have a change of heart. So, the invitation to return was totally out of deepest left field. Leuenberger said he had received a contract, which he had sent to me in Zurich, where he had presumed I was. The show wanted me not only to return but they were planning, they said, a gala season built around me -- it would celebrate my fortieth year with the Ice Follies.

I was a little skeptical, but still excited. I went from Las Vegas to San Diego where the show was next scheduled to appear. While I waited for the Ice Follies to arrive in San Diego, I talked with some old friends who had been urging me to join them in the real estate business in Southern California. A few years before, on a whim, I had studied for the California Real Estate License and I had taken and passed the exam. So, I was licensed to do business in the state, and these friends -- my business partner, Tom Thompson and his wife, Judy -- had been trying to persuade me to make that my new career.

But I was an ice skater first and foremost, and if there was a chance to do that again, I would jump at it.

Then the show arrived. In the coffee shop of the Catamaran Hotel in Pacific Beach, a San Diego suburb, I found Jill Shipstad having breakfast with Richard Dwyer [85-86 201-202]. He had been the company manager, as well as a leading skater, since 1975 and was now a vice-president, too. That morning in the coffee shop he was friendly enough.

"Hi, Frick," he said, and he shook my hand warmly. Jill gave me a big kiss. Dwyer said, "I've been hearing about all the things you've been doing in the year away from us. You are really an amazing fellow!"

He waved me into a seat in his booth and began talking about possible skaters to be my partner in my act for the coming season. Together, we produced a list of six names and then pared that down to four.

Later, at the San Diego arena, I saw Don Hunter. He too, was warm and friendly. I saw Bob Shipstad, who had driven down from his home in Los Angeles just to say hello to me. I appreciated that gesture enormously. I had a reunion with many old friends who were still with the show, and met some of the new faces. I looked at them all as potential partners. I did some testing of these skaters -- thirty minutes with each of the four, to assess their abilities.

It was agreed that I would join the show again the following August in Sacramento where they would be rehearsing for the new season. So, I went back to Switzerland for the rest of the spring and the early summer.

During that period, there were some more surprises. Bob Shipstad sent me a selection of color photos of myself in action and asked which one I would like them to use in the new program. That had never happened to me in my entire thirty-nine years with the show.

He also sent along a longer list of candidates for the job of my new partner.

I began to get excited about my return to action. It seemed that something had caused them to have a change of heart. I didn't know for sure what it was -- I still don't -- but I had some theories.

One reason may have been their new tie-in with the Baskin-Robbins ice cream people. That company had begun a major promotion involving the Ice Follies and had apparently insisted that I be part of the package. They were planning to have "Frick's Anniversary Parties" wherever we played, with a small portable rink set up in prominent places near one of their stores, and me and some others doing a pocket show to help promote their products and at the same time, to help promote our show.

Another possible reason for them asking me back was -- I learned later -- that when I was not with the show, a lot of fans had protested. They had asked, "Where is Frick?" and when they were told that Frick wasn't with the show any more, they had gotten angry. A few had asked for their money back.

The rumor had gotten around for a while, that I had died, some of my old friends in the company told me. My pals had put a stop to that as quickly as they could.

There was a third reason why they rehired me, and I think this was the strongest of all. In the year or so I was away, I continued to work and my TV appearances with Donny and Marie Osmond and with Charles Schulz and the "Peanuts" gang had been enormously popular. I feel that the show thought they would reap some financial benefit in having me back and exploiting my new-found TV stature.

Whatever the reason -- and it probably was some combination of all of the above -- I was grateful. When August came and I went to Sacramento, the first day I was approached by a skater named Ted Barton, whose name was on the list of potential partners. He was enthusiastic about skating with me and he said he knew the act very well. He told me he had been watching it for several years and was confident he could handle the job. I decided to let him try, and Shipstad agreed with me.

Ted happened to get married that week and there was a gala wedding party and he put me at a table with five beautiful new Folliettes and I danced all afternoon. I could have danced all night and perhaps I did, but I truly don't remember.

When I began skating again, it was as though I had never left. It all came back to me with a pleasant rush, and I enjoyed that sensation enormously. I also enjoyed the fact -- which surprised me -- that the Follies people were now promoting me more than they ever had in the past. They put "Mr. Frick Is Back!" posters on billboards and on buses and large signboards with my photograph all over town.

When Yvonne flew into San Francisco -- our next stop after the Sacramento debut -- she was greeted by those posters in the airport. She was stunned and thrilled by that sight.

I dedicated my performance to her and she had tears in her eyes. It all seemed too good to be true. After those last few years of jealousy and intrigue, this new era made us feel like we were living in some sort of fairy tale and we all know that fairy tales don't happen in real life. But it was actually happening; I was getting respect.

That felt good.

We had rehearsed for six weeks and it was hard work -- a new partner, new technicians on the lights and the sound equipment, a new orchestra leader and, of particular importance to me and my act, a new drummer. But everyone did his best and in most cases, that were far more than merely adequate.

The Sacramento opening had been warmly received. Sacramento had always been a good town for me. On this opening night, I was pleased when the audience responded to my performance and gave me a standing ovation. We had all felt the opening was a smash. There was the usual post-premiere party, and that was another success. I even found myself standing at the bar, at one point, next to Don Hunter, and we clinked glasses, toasted our mutual happy futures, and had a very pleasant chat.

I invested in a new wooden crate to house all my props. And profiting from experience, I had it built large enough so it could also carry a few of my personal suitcases. That would free us from carrying those over-stuffed bags as we travelled from one City to the next. It made our future travels much easier.

Thus, began a pleasant tour. It was even more pleasant because it followed so closely on the heels of that terrible moment when I was fired. It was almost an anti-climax, and they can be even more enjoyable than climaxes.

In each City, because of the show's tie-in with Baskin-Robbins, I was part of that special promotional show. They played up the theme of "Mr. Frick's Fortieth Anniversary" very heavily. They had devised that miniature rink with sticky mock ice which was barely adequate for a little skating, but not much. We put on fifteen-minute shows which were only hors d'oeuvres, a tiny sample of what our real show had to offer.

In many of the cities, beginning with San Francisco, they arranged for mayors to sign proclamations -- "Mr. Frick Day" -- which were pleasing to my ego I must admit [¶3-4 📄 228-229]. And it was also pleasing the way the public responded with obvious affection for me.

The new management of the show -- it was now owned by the Felds, the same people who owned the Ringling Brothers Circus -- wanted me to sign a new contract. I said I would, but I

Chapter 11

asked for a hefty raise and -- another surprise! -- They agreed, without any hassle or discussion or negotiations.

They said they wanted new photographs. Over the years, I had once or twice been disappointed in the quality of the pictures taken by Ice Follies photographers. So, it was without much enthusiasm or hope that I showed up at the rink this time. I went through my routines for him and -- one more surprise: -- the shots were excellent. In fact, they were the best I had ever had taken.

I started thinking that I must have died and gone to Heaven. Things were going too well. And they continued to go well for many months, many performances in many cities before many thousands of people. But nothing ever lasts or stays the same. Change is part of our life, and change is not always good.

So, there came a day when they switched the program around and, as I have written, I was asked to follow a dog act on the bill. I have nothing against dogs, as a class. My love for Lulu knew no bounds, and I also respected her. But sharing my wife with Lulu was one thing; following a dog act on the Ice Follies program was an entirely different situation.

In addition to the degradation of it, and the danger, a dog act is also hard -- probably impossible -- to time precisely. Dogs aren't people and so their act runs a few minutes longer one day, a few minutes shorter the next. It is almost an ad lib situation.

So, the act that follows the dog act -- in this case, that would be me -- is never sure exactly when it will go on. My entrance that year was inside a giant hunk of cheese. So, I would have to stay inside my giant hunk of cheese like a time pill inside a capsule, and wait and wait and wait, and never really be sure when I would be going on. I couldn't see anything and I couldn't hear what was going on the rink. The first thing I would know that I was about to have to start performing was when I would feel me and my cheese catapulted onto the ice. The stagehands would be shoving me out onto the ice at twenty-five miles an hour and I would have to start my act.

It was nerve-wracking, to say the least.

1954 - Mr. Frick's Cantilever Spread Eagle
Ice Follies

Picture 54 ✦ Page 161

1954 - Mr. Frick & Nancy Travis
Ice Follies

1954 - Mr. Frick & Nancy Travis
Ice Follies

Picture 56 ✦ Page 161

1955 - Mr. Frick & Nancy Travis
"Antarctic Adventurer"
Ice Follies

Picture 57 ✦ Page 161

1955 - Mr. Frick Ice Comedian
Ice Follies

Picture 58 ✦ Page 161

1955 - Mr. Frick's Cantilever Spread Eagle
"Antarctic Adventurer"
Ice Follies

1956 - Mr. Frick, creator of laughs
"Park Bench Ambassador"
Ice Follies

Picture 60 ✧ Page 161

1957 - Mr. Frick & Doris Meyers
Ice Follies

Picture 61 ✤ Page 161

1957 - Mr. Frick
"Geiger Counter Capers"
Ice Follies

Picture 62 ✧ Page 161

1958 - Mr. Frick & Gail Foster
"Alpine Antics"
Ice Follies

1958 - Mr. Frick-The best in ice comedy
"Alpine Antics"
Ice Follies

Picture 64 ✦ Page 161

1958 - Mr. Frick-USS Nautilus SSN - 571
Ice Follies

1959 - Mr. Frick & Gail Foster
"Antarctic Scientist"
Ice Follies

1959 - Mr. Frick's Cantilever Spread Eagle
"Top Banana"
Ice Follies

Picture 67 ✧ Page 161

1959 - Mr. Frick-Makeup Backstage
Ice Follies

Picture 68 ✦ Page 161

1960 - Werner Fritz Groebli
Businessman
Ice Follies

Picture 69 ✧ Page 161

1960 Mr. Frick
Ice Comedian
Ice Follies

1961 - Mr. Frick & Doris Skillings
"Traveling Light"
Ice Follies

1961 Mr. Frick & Doris Skillings
"Traveling Light"
Ice Follies

Picture 72 ✦ Pages 161, 220, 227

1962 - Mr. Frick's Nine Thousandth Performance
from left to right: Oscar Johnson, Roy Shipstad, Mr. Frick, wife Yvonne & poodle Lulu
Ice Follies

1962 - Mr. Frick-Backstage
Ice Follies

Picture 74 ✧ Page 161

1963 - Mr. Frick's Cantilever Spread Eagle looks so easy. The gravity-defying backbend, with feet akimbo, has been a trademark of his years as a professional performer on ice.
Ice Follies

1964 - Mr. Frick & Ina Bauer
The three-time German champion Ina Bauer
Ice Follies

1965 - Mr. Frick
Ice Follies

Picture 77 ✧ Page 161

1966 - Mr. Frick & Ina Bauer
Ice Follies

Chapter 11 -193-

1967 - Mr. Frick on the Tramp
Ice Follies

1968 - Mr. Frick's Cantilever Spread Eagle or Gravity Defying Backbend
Mr. Frick, the genial gentleman of the ice
Ice Follies

Picture 80 ✧ Page 161

1969 - Mr. Frick & Susan Berens
"The Ice Follies Ranch"
Ice Follies

1969 - The hilarious Mr. Frick still performs his incredible Cantilever Spread Eagle
Mr. Frick with Kettledrum
Ice Follies

Picture 82 ✧ Page 161

1970 - Mr. Frick
"Frozen Arctic"
Ice Follies

1971 - Werner Groebli
Now Playing: Walter Matthau & Elaine May "A New Leaf"
Ice Follies

Picture 84 ✦ Page 161

1971 - Mr. Frick's Cantilever Spread Eagle
"The new Ice Age"
Ice Follies

1971 - Mr. Frick & Jill Shipstad
Ice Follies

Picture 86 ✦ Pages 161, 166

1972 - Mr. Frick & Richard Dwyer ("Mr. Debonair")
Ice Follies

1972 - Mr. Frick's Cantilever Spread Eagle
Ice Follies

1972 - Mr. Frick & Snoopy
Snoopy admires Mr. Frick's Cantilever Spread Eagle
Ice Follies

Picture 89 ✧ Page 161

1973 - Mr. Frick hands over a bouquet to Janet Lynn
Ice Follies

1974 - Mr. Frick's Cantilever Spread Eagle
Ice Follies

Picture 91 ✦ Page 161

1974 - Mr. Frick
Thirty-five years with the Ice Follies
Ice Follies

Picture 92 ✦ Page 161

1975 - Swiss Jewel Mr. Frick
Mr. Frick is one of the most enduringly funny men in the entertainment world
Ice Follies

Picture 93 ✧ Page 161

1976 - Mr. Frick's Cantilever Spread Eagle
Ice Follies

Picture 94 ✦ Page 161

1977 - Mr. Frick
Attention Please!
Ice Follies

Picture 95 ✦ Page 161

1978 - Ice Comedian Mr. Frick
Ice Follies

Picture 96 ✦ Page 161

1979 - Mr. Frick and Sesame Street's Big Bird
Ice Follies

Picture 97 ✦ Page 161

Mr. Frick, the most enduring comic on ice, celebrates 41 years of superior shenanigans with the 44th Edition of Shipstads and Johnson Ice Follies. (FOL/80-40)

1980 - Mr. Frick
"The most enduring comic on ice"
Ice Follies

1980 - Mr. Frick
"Funnier than ever"
Ice Follies

CHAPTER 12

When I was fired, I may have worried about my ego, about what I would do with my time, about my pride and my sensitivity, about many things, but I didn't have to worry about money.

People sometimes say that it is because I am Swiss, and perhaps because of my early training -- having to watch each franc, each pound, each dollar very carefully and wisely. All that may have had something to do with the way I came to regard financial considerations. It may also have been something of an ethnic, genetic thing. We Swiss are a nation of people who are inherently cautious about money, and yet we can be daring in our investments. I grew up realizing that money is serious business. I still feel that way.

As soon as I began to earn reasonably good money, after I first came to the United States, I started a program of investments. I had arrived in 1938 with only fifty dollars. Beginning in 1941, I started purchasing shares of stock, a few at a time in the beginning. I have become a vigorous investor. One of my New York brokers was quoted as calling me "a wizard."

Hardly that, but I have had my successes as well as, quite naturally, some failures too, in the forty-five years or so that I have been dabbling in the stock market. Many financial columnists have written about me and my investments, as well as sports writers who wrote about my skating talents.

Some of my colleagues on the show used to snicker about how I watched every nickel. But if you watch enough nickels, pretty soon you are watching a dollar, and enough dollars can be serious money. Yvonne and I have taken several trips to Hawaii on money we have saved one way or another.

When we played in Canada, I became something of a private banker for the company. The cast members would give me an American dollar and I would give them a Canadian dollar in exchange. Each one of those transactions resulted in an eighteen cent profit for me, because I had purchased the Canadian dollars in large amounts at the discount, before we entered Canada. This, of course, was more than twenty years ago; I doubt that that could be done today.

I was also known as a tough negotiator for my contract. As I have written, Frack and I did use an agent for a season or two, but mostly I did the negotiating for both of us and after Frack left the show, I negotiated my own contract every year. I often felt that I settled for less than I should have received, but I suppose every negotiator feels that way. I do believe that I did better than most of the skaters. I would try for side benefits -- hotel-room-breaks, travel for Yvonne -- in addition to my salary. And, having travelled a lot, I knew that often those side benefits cold results in real money in my pocket over the long run.

I was frugal, but I like to think I was frugal like the character Jack Benny played was frugal -- in fact I was often called "The Jack Benny of the Ice." Like the real Jack Benny, however, I was not a total penny-pincher. I was, in fact, a very generous tipper. Whenever I would board a train, I would tip the porter generously -- both in advance and later, as I left -- and I got excellent service as a result. I once tried to figure up how much I had spent in tips on my trusty old Hartman suitcase -- forty years old when I retired it -- and, to the best of my reckoning, I must have laid out $3,000 in tips to porters and Red Caps and Sky Caps and Bell Boys to carry that bag in its lifetime.

My investments are a combination of serious and scientific study of the market, hunches, and a little inside information from time to time. I do study the market very thoroughly. I have tried many of those "insider information services" and publications, and I have found that the best information comes from the daily newspaper. So I buy several every day, read the financial sections thoroughly, and digest what I have read.

But I also play hunches. You have probably heard of the financial wizards who throw darts at the stock market listings and buy whatever stock the dart hits -- and do very well with that system. I don't go quite that far, but I do play my hunches and I have done pretty well with them.

I like to buy stock if I know somebody whose name is similar to a listed issue. When Karen Kresge joined the show, I bought shares of Kresge, which has done very well, first with its Kresge stores and later, with the K-Mart stores. When Peggy Fleming became a member of our group, I noted there was a Fleming Company listed, so I bought some shares in Fleming, and it did reasonably well. When I began using Ozite carpets in the number -- that new indoor-outdoor carpet material -- I thought the stuff was pretty good so I went out and bought Ozite shares. And it has done well, too.

But I also tried to do research. My late brother-in-law in Switzerland, Ernst Oertli, was a manufacturers' representative and dealt mainly with high-tech items. He gave me tips on companies he felt were comers and I often took his advice, but I would always try and check them out first, before I bought.

One year, he told me about a new company he thought had promise. It was called Texas Instruments. He suggested I look into it the next time I was in Dallas. I had been on vacation in Zurich at the time, so I booked my flight to San Francisco via New York and Dallas, and stopped in the Texas City and went to the Texas Instruments plant to look it over.

I learned that the head of T.I. was a man named Eric Jonnson, and that he was an ice skating enthusiast. I had trouble reaching him -- an officious secretary -- so I crashed his office, going up a back stairway to avoid that secretary. I began talking to him about ice skating. He knew my name, which helped considerably, and he had a daughter with ice skating ambitions, and that didn't hurt either, when I promised I would see that she got a fair audition.

Then we began talking about his company, and he wound up showing me around. I liked what I saw. I even liked the cafeteria, and my decision to invest, based partly on the fact that the firm had a well-run cafeteria, was not too far-fetched. Not long ago, an expert wrote, "If the cafeteria is well-run, that is an excellent sign."

I wound up investing in T.I., and did very well as a result. And I also talked about Ernst to Eric Jonnson, and my brother-in-law ultimately got an excellent contract to represent T.I. in Switzerland.

Naturally, some of my purchases have turned out poorly. I bought Douglas Aircraft when it was $105 a share and eventually bailed out when it was $83. I took my losses like a good Swiss, entering them as a loss on my income tax return. You can't win them all.

We have a joke, Yvonne and I, and on days when the Stock Exchange plunges we say, "Well, it's hamburger time today." And often, we will actually eat hamburgers that night, just to prove a point. On the other hand, on days when the market -- and hence, my on-paper worth -- has soared, we talk about champagne and caviar.

I own some real estate, too. My first investment in that area was a duplex in Los Angeles. There were two tenants in the building, and they were both demanding types. When I went to visit my building, I would park a few blocks away and look at the place through a pair of binoculars to see what the condition of the roof and the siding was. That way, I could avoid personal contact with the tenants; I owned the building several years, and only went inside a few times during that time.

I have owned other real estate. There was an apartment building in the Silicon Valley, where my tenants were three elderly couples. We had had a few more-or-less discussions, as landlords and tenants are bound to have, so I was a little worried one evening when I saw all six of them sitting in the front row as I skated out on the ice at the San Francisco Winterland. The thought went through my mind that they were going to cause some sort of scene or disturbance. But no, as it turned out, they had just decided to go and see their landlord skate.

I still own some real estate, and I have other investments besides my stock market holdings. I have always believed in U.S. Government Bonds as the safest and surest of investments. I realize that the stock market is a gamble and, like all gambles, you can lose as quickly as you can win. So I always convert a portion -- about forty percent -- of my stock market profits into government bonds, which are not a gamble.

People have often asked me if I own any of the Ice Follies, and when I say I don't, they wonder why not. They know that I am a big investor, and they obviously jump to the conclusion that I should have invested in the Ice Follies. The problem has been that through most of the show's torturous financial career, it has been owned by closed corporations. No outside investors were welcome.

It was owned first by the Shipstads and Johnson; that was totally closed. Then Shasta Corporation bought it; that, too, was a closed outfit. Then a group of investing doctors of Minneapolis -- Medical Investment Corporation -- bought it, and only doctors were eligible to own shares. (Eventually, some shares were traded Over-The-Counter, and I did buy some of them, but at the wrong time; it slid down and I wound up losing a lot.) Later, the show was bought by Arthur Wirtz and then by the Felds, and each time, it was unavailable to outside investors.

Finally, it was purchased by the Mattel people, the toy manufacturers. Mattel's stock was available, so I did buy some shares, and made a profit, small, but in the black.

I also bought shares in Metromedia, which owned our chief rival, Ice Capades. I didn't feel the least bit treasonous about that and, in fact, was very happy when I met Metromedia's president, John Rouge, and he advised me to hold on to my stock in his company.

"It can only go higher, Frick," Kluge told me. And in the following six years, my Metromedia stock increased in value ten-fold -- actually, the value was nearly fifty times its low of around $7 a share.

I had a lucky break in the '50s -- and had the good sense to capitalize on it. My old Swiss friend, Herman Faenger, the engineer who, as I wrote earlier, worked with Alexandre M. Poniatoff in developing the first video cassette recorder, tipped me off and I bought Ampex stock.

Then Poniatoff, visiting me in my dressing room, told me the price of the stock was too high. He said he was selling his shares and getting into real estate, so I figured if the company president was bailing out, I would be smart to do the same thing. So I sold, and took my profits and was not hurt when Ampex plunged a few months later.

Picture 99

Werner Fritz Groebli retired in the 1990s

CHAPTER 13

My last few years as a professional ice performer -- or ice comedian or whatever you choose to call me -- were not entirely happy ones. Being invited back to re-join the show was not, as it turned out, enough to guarantee happiness.

But those years were certainly far from unhappy ones. Actually, they were years like most years -- a bit of good, a bit of bad, and plenty of in-between.

I received an award -- the Ice Skating Hall of Fame award -- in 1978 [🏆1 📄 226]. I certainly feel that falls in the "good" category. In fact, I would even go so far as to classify that particular moment as beyond "good" -- perhaps even "great." There were other awards, too, such as the one the Swiss Club in San Francisco gave to me in honor of my forty years with the Ice Follies [🏆3-4 📄 228-229].

And there were many other "good" or borderline "great" moments. One such was getting to-know Charles (Sparky) Schulz, who has always been a tremendous ice skating enthusiast. He put together an ice skating special for television and invited me to perform on it with Snoopy and some others [🖼88,100-101 📄 204, 230-231]. Not only was that good fun, but it was financially very rewarding and gave me added prestige with the show, for a few fleeting moments. (Prestige is, I have found, a very ephemeral thing; here today, gone tonight.)

I also did a TV special with Donny and Marie Osmond and it, too, was a pleasant and financially profitable experience. I appeared on other television shows, too, such as Mike Douglas' talk show which at the time was one of the most popular shows on the air.

In and among my performances and the honors of all, there were a few trips back to Switzerland for one reason (vacation) or another (the health of either Yvonne or me, or both). I flew over the Atlantic Ocean so often I got so I could recognize the waves, and knew many of them by their first foam. When the Jets came in, however, they would fly so high that it was no longer possible to make out any waves at all. For me, that made the trip considerably less fun, but, of course, considerably quicker.

For a year or more, the Baskin-Robbins ice cream company's promotion was in full bloom. This was a delight for me, as it enabled me to stay in personal touch with my fans. In City after city, they put up their small rink in some downtown location where a few of us would stage our miniature ice show. Mostly, the experience was enjoyable -- it was certainly good for both our show and for the sale of the company's ice cream -- although skating on that tiny rink with its poor surface was difficult and dangerous.

There were some personal pleasures, too, during that last tour. One was the wedding of my latest partner -- as it turned out, Ted Barton was also my last partner. He was married in Sacramento.

One of the in-between experiences I lived through during that era was, at best, a mixed pleasure. It was then Irwin Feld, of the circus-owning Feld family and the current owner of the Ice Follies, acceded to my request for a raise, and it was a hefty one -- forty percent. But he denied, at the same time, my request that Yvonne's transportation be paid for by the company. The raise more than made up for that amount of money and yet the refusal made Yvonne feel that she wasn't wanted and that hurt her deeply. In the past, her transportation had always been part of my pay package, so the action by Irwin Feld really wounded her. It made her feel as though she were an outsider with the show.

Nevertheless, I did sign again for the '79-'80 tour, and then I received a blow that was equal to the one Yvonne had gotten. I learned that my act was once again being shoved around and placed in an unfavorable spot on the program. I asked everyone -- from the people who were running the show on a day-to-day basis to the Felds, who owned it -- to put me back where I felt I belonged, but no luck.

The show had some problems of its own. We had been scheduled to appear at the Kemper Arena in Kansas City. That structure had once won an award for its architectural design, but the award didn't prevent it from collapsing a few weeks before our date to appear in it. So, naturally, that week was cancelled. On a tour such as ours, a cancelled week without any income is a disaster. The huge payroll rolls on, but there is no revenue to offset the expenses.

Most major events in people's lives happen with unexpected suddenness. They are like earthquakes; unpredictable in the extreme.

On our first Saturday performance in Chicago one day in 1979, we had had some problems. Mainly these were because we were breaking in a new lighting director for the show and he was still a bit slow responding to the cues. Our show was always a teamwork production and it depended on many people doing many things, and all of it meshing smoothly. When there was a new person in a key role, that teamwork suffered. And on this day, I was the chief sufferer.

I was in the midst of my climactic stunt -- the backbend spread eagle. I was bent over backwards, staring UD at the ceiling, skimming around the surface of the ice at my usual twenty-five miles per hour speed, and depending on the lights to judge where I was and when I should turn. But the lights were just a touch off and so I misjudged the location of the bang board and rammed into it. They were low, made of metallic frames, and when I hit those knees first, I fell. It wasn't a long fall -- perhaps ten inches, because I was so low to the surface of the ice at the time -- but it was my knees that bore the brunt of the accident.

That was the end of my career. I could tell it almost at once. When you are young, you can recuperate rapidly from such injuries. I had had broken knee caps before, as well as many other lesser injuries and wounds. But I was now in my middle sixties and, while my doctor said I had the condition of a fifty year old, still the body does change. Things heal slower, if at all. So, I hobbled off the ice, had my knees patched, and set about recuperating.

Another indication of my mortality came about six months before that injury when I learned that Frack had died. I knew, of course, that his illness was possibly fatal; still I was stunned and terribly saddened to hear of his death. I remembered so clearly him as a boy --

some years younger than me -- and so full of life, so physically fit, so agile, so spry and so young. And now he was gone forever.

Frack was only sixty years old when he died. I was already sixty-four -- and still out there two or three times a day until that final, career-ending injury.

By the time I stopped skating, I had been a professional ice skater for forty-three years. I think I had performed more than 15,000 times [72 188]. I suspect that I was seen in action by more people than any other performer who ever lived, except possibly for a few old circus clowns. I had become an institution -- as someone said, I was "a legend in my own time."

I knew that as a person gets older, he simply no longer has the energies he had before. A doctor once told me that a young man and an old man might both be able to run up a flight of stairs in the same time, but it would take the older man twice as long to recover from that exertion as the younger man. In the last few years I skated, I had restaged my act, because it made sense at my age to do fewer but bigger tricks. I would no longer waste what energy I had left on small tricks, because (a) the audience remembers primarily the big things to you, so (b) why spend my strength on things they won't remember anyhow? I believe all that contributed to an improvement in my act.

I had been fueling my ego for a few years with a cute saying, "When you are over the hill, you pick up Speed" and the old Pennsylvania Dutch remark, "You get too late schmart and too soon old."

It gives me great pleasure to be able to help younger skaters. I believe that all of us, as we grow older, have an obligation to pass on what knowledge we have accumulated to the next generation.

There was a subtle change in my attitude I began to recognize, too. This contributed to my decision to retire after that final injury. I gradually realized that I no longer had that burning urge to perform that I once had had. When it penetrated my conscious mind that that was the case, I knew the time had come to quit.

Why not quit when I was on top? That seemed to me the sensible thing to do.

Yvonne was ecstatic with my decision. It

meant that we could have something approaching a normal life, for the first time in our years together. I think she had been secretly hoping for years, that I would retire, but she had never pushed it.

I was certainly still in good condition -- I didn't smoke or drink anything stronger than beer or wine (except for that shot of bourbon I poured over my breakfast grapefruit) and I maintained my weight at an acceptable figure. So, I knew we could have some years -- perhaps many years -- of the good life together. We have our pied-a-terre in Switzerland and we had a lovely home on Lake Tahoe until the day it collapsed under a load of snow and' was totally destroyed.

We spend our summers in Switzerland, our winters in Palm Springs, California. It is a very nice way to live.

As soon as I left the show and knew that, as a consequence, I would not have that daily performance to exercise my body, I began a program of physical conditioning to stay in shape. I do some brisk walking some time every day. I believe in stair-climbing as a good exercise and try to do some of that every day, too, or a few laps in a swimming Pool.

It is gratifying to reflect, as I climb those stairs or walk that walk or swim those laps, that I have made some impact on the world I live in.

I believe it is not a false boast to make that statement. After all, The World Almanac lists me among its "Prominent People." I am in the Skating Hall of Fame and Who's Who in America. Articles about me are in the morgues of most of the great newspapers in America, and in many papers around the world.

And my name has become part of the language. Johnny Carson once introduced two opera singers as "the Frick and Frack of the Metropolitan Opera." Dean Martin put his arm around Frank Sinatra once on TV and said, "We're just like Frick and Frack." Just this past Christmas, I received a Christmas card with a reference to Frick and Frack.

Of course, I am realistic enough to understand about fame. I realize that next year or maybe the year after that, my name will be dropped from that "Prominent People" list in The World Almanac and from Who's Who in America, as my prominence fades away. And someday my clippings in those newspaper morgues will be burned to make room for newer and more up-to-the-minute people. I think my appearance in the Skaters' Hall of Fame has a good chance of hanging around for some time, but even that is bound to be only temporary -- providing they clean my shirt periodically.

Nothing lasts forever, and certainly fame doesn't.

However, at the moment, as I write this book, there are many thousands -- perhaps even millions -- of people who know me. I have given them some moments of happiness and I will always be proud of that fact. I have enjoyed performing, but it is even more gratifying when the public tells me, as they have on many, many occasions, that I have given them a great deal of pleasure. It was also fun to be funny.

It is nice to know, too, that my work has been the inspiration to young skaters. Beginning in 1984, I began reading in the newspapers about a fine young figure skater named Debi Thomas. And in all her interviews, she would give me credit for inspiring her.

She was interviewed when she skated in Tokyo in 1984 and the interviewer asked her the obligatory question, "How did you get started skating?" Debi's answer was, "I saw Mr. Frick skate and I thought the man looked drôle, so I decided to skate myself."

About a year later, I was at Charles Schulz's rink in Santa Rosa for his ice production, when I suddenly felt someone kiss me on my cheek. I turned and there was this pretty girl smiling up at me.

"I am Debi," she said.

So, I have been following her meteoric career with almost paternal pride. Debi won her first U.S. title in February 1986 and her first world title the next month. I was in Geneva to root for her as she won that first world title. I would have liked to have been in Moscow later in '86 when she was featured partnered with a Russian skater, in the Friendship Games. (For the TV coverage of that event, Peggy Fleming was the commentator and she offered a brief history of skating, and included six skaters -- and I was one of the six.)

That was another pleasant moment. There

have been many of them in my life, and in Yvonne's life, and in the life, we currently share. We take particular pleasure in new ice skating rinks being built and old ones being refurbished, which means a new generation of ice skaters will be forthcoming.

I read with great satisfaction about the reopening [November 13, 1986] of the Wollman Memorial Ice Rink in New York's Central Park, which has always reminded me of a Currier & Ives print. I think we have real estate tycoon Donald Trump to thank for that -- and he doesn't even skate.

Our friends, Walter and Carol Probst -- she was the former Ice Follies star, Carol Caverley -- have built an especially lovely rink, Ice Castle, in Blue Jay, near Lake Arrowhead in California. It is nestled in the pine woods of that beautiful mountain resort. We were invited for the opening, a $500-a-plate charity affair, with fifty-six musicians playing for the skaters while the diners watched in obvious delight. Walter really built it for Carol who still loves to skate, but she is so busy running the place now that she seldom has the time to skate herself. Incidentally, the greatest flight I ever took was in Walter Probst's private plane, a BAC 111. We drank champagne while the pilot let us view the Greenland glaciers. Yvonne reported that the toilet in the ladies' room was so ornate she had a lot of trouble finding the handle to flush the john.

Despite the new and renovated rinks, we have lost a few, too, notably the old Squaw Valley rink in California, the site of the '60 U.S. Olympic hockey triumph over the Russians.

That arena was dynamited into oblivion -- I witnessed that tragedy -- when somebody decided they would rather have a parking lot than a rink.

Fortunately, the good moments outweigh the bad. I think my future will see more good -- even great -- moments. I am fortunate in having Yvonne and fortunately, her health these days is better than it has been in years. We are in good shape physically -- she still watches over my diet like a hawk, and I am managing to stay at or near 177 pounds [80.3 kg].

And we have good friends all over, and friends are very important in our idea of the full life.

One of those friends is Charles Schulz -- we are in that intimate circle who can call him Sparky. He has built what is probably the world's finest ice rink near his home in Santa Rosa, California [Snoopy's Home Ice|Redwood Empire Ice Arena]. The rink is in a park-like setting with lovely features such as a Spanish well and autographs of his friends in cement and his Puppy Bar and a restaurant. Every morning, you can find Sparky at his usual table in the restaurant reading the morning paper before he goes off (past his tennis court and his pool) to his office to work on the next day's "Peanuts" cartoon strip.

Each year, that rink is the site of a gala ice show, and Yvonne and I are always invited. We sit at a rink side table, drinking champagne and watching the show.

I was pleased recently when Schulz came to Basel when I was there, and I was able to reciprocate, after a fashion, by showing him my home City and entertaining him there. We even went on a ceremonial ride on a Basel fire engine.

Schulz says he has long been a Frick and Frack fan and that makes it nice for me. It was always pleasant to be appreciated, and even more pleasant to be appreciated by someone who is an expert. Schulz is certainly that. You would have to classify him as a world-class hockey fan.

During his visit to Basel, we stopped for a while in our Rathaus -- the town hall -- and Schulz was fascinated to observe the passing parade. He watched the people go by for a while and then laughed.

"You know, Frick," he said, "these people could be in New York or London or anywhere. People are people, the same the world over."

Maybe it is his grasp of that simple fact that has helped make "Peanuts" loved internationally. It is as popular in Basel as it is in Santa Rosa.

Schulz has used my name in, at last count, four of his comic strips [1-4 232-233]. He gave me the original of two of them, which are now one of my proudest possessions. In it, Snoopy, who was about to try out for the Olympics said, "I'll disguise myself as Mr. Frick [1975]." That, too, is a form of immortality. Somewhere there must be a file of all the "Peanuts" strips -- in the United Features office in

New York, if nowhere else -- and so that particular strip exists somewhere forever. Or as long as forever can be these days.

The Schulz/Frick association has been good for me. For one of the early specials and which I appeared, Yvonne and I flew back from Zurich to Santa Rosa, only to be told that the sequence I was doing on the show was going to be filmed in Switzerland.

"I could have left my laundry in Zurich," I said, as I packed again after unpacking only an hour before.

That was the trip, I remember, where I carried a wooden prop gun, and those were the times when the world -- and particularly the airlines -- were very jittery because of hijackings and rampant terrorism. That gun may have been made of wood, and harmless, but it looked very real. I had Yvonne carry it as we headed for the TWA checkpoint. (I may be wrong, but I don't think they are as careful with their inspection of women passengers as they are with men which, if true, is a mistake, but that's another book.)

I went through first and then turned to see how Yvonne would do. She made no effort to hide the gun. It was there in plain sight. And the guard must have seen it, but he just smiled at Yvonne and she waltzed through without any trouble at all.

The Snoopy you see on those TV skating specials isn't a dog at all. Inside that Snoopy suit is a human being. And it isn't always the same one, either. I know, because when we were in Switzerland, and I skated with Snoopy, he was talking German -- but she had spoken English when I skated with "him" in California. Actually, in Switzerland [1974], we hired a champion skater to put on that Snoopy costume and skate with me.

They filmed Snoopy in all sorts of situations. They wanted him filmed with a herd of cows, so we contacted a farmer near Arosa [canton Grisons]. His cows were on a tight, regular schedule -- they left the barn every morning at seven. But our crew couldn't get there until eight, so the farmer reluctantly agreed to hold the cows an hour later the next morning. But nobody told the cows. So, when we were finally set up with cameras and lights and actors, and they turned the cows loose to come out and mingle with Snoopy, they were angry. Instead of their usual cow-like amble, they rushed out of the barn, mooing in protest, and charged the cameras and the crew. We all ran and the director never did get the shot of Snoopy and the cows.

At the Arosa station [📷 52 📄 154], a train was poised to leave as our company arrived. Some of our crew had gone ahead to the next station to film Snoopy getting off the train. We barely had time to buy tickets for the short run to that next station. The actor in the Snoopy costume was already on board the train when I rushed up to his window and handed him his ticket.

"Put on your head," I shouted to him above the chug of the train starting to move. "All dogs ride for half-fare on Swiss railroads."

It gave me a great inner satisfaction to find out that he followed my advice, and I had another triumph of out-witting a transportation company.

I treasure my association with Schulz and Snoopy and the others. I hope it will continue in the years to come. Sparky Schulz' philosophy -- he frequently talks about man's ability to laugh at himself -- is, I think, a very upbeat, positive one. I like to think that my work on the ice, in front of millions, has helped them to laugh at themselves. From time to time, I think that perhaps I have taken my own life and my own work too seriously in the past. I hope to change that in the future, and enjoy my retirement.

Now that I am simply one of the spectators, I believe I will have more time to find the humor in what I see, and even find the humor in myself.

With Yvonne (who has been a spectator far too long) at my side, we can now celebrate each day. As Yvonne has so often said, the mere fact of waking up and realizing you are alive is a form of celebration.

I have the satisfaction of realizing I quit when I was at the top, so I can look back on a career with no weaknesses, no regrets and no embarrassments.

Our life now is not one of standing still. We plan to move forward as we always have done. We have skated over much thin ice, and we probably will encounter much more. But the thing about thin ice is that you have to keep moving, and leave the cracks behind.

Chapter 13

North Lake Tahoe Bonanza
Wednesday, May 30, 1984

"Frick" chosen for Skating's Hall of Fame

This year's choice for the honor
By Rick Folstad

With half the legendary ice skating duo known as Frick and Frack still roaming the world and reminiscing of 41 years on ice, which included 15,000 performances and the watching of a nation grow from the window of a Pullman, induction into the United Figure Skating Association's Hall of Fame would seem both overdue and appropriate.

It was May 19 when Swiss-born Werner Groebli received letter from the USFSA's Ben Wright informing him he was this year's choice for the honor. When and where remain uncertain, but the specifics are meaningless. The honor is bestowed on one individual each year, and this year belongs to Groebli.

"My old costume and a pair of my skates are at the USFSA's museum in Colorado Springs, Colo. right now," said Groebli. "They've been there for five years, right next to Sonja Henie's display. Groebli is the Frick half of the former duo and he's a resident of Incline Village where he calls both the air and people beautiful.

"I came up here many years ago when the show was in Sacramento," said Groebli. "And I fell in love with the mountains, the climate and the people."

Entering his fourth summer at Incline, Groebli, 69, says the Tahoe winters are a little hard, so in the past, he and his wife Yvonne have left the hill in winter. This year, they may stay.

"Yvonne is both Swiss and French, a good combination," said Groebli. "We were married Dec. 30, 1954 so we could split our income tax."

Holding onto the humor that made the Frick and Frack act one of the premier attractions of Shipstad and Johnson's Ice Follies, Groebli left the show in 1980 after slamming into the boards of an ice arena and injuring his knee. His partner Hans Mauch, better known as Frack, died in 1979 shortly after the team had been inducted into the Ice Skating Association of America's Hall of Fame in 1978 [🏆1 📄 226].

"Hans and I were next door neighbors in Basel, Switzerland," said Groebli. "We did a lot of skating but had no intentions of being comedians. But we had a sense of humor and we both had a unique style and some eccentric moves and at the request of an ice rink manager in Switzerland, we started performing at social events. After me moved onto St Moritz and did some performances, we left school and went first to England and then to America. And we never came back."

Groebli and Mauch came to America in 1938, joining the 2-year-old Ice Follies in 1939. Forty one years later, Groebli left the show after seeing the coming and going of more than 800 Follies performers, visiting countless cities, and experiencing a new country by way of railroads and short layovers.

"I saw a lot of cities and arenas," said Groebli. "We did regular performances in Providence, New Haven, Minneapolis, San Francisco and Sacramento and all over. We performed in San Francisco up to 14 weeks each year and during the last years of the Ice Follies; we set up a base in Sacramento where we rehearsed new shows."

Like its oldest and most notable performer, the Ice Follies no longer perform on ice. According to Groebli, a declining interest in the Follies and competition from other entertainment centers and concepts made the show financially impractical. But the disbanding of the show has not lessened the memories.

"We listed 170 skaters," said Groebli. "But there were usually only 65 or 70 skaters traveling the show. Sometimes we took up 15 railroad cars across the country and we would sometimes hook up with the president's car and party. That era is gone now, but we still consider ourselves all part of the Follies family. From the time, it was founded in 1937 to its closing, we had three generations of skaters."

Some of those skaters, some who traveled the country with Groebli and some who joined the Follies shortly before Groebli left, will have the opportunity to renew old friendships, form new ones and remember past times when former Follies skaters reunite June 20, and 21 at the MGM Grand in Reno.

"We've sent out hundreds of invitations," said Groebli. "But a lot of addresses have been lost and some of the performers have died. We're still hoping for 300 or 400 people." According to Groebli, the reunion will include a banquet and cocktail party and will be a return trip to Reno for some of the Follies people who used the audition potential skaters in Reno.

"Though we held auditions there, we never played Reno," said Groebli. "And I always wished we had."

At the present, Groebli, who weights the same 174 pounds he weighed when he came to America in 1938, is working on his memoirs for a book he hopes to have published sometime in the near future. And he continues to travel; having made more than 55 trips to Switzerland over the years and is now making plans for a trip to Montreal to honor the son of a former Follies skater.

"I'm doing the things now which I couldn't do when I was traveling with the show," said Groebli.

Yet along with the free time, come memories of those changes which Groebli didn't like to see or remember.

"I watched them demolish Blythe Arena (in Squaw Valley) last year," said Groebli. "And it was very sad, a shame. I kind of sang a swan song when they took it down. They just don't build ice arenas like that anymore. My knees have outlasted most refrigeration pipes in mot arenas. There's very few of those old arenas left."

But Groebli doesn't hang onto the past too long. Too many trips and too many plans don't allow for down time.

"Along with working on the book, I'm doing some correspondence," said Groebli. "And I'm preparing for the Montreal trip and the reunion in Reno."

And sometime in the near future, there's an induction into the USFSA Hall of Fame.

ICE SKATING HALL OF FAME

Be it known by all here present

That the great Swiss ice comedians, FRICK & FRACK (WERNER GROEBLI AND HANS MAUCH) have been elected to membership in the ICE SKATING HALL OF FAME on this eleventh day of May in the year 1978;

That this membership has been awarded to them for providing entertainment to millions of people throughout the world with their great skill and total dedication to ice skating.

In honor of these achievements, membership in the ICE SKATING HALL OF FAME is hereby declared.

President, Ice Skating Institute of America

Chairman, Awards and Citations

1978 - Frick and Frack
Ice Skating Hall Of Fame

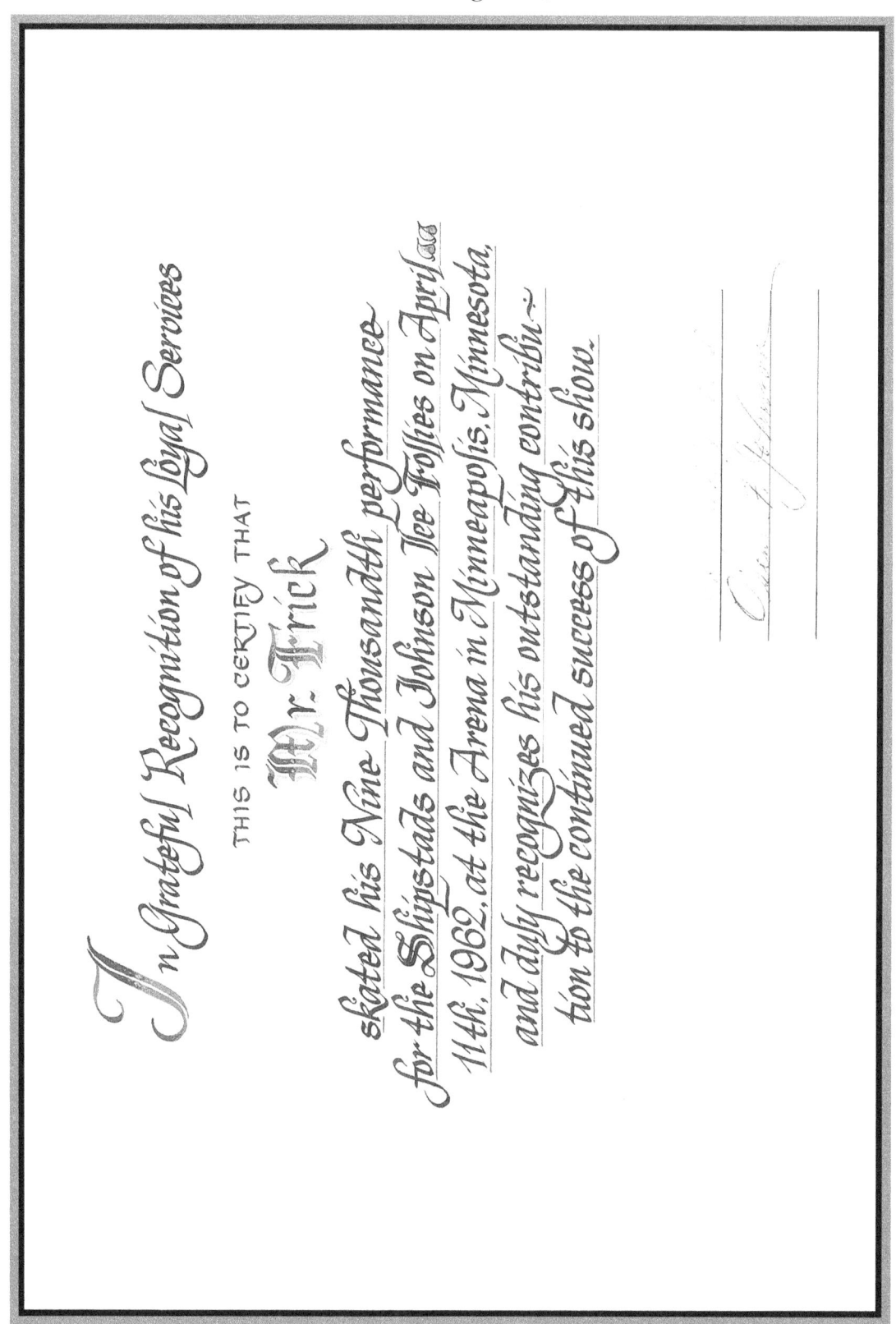

1962 - Mr. Frick's Nine Thousandth Performance
Shipstads and Johnson Ice Follies

Honor 3 ✦ Pages 167, 219

OFFICE OF THE MAYOR
SAN FRANCISCO

GEORGE R. MOSCONE

Proclamation

WHEREAS, ICE FOLLIES skating spectacular has been entertaining families for forty-three years with an exciting combination of music, costumes, comedic classics and precision skating; and

WHEREAS, The all-new ICE FOLLIES is appearing in San Francisco August 16 through September 3, 1978, at the Civic Auditorium; and

WHEREAS, Internationally-known skating comedian Mr. Frick, the original half of the favorite Frick and Frack comedy team, is celebrating his Fortieth Skating Anniversary with the ICE FOLLIES; and

WHEREAS, Mr. Frick has skated before more than 70 million fans in more than 16,000 performances and is internationally renowned for his extraordinary showmanship; and

WHEREAS, At sixty-three years of age, Mr. Frick continues to bring happiness and laughter to audiences throughout America; and

WHEREAS, Baskin-Robbins Ice Cream Company, also bringing fun and happiness to families across the nation with their unique ice cream flavors, is holding a special Fortieth Anniversary Celebration for Mr. Frick on August 31, 1978, in Union Square;

NOW, THEREFORE, I, George R. Moscone, Mayor of the City and County of San Francisco, do hereby proclaim Thursday, August 31, 1978, as MR. FRICK DAY in San Francisco; do compliment Mr. Frick on the accomplishments of his extraordinary career, and do wish him good health, happiness and success in his unique role with the ICE FOLLIES through many rewarding years to come.

IN WITNESS WHEREOF, I have hereunto set my hand and caused the Seal of the City and County of San Francisco to be affixed this twenty-fourth day of August, nineteen hundred and seventy-eight.

George R. Moscone
Mayor

1978 - Mr. Frick Day
Proclamation
Office of the Mayor San Francisco

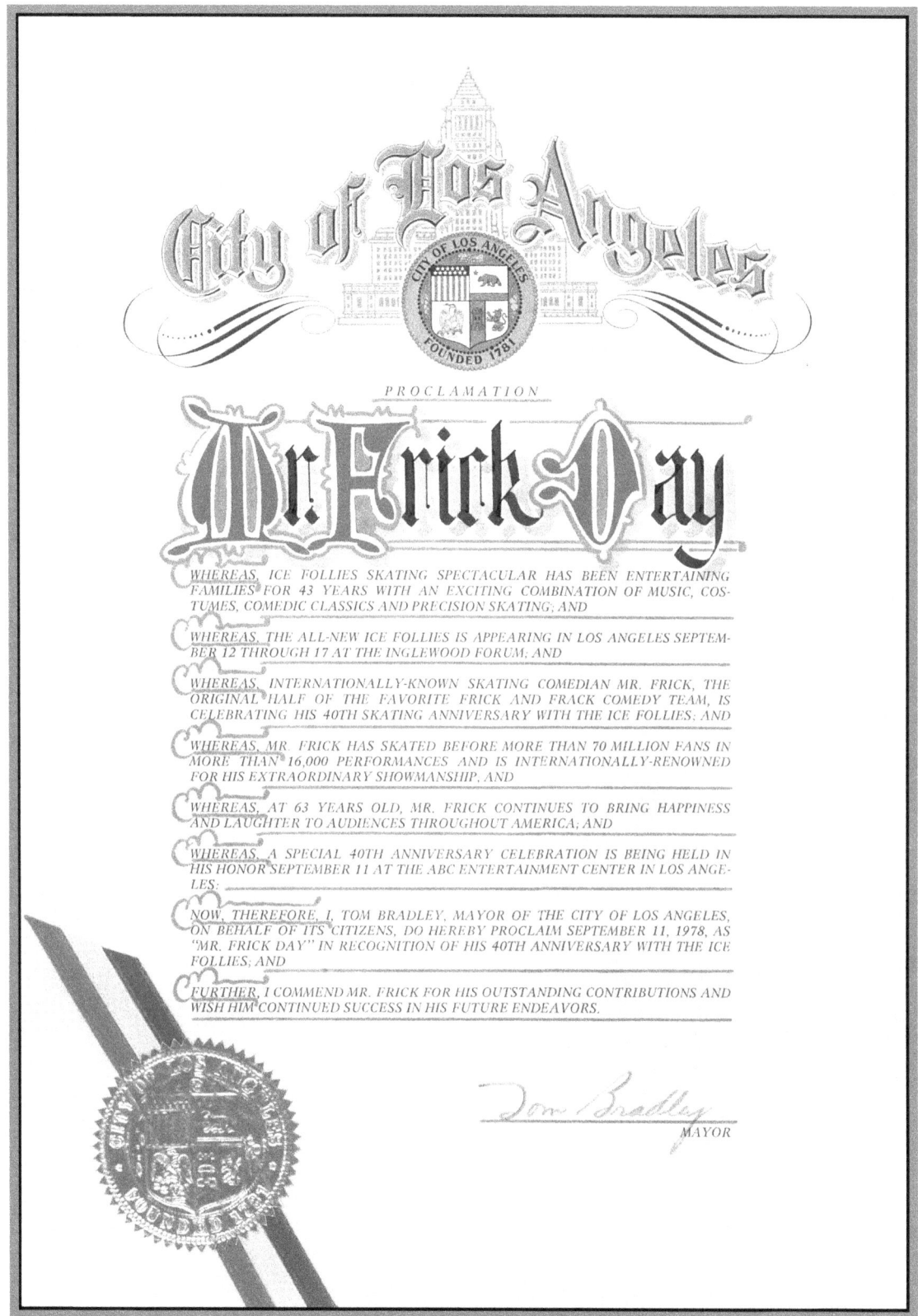

1978 - Mr. Frick Day
Proclamation
City of Los Angeles

1972 - Mr. Frick, Karen Kresge & Snoopy
Ice Follies

1973 - Mr. Frick & Snoopy
Ice Follies

Peanuts 1 ✧ Page 222

1975 - Peanuts by Charles M. Schulz
"I'LL DISGUISE MYSELF AS MR. FRICK"

Peanuts 2 ✧ Page 222

1977 - Peanuts by Charles M. Schulz
"FOR A MOMENT THERE I HAD MR. FRICK WORRIED"

Peanuts 3 ✧ Page 222

1978 - Peanuts by Charles M. Schulz
"I'D EVEN INTRODUCE YOU TO MR. FRICK"

Peanuts 4 ✧ Pages 161, 222

1980 - Peanuts by Charles M. Schulz
"I SHOULD BE IN AN ICE SHOW"

Cartoon 1

Mr. Frick the most imitated comic on ice

Cartoon 2

Mr. Frick performs one of the most difficult and imitated skating tricks

Chapter 13

-235-

1946 - Mr. Frick-"Helvetian Ambassador of fun to patrons of the Ice Follies"

Epilogue

Werner's final years alone in Switzerland

"Carola; Yvonne just died (December 2, 2002)!" My mother was completely confused after this phone call, which she had received by Werner from the USA and so she immediately called me. "Werner will return to Switzerland definitely!" Yvonne and Werner got used to the idea about 2001 to dissolve their American household, because of their bad feelings concerning Yvonne's health. However, her passing came for all of us unexpectedly.

Some weeks later Werner came back to Switzerland, accompanied by two good "fairies." Now he was alone in his "eyrie" (attic home) in Seefeld, a treasured living quarter on wonderful side of Lake Zurich. Next to him, lived two single widowed neighbors, first a former opera singer and second a lovely woman, who had watched their attic home for many years, during the Groeblis absences in the winter months.

At the beginning my mother constantly checked if all was in order and helped Werner get domestic again in Zurich. Furthermore, many relatives and friends supported him in dealing the loss of his beloved wife. After a while, my seventy years old mother was overwhelmed by the work it took to take care of all the small and large tasks, which were requirements of Werner's everyday life. As Werner was to me like a dear uncle, I accepted instantly to support him.

Usually we had a beautiful time together. I reserved one day during the week, to have everything well organized for him. But if worse came to worst, my sons and I stopped by early in the morning, to change a lightbulb or to give a hand with the microwave.

Werner wooed his lovely neighbors for attention as only a comedian would. For example, he placed an apple pie with one of his star photos, with dedication and signature, in front their doors or brought them the newspaper, when he was going to fetch his own daily paper. Another day, when there was not much going on, Werner devised an experiment. He placed an apricot in the elevator and watched how long it will take before the delicate apricot was taken by someone. There were some moments, which were too much for the opera singer. As a reply to Werner's antics she bounced back an apple, which was placed in front of her door, when she faced Werner's head in his doorframe. The apple then hurled back and forth like a tennis ball between them, she told me someday laughing.

Two levels below lived Nello Santi, a longtime maestro at the Opera House of Zurich. Furthermore, Nello Santi had conducted the Metropolitan Opera in New York during twenty-nine years. During this time, a longstanding friendship connected the family Santi with the Groeblis. So, after Yvonne's death the Santis assisted Werner at the beginning with her domestic aid as well.

Weekly there was scheduled a visit to his bank at famous Bahnhofstrasse in Zurich. The front desk lady recognized him immediately in the entrance hall, probably because she thought that Werner must be already part of this financial institution. Sometimes I accompanied him to the bank. When we were seated in one of the conference rooms and waited for his administrator, who was a good friend of his, he suddenly stood up and delivered a funny speech to the directorate of the bank or he simply sang a ditty.

Despite his age, Werner was always dressed in bright colors. His 90th birthday was celebrated in "Don Giovanni" near by the Opera House of Zurich. He came with a glowing red jacket and a fancy tie designed by Rolf Knie, an offspring of the oldest and most famous circus dynasty of Switzerland.

Over time Werner needed more professional care and so we made use of an aid-organization, which enabled him to stay at home as long as possible. Werner had his own precise ideas concerning the aid-ladies, who took care of him, which made looking after him a bit more difficult.

The many phone calls Werner received from the USA and from Switzerland every day made a major contribution to his quality of life in his last years. A part of his heart always remained in the USA and he enjoyed hearing the news of his friends. I like to recall when we organized his 90th birthday that we had to make sure he was back at 77 Wildbachstrasse by three o'clock sharp so as not to miss any calls from the USA.

For many years, he was a regular at the "Mövenpick" restaurant, where his table was always reserved for him and he was looked after with a lot of loving affection. It was quite common for him to be given a free package of cakes to take home for his afternoon tea. Of course, Werner enjoyed very much the attention they paid him there. There he had his performances, as every visit invariably turned into a performance. He loved making people laugh or just smile.

Every year he was very happy, when his friends sent newspaper cuttings on his birthday, the 21st of April. They described who will celebrate a birthday that day. In his final years, he was written up in the list before Queen Elisabeth. Then he told me this story over again and again, that when he was in London in 1939 music was playing in front of the Buckingham Palace on his birthday. He thought it was in honor to his birthday, but the guard clarified: "It's not for you, but for the Queen." So, he knew that his birthday was on the same day as Queen Elisabeth's birthday.

A constant companion was also the NZZ (Neue Zürcher Zeitung) and the International New York Times, which he studied until a short time before his death so that, he would always up-to-date with the stock market prices.

He had kept his "eyrie" (attic home) up until November 2005, when he had to give it up due to the increasing ailments of old age and move into the Bethesda Old People's Home, where he could be given the care he needed.

In his room at Bethesda he had a wonderful view of the Alps and he loved looking out from his balcony to the pond with the ducks and the goats at the water's edge. Beneath his room a small flower-bed and herb garden were a delight to his eye. He really had "a Room with a View," which he loved telling everyone about. We are all glad that Werner had such a beautiful last place of residence! Werner lived from meal to meal at Bethesda. His favorite was ice cream, which he ordered at least once a day.

Werner's end came quite unexpectedly, even though he had mentioned death time and again in his last weeks. I like to recall how he was sitting in the armchair on the Friday before he went into hospital and said to me: "All right, and now I'll die!" I laughed and said: "Werner you'll have to place that order with the Lord."

On Saturday night Frick fell in his room and broke the neck of his femur. Nobody knows how he got back into bed by himself. It was only during the morning ablutions that they noticed his leg was broken. Werner was already very dazed when he was driven to the hospital for the operation. The operation went well, but Werner was as if he was no longer properly awake again and could only answer "Yes." For a long time the doctors thought it was an after-effect of the anesthetic. Since he could no longer swallow either he would have had to be fed artificially through a stomach tube. This decision, which would have enabled him to return to Bethesda, was postponed, but Werner voided the decision by passing away. He passed away with a smile on his lips. At the right time, he had successfully placed the order to be taken up into kingdom of heaven.

We have lost a lovable man, who remained a comedian with all his heart and soul until the end.

Carola Klinkert-Huegin

Index

A

Admiral Felix Gygax
 75
Accident
 30,117-118,220
 * Beer Puddle
 99
Adolf Hitler
 27,108,151
Airline
 78,123-124,126,128,158
Airline Stewardess
 98,140
Aja Zanova (Alena Vrzáňová)
 142-143
Albert Einstein
 23
Alexander M. Poniatoff
 125,217
Alps
 13 54
 9,15,17,110,133,238
 * Alphorn
 17
 * Foothills Of The Alps
 15
 * Skiing
 39,110,133,148
America | United States
 4,27,32,37,40,77,85-86,97,
 100,108-109,111,120,127,
 128,133,142-143,153,221,
 224-225
 * Life Magazine
 79
 * North America
 32,102
 * South America
 9,163-165
American
 12,17,21,37,78,102,107,
 119,151-152
 * American Boy
 12

* American Brunch
 14
* American Car
 128
* American Champion
 119
* American Citizenship
 102
* American Continent
 102
* American Custom
 80
* American Girl
 98
* American GIs (Soldiers)
 152
* American High School
 21
* American Hospital
 108
* American Household
 237
* American Language
 82,129
* American Milk
 14
* American Naval Officer
 75
* American Railroad
 145
* American Soldier
 152
* American Way Of Life
 103,152
* American Workmen
 108
Americanized
 37
Ambassador
 38
 * Helvetian Ambassador
 ☺ 3 236
 * Park Bench Ambassador
  59 175
Amish
 147

Ampex
 125,217
Andrée And Pierre Brunet
 29
A.P. Giannini (Founder
Of The Bank of America)
 85,103
Architecture Study
 22,24-25,88
Armand Perren
 24
Army
 * Army Buddies
 143
 * German Army
 81
 * Ice Follies
 139
 * Swiss Army
 13,15,24-25,86
 * U.S. Army
 151-152
Arosa | Switzerland
  52 154
 223
Arthur Wirtz
 34-35,217
Athlete
 5,79,82,84,87,127,134,
 143,164
Attraction
 25,161,224
Audrey Hepburn
 31
Aunt (Tante) Celly
 17-18
Aunt (Tante) Emmy
 13-14,18

B

Babe Ruth
  4 45
 34

Index
-239-

Backstage
- 🖼 8 📄 49 | 28 📄 69 | 67 📄 183 | 73 📄 189
- 📄 31,38,77,86,104-105,107, 119,142,144,157,162-163, 165

Bad Ragaz | Switzerland
- 📄 13

Ballet Russe
- 📄 83

Bank Of America
- 📄 85,103

Barbara Walters
- 📄 81-82

Basle (Basel) | Switzerland
- 📄 9-13,15-27,36,40,88,94,117, 144,152,222
* Basle Cathedral (Münster)
  - 📄 17
* Church Chimes
  - 📄 22
* Frobenstrasse
  - 📄 9,11-15,18-20,25,88,117, 155
* Gempenfluh
  - 📄 15
* Gundeldingerstrasse
  - 📄 12
* Kunsteisbahn Basel (Artificial Ice Rink Basle)
  - 📄 18,25
* Margarethenpark
  - 📄 12-13,17-18,20,23-24, 40,97
* Pharmacy
  - 📄 11
* Rhine (Rhein)
  - 📄 11,19
* Rathaus (Town Hall)
  - 📄 222

Basle News (Basler Nachrichten)
- 📄 25

Beer
- 📄 23,83,99,101,104,127-129, 143,165,221

Berne (Bern)
- 📄 88

Bert Lundblad
- 📄 102-103

Bette Midler
- 📄 136

Betty Grable
- 📄 33,77

Beverly Hills | California
- 📄 11,77,103,108

Blackpool | England
- 📄 29

Bob Hope
- 📄 77

Bob Leduc
- 📄 140

Bob Shipstad
- 📄 104,162,166

Bourbon
- 📄 79,221,252

Brigitte Amann
- 📄 145

Boston
- 📄 108,118,128-129

Boston Garden Arena
- 📄 36

Brighton | England
- 📄 27-30

Buffalo | New York
- 📄 75,118,134,144

Businessman
- 🖼 68 📄 184
- 📄 18,81,86,143

C

Canada
- 📄 30,36,98,215

Cantilever Spread Eagle, Cantilever Backbend
- 🖼 34 📄 89 | 39-41 📄 94-96 | 49 📄 138 | 53 📄 169 | 58 📄 174 | 66 📄 182 | 74 📄 190 | 79 📄 195 | 81 📄 197 | 84 📄 200 | 87 📄 203 | 88 📄 204 | 90 📄 206 | 93 📄 209
- 📄 3,5,24,29,88-89,94,163,220

Carol Caverley
- 📄 222

Cartoons
- ☺ 1-3 📄 234-236
- 📄 4,222

Cécile (Yvonne's Sister)
- 📄 102,108,110-111,155-156

Celebrities →
Mr. Frick & Celebrities
- 📄 4-5,77,103

Charles Schulz (Sparky) →
Snoopy
- 🐾 1-4 📄 232-233
- 📄 4-5,141,164,167,219, 221-223

Champion
* California Champion
  - 📄 161
* Canadian Champion
  - 📄 119
* Champion Amateur Skater
  - 📄 24
* Champion Packer
  - 📄 123
* Champion Skater
  - 📄 223
* French European Pair Champions
  - 📄 29
* German Champion
  - 🖼 75 📄 191
  - 📄 141
* North American Champion
  - 📄 119
* Olympic Champion
  - 📄 5,98
* Ontario Champion
  - 📄 119
* Skating Champion Of Czechoslovakia
  - 📄 142
* Swiss Junior Champion
  - 📄 38
* Swiss Skating Champion
  - 📄 20
* U.S. Championship
  - 📄 140
* World Champion
  - 📄 98

Charlie Chaplin
- 📄 34,80,119

Cheese
- 📄 80,84,103
* Bread And Cheese
  - 📄 16,141

-240-

* Cheese, Chocolate, Watches, Bank Accounts, Swiss Army
  📄 24
* Entrance Inside A Big Cheese
  📄 84,168
Chicago | Illinois
  🖼 43 📄 114
  📄 32,36,99-102,105,108,118, 129,134,145-146,157-158
Children → Kids
  🖼 52 📄 154
  📄 9,12-13,16-17,39,98,109,111, 129,140,148,155-156,161
Christmas
  📄 78,80-82,106,109-110,147, 162,221
* Christmas Cards
  📄 109,147,221
* Christmas In New York
  📄 80-82
Chuck Davidson
  📄 119
Church
  📄 108,152
* Church Bells
  📄 17,22
* Church Chimes
  📄 22
* Church Services
  📄 26
* Protestant Churches
  📄 17
* Reformed Church
  📄 17
* Rockville, Maryland
  📄 106
Cincinnati | Ohio
  📄 106,108
Claude Langdon
  📄 27-28,30-31
Cleveland | Ohio
  📄 75,108,110,141,144
Colorado Springs | Colorado
  📄 83,147,224
Comedian
  📄 34,88,126,136,237-238
* Ice Comedians
  🖼 1-2 📄 42-43 | 57 📄 173 | 69 📄 185 | 95 📄 211
  📄 4-5,219

* Skating Comedians
  📄 41,88,94
* Swiss Comedians
  🖼 22 📄 63 | 34 📄 89
  📄 88,94
Comedy Skating
  📄 79-80,82,159,161
Contracts
  📄 5,28,36-37,88-89,143, 159-160,162,164,166-167, 215-216
Customs
  📄 17,156
* Spanish Customs
  📄 158
Customers
  📄 100,127,135
Costumes
  📄 36,80,82,89,144
* Copying Frick And Frack Costumes And Maneuvers
  📄 83
* Costumes Attached By The Sheriff
  📄 36
* Fresh And Clean Costumes
  📄 77
* Geisha Costumes
  📄 126
* Good Costumes (by Academy Award winner Helen Rose)
  📄 35
* New Costumes
  📄 77
* Skating Costumes
  📄 18
* Snoopy Costumes
  📄 251-252
* Swiss Folk Costumes
  📄 26,83,133

D

Dad (Bappe)
  📄 11,14,17-19,22,28
Dallas | Texas
  📄 216
Danse Macabre
  📄 30

Dave Thomas
  📄 81,104,119
Dean Martin
  📄 221
Death
* Frack, Hansruedi Mauch
  📄 37,121,220,224
* Frick, Werner Groebli
  📄 238
* Sonja Henie
  📄 35,77
* Yvonne Groebli
  📄 107,237
Debi Thomas
  📄 221
Denver | Colorado
  📄 75,105,126,137
Detroit | Michigan
  📄 126,144,148
Dick Dwyer
  📄 142
Disease → Illness
* Bone Disease
  📄 4,38,118
Disney
* Disneyland
  📄 85
* Disney On Ice Show
  📄 104
Dogs
  📄 76,111,155,223
* Dog Act
  📄 86,155,158,168
* Frick And Frack
  📄 82,129
* Lulu
  🖼 45 📄 116 | 72 📄 188
  📄 109,111,155-158,168
* Snoopy
  📄 223
* St. Bernard Dogs
  📄 135,155
* Travelling With A Dog
  📄 111,155,157
Dollar
* American Dollar $
  📄 26,28,33,36,40-41,78,82, 119,127,160,164,215
* Canadian Dollar
  📄 215

Donald Trump
- 222

Don Hunter
- 162,166-167

Donny And Marie Osmond
- 120,137,163-164,167,219

Doris Meyers
- 60 176

Doris Skillings
- 70-71 186-187

Dorothy Ann Nelson
- 47 131

Doug Maxon
- 128,162

Dr. Arthur Brandt
- 27,32

Dr. Grantley Taylor
- 108

Dr. James Koch
- 25

Dr. John Raker
- 108

Dr. Tenley Albright
- 129

Dutch
* Dutch Countryside
  - 147
* Dutch Language
  - 105
* Dutch Remark
  - 224
* Dutch Waitress
  - 135

Dwyerites and Frickites
- 161

E

Eddie Shipstad
- 77,83

Editions Of Swiss Movements
* eBook, Paperback (6x9)
  - 259
* Special Edition (8.5x11), Deluxe Edition (8x10)
  - 260

Edward Koch
- 99

Eleanor Roosevelt
- 78

England
- 27-31,37,41,97-98,133,224

Eric Jonnson
- 216

Eric Wait
- 30

Ernst Oertli (Brother-In-Law)
- 102,108,110,156,216

F

F.B.I. (Federal Bureau of Investigation)
- 84-85

Figure Skaters → Skaters

Folliettes
- 79,85,97-100,119,128-129, 137,139,141,145,157,167

Frack → Hansruedi Mauch
- 41 96
- 5,26,28-41,75-80,82-86, 88-89,98,101,103-104, 117-121,129-130,133-135, 159-160,215,220,224

* Bone Disease
  - 4,38,118,252
* Frackless
  - 252
* Frack's Rocking Chair Routine
  - 40
* Jacket
  - 26
* Rubber Legs
  - 5,80,119

Fran Claudet
- 99,143-144

Frank Libuse
- 126

Frank Sinatra
- 221

Frankie Sawyers
- 21 62
- 41

Franklin Roosevelt
- 79

Fred Astaire
- 38 93

Fred Leuenberger
- 162-163,166

Fred The Cabbie
- 105-106

Frick And Frack
- 1-20 42-61 | 23-33 64-74 | 34 89 | 40 95
- 🏆 1 226
- 3-5,26-29,34,38,76,79-80, 82-83,88,94,103,125, 129-130,133-135,152,161, 221-222,224,252

* Frick And Frack Sandwich
  - 82
* Swiss Idiots, Iced Nuts
  - 35
* Swiss Team Of Comedy Skaters
  - 76

Frol Koslov
- 85

G

Gail Foster
- 62 178 | 65 181

Gary Johnson
- 81,119,123,160

Gerald Graham
- 36

Government
* Government Of The United Kingdom
  - 33
* Japanese Government
  - 151
* Swiss Government
  - 15
* U.S. Government
  - 21,75,151,216

Graf Zeppelin
- 9

Grandfather (Grossvater)
- 16

Grandmother (Grossmutter)
- 16

Grapefruit
- 79,123,221,252

Gravity
 🖼 22 📄 63 | 34 📄 89 | 74 📄 190 |
  79 📄 195
 📄 25,34
Gstaad | Switzerland
 📄 108,110,147
Gun
 📄 18,84-85,223
Gymnasium
(Academic High School)
 📄 18,21

H

Hall Of Fame
(Colorado Springs)
 🏆 1 📄 226
 📄 83,120,147,219,221,
  224-225
Hansruedi Mauch → Frack
 📄 4-5,19-20,23,25,88,94,
  117,120,224
Hawaii
 📄 215
Hawaiin Hula Dancer, Maiden
 📄 35
Hellzapoppin
 📄 126
Herbert "Papa" Yates
 📄 133
Herman Faenger
 📄 125,217
Hershey | Pennsylvania
 📄 129,146-147
Hockey
 * Montreal Canadians
  📄 251
 * Wacky Hockey by
   Frick and Frack
  🖼 📄 251
Hoffman LaRoche
 📄 11,21
Holiday On Ice
 📄 76,140,162-163
Hollywood
 📄 30,32-37,77-78,133-135,137
Honor
 🏆 1-4 226-229
 📄 4,26-27,30,84,102,145,
  219,224-225
Hospital
 📄 30,108-110,118,238
Hotel
 📄 37,78,80,86,98,105-106,
  108-109,111,118,120,124,
  127-129,135,140-141,143,
  146-148,156-158,164-165
Hotel Room
 📄 80,86,101,107,109,111,119,
  127,129,135,140-141,143,
  146,148,155,215
Hotels:
 * Allerton | Chicago
  📄 101
 * Beverly Hills | Los Angeles
  📄 77,103
 * Bismarck | Chicago
  📄 99
 * Broadmoor | Colorado Springs
  📄 83,147
 * Brown Palace | Denver
  📄 105
 * Canterbury | San Francisco
  📄 103
 * Catamaran | San Diego
  📄 166
 * Claremont | Berkely
  📄 103
 * Curtis | Minneapolis
  📄 98,128
 * Elite | Zurich
  📄 102
 * Fairmont | San Francisco
  📄 142
 * Fleabag | Mexico
  📄 36
 * Gaylord | San Francisco
  📄 128
 * Hershey Inn | Pennsylvania
  📄 146-147
 * Kulm | St. Moritz, Switzerland
  📄 26
 * Manger | Boston
  📄 129
 * MGM Grand | Reno
  📄 225
 * Olympic | Seattle
  📄 102,148
 * Palace | Gstaad, Switzerland
  📄 108,110,147
 * Palace | St. Moritz, Switzerland
  📄 26
 * Portland | Portland
  📄 119
 * Royal York | Toronto
  📄 144
 * Sahara | Las Vegas
  📄 120
 * The Conrad Hilton | Chicago
  🖼 43 📄 114
 * Victoria | New York
  📄 127
 * Waldorf-Astoria | New York
  📄 78
 * Windsor | Montreal
  📄 143
Hubert Humphrey
 📄 78-79,106
Humphrey Bogart
 📄 133-135

I

Ice Capades
 📄 35-36,99,140,143,159,217
Ice Comedians → Comedian
Ice Follies
 🖼 3-10 📄 44-51 |
  17-21 📄 58-62 |
  23-33 📄 64-74 | 34 📄 89 |
  35-38 📄 90-93 | 41 📄 96 |
  42 📄 113 | 46 📄 122 |
  47-48 📄 131-132 | 49 📄 138 |
  50-51 📄 149-150 |
  53-99 📄 169-214 |
  100-101 📄 230-231
 🏆 2 📄 227
 ☺ 3 📄 236
 📄 4-5,30,36-39,41,75-77,79-81,
  85-86,88,94,97-98,101,105,
  120,123,126,129,134,136,
  139-146,151-152,156,
  159-160,165-166,168,216,
  219,222,224

Ice Rinks, Artificial Ice Rink
Ice Skating Rinks (Kunsteisbahn)
 📄 9-10,12,17-18,20,24,30-34,
 36,40,75-78,80-85,88,94,99,
 125,133-135,137,140-142,
 155,160,166-168,219,
 221-222,224
* Charles Schulz Rink |
Santa Rosa
 📄 221-222
* Ice Rink | Tokyo
 📄 81
* Richmond Rink | London
 📄 81
* Rockefeller Center Rink |
New York
 📄 80-82
* Stradivarius Rink | Minneapolis
 📄 75
* Winterland Rink | San Francisco
 📄 76,85,151-152,216
* Wollman Memorial Ice Rink |
New York
 📄 222
Ice Skaters → Skaters
Ice Skates → Skates
Ice Shows | England
* Danse Macabre
 📄 30
* Rhapsody On Ice
 📄 30-31
* Switzerland
 📄 29-30
* The Great Charlotte
 📄 31
* Wintersport
 📄 31-32
Ice Shows | Ice Follies
Frick And Frack, Mr. Frick & Co
* Alpine Antics
 🖼 62-63 📄 178-179
* Antarctic Adventurer
 🖼 56 📄 172 | 58 📄 174
* Antarctic Scientist
 🖼 65 📄 181
* Frozen Arctic
 🖼 82 📄 198
* Funnier Than Ever
 🖼 98 📄 214

* Geiger Counter Capers
 🖼 61 📄 177
* Get In The Driver's Seat
 🖼 19 📄 60
* In The Bahamas
 🖼 29 📄 70
* Park Bench Ambassador
 🖼 59 📄 175
* Sea Foot
 🖼 25 📄 66
* Swiss Jewel Mr. Frick
 🖼 92 📄 208
* The Admiral And His Aides
 🖼 21 📄 62
 📄 41
* The Ice Follies Ranch
 🖼 80 📄 196
* The Most Enduring
Comic On Ice
 🖼 97 📄 213
* The New Ice Age
 🖼 84 📄 200
* Top Banana
 🖼 66 📄 182
* Traveling Light
 🖼 70-71 📄 186-187
Ice Skaters → Skaters
Ice Skating Rinks → Ice Rinks
Illness → Disease
 📄 5,220
Ina Bauer
 🖼 75 📄 191 | 77 📄 193
Income Tax
 📄 83,216,224
Inge Manger
 📄 20
Interviews
 📄 136,221
* Debi Thomas
 📄 221
* Financial Editor Of The
Milwaukee Paper
 📄 127
* Mike Douglas In His Heyday
 📄 136
* NBC Barbara Walters
 📄 81-82
* NZZ Neue Zürcher Zeitung
 📄 165

* WMAQ-TV
 📄 157
Investments
 📄 107,109,215-216,252
Irma Thomas
 📄 35
I.R.S.
(Internal Revenue Service)
 📄 141
Irwin Feld
 📄 219

J

Jack Benny
 📄 136,215
Jackie Coogan
 📄 33-34
James Stewart
 🖼 36 📄 91
 📄 77,136
Janet Lynn
 🖼 89 📄 205
Japanese Americans
 📄 152
Jay Humphrey
 📄 119
Jeannie Simms
 🖼 8 📄 49
Jill Shipstad
 🖼 85 📄 201
 📄 166
Jim Jones
 📄 152
Jim Reid
 📄 252
Joan Crawford
 📄 33,77
Joe Maxwell
 📄 109
John F. Kennedy
 📄 21,75,152
John F. Kennedy International
Airport (New York)
 🖼 44 📄 115
 📄 110
John Hadlich
 📄 119

John Hall
  📄 87
John Harris
  📄 36,143
John Nance Garner
  📄 78
John Rouge
  📄 217
Johnny Carson
  📄 221
Josef Stalin
  📄 85
Judi Denton
  🖼 47 📄 131
Julie Andrews
  📄 31

K

Karen Kresge
  🖼 50-51 📄 149-150 | 100 📄 230
  📄 141,216
Kennel
  📄 111,155-157
Knee
  📄 13,18-19,24,38,88,109-110,
  118-119,146,220,224-225
* Knee Cap
  📄 38,118-119,220
Kids → Children
  🖼 49 📄 138
  📄 13,25,34,39,140,143-144
Kurt Neumann
  📄 31

L

Lady, Let's Dance → Movies
  🖼 13-16 📄 54-57
  📄 4-5,37,134-135,137
Lake
* Lake Arrowhead
  📄 226
* Lake Constance
  📄 9
* Lake Erie
  📄 168
* Lake Tahoe
  📄 135,154,221,224
* Lake Zurich
  📄 237
Lake Tahoe
  📄 135,221,224
Language
  📄 5,28-29,82,88,105,
  129-130,151
* Dutch
  📄 105
* English
  📄 25,28-29,37,89,101,125,
  142,223
* French
  📄 25,105,151
* Frick And Frack
  📄 5,82,129-130
* German
  📄 4,29,142,151-152,223
* Italian
  📄 89,105
* Romansh
  📄 105
* Swiss German
  📄 4,29,105,152
Las Vegas | Nevada
  📄 120,166
Lawrence Welk
  🖼 37 📄 92
  📄 77
Legendary
  🖼 4 📄 45
  📄 31,38,76,83,103,105,159
* Frick and Frack
  📄 3,134,224
* Mr. Frick
  📄 161,220
Life Magazine
  🖼 22 📄 63 | 39-41 📄 94-96
  📄 79,94
Liverpool | England
  📄 32
London | England
  📄 29-30,81,94,124,222,238
Los Angeles | California
  🖼 1-2 📄 42-43
  🏆 4 📄 229
  📄 32-33,36,77,83,85,103-104,
  108,118-120,124,126,135-
  136,145,148,166,216
Los Angeles Times
  📄 87
Luggage
  📄 80,83,123-124,158
* Suitcase
  🖼 42 📄 113
  📄 123-125,167,215,252
* Trunk
  📄 83
Lulu
  🖼 45 📄 116 | 72 📄 188
  📄 109,111,155-158,168

M

Madison Square Garden
  🖼 28 📄 69 | 34 📄 89 | 47 📄 131
  📄 34,41,76,81,88,125,163
Maria Belita Jepson-Turner
  🖼 15 📄 56
  📄 30,133-135
Marriage
  📄 5,98-99,102,106-107
Mary Elchlepp
  📄 98
Matterhorn | Switzerland
  🖼 13 📄 54
  📄 15,133
Maturität (Higher Education
Entrance Qualification)
  📄 21
Maurice Chevalier
  🖼 35 📄 90
  📄 77
MCA
(Music Corporation of America)
  📄 38-39,77-78
Medal
  📄 141
* Gold Medal
  📄 162
* Gold Medal Winner
  📄 139-140
* Olympic Gold Medalist
  📄 129
* Silver Medal
  📄 25

Index

*Swiss Junior Champion
  📄 38,252
MGM (Metro-Goldwyn-Mayer)
  📄 33
Mike Douglas
  📄 136,219
Milton Berle
  📄 160
Milwaukee | Wisconsin
  📄 99-101,127
Minger
  (Cantilever Spread Eagle)
  📄 24
Minneapolis | Minnesota
  📄 75-76,78,98,101-102,128,
  160,224
Mom (<u>Mamme, Muti</u>)
  📄 9,11-12,27-28
Monogram Studio
  📄 133-134
*Monogramish
  📄 134
Montreal | Québec
  📄 134-135,143-144,225
Movies
  📄 4,32-33,37,39-40,77,130,133
*Chance To Do Movies
  📄 32,37,133
*Lady, Let's Dance
  🖼 13-16 📄 54-57
  📄 4-5,37,134-135,137
*Silver Skates
  🖼 11-12 📄 52-53
  📄 4-5,37,133-155
Movie Star
  📄 32,77,133
Mr. Frick
  🖼 21 📄 62 | 42 📄 113 |
  44-45 📄 115-116 | 46 📄 122 |
  47-48 📄 131-132 | 49 📄 138 |
  50-51 📄 149-150 | 52 📄 154 |
  53-67 📄 169-183 |
  69-82 📄 185-198 |
  84-98 📄 200-214 |
  🏆 2-4 📄 227-229
  ♟ 1-3 📄 232-233
  ☺ 1-3 📄 234-236
  📄 4-5,33,75,82,119,128,
  145-146,162,164,167,
  221-222,252

*Mr. Frick's Cantilever Spread
  Eagle, Cantilever Backbend
  🖼 34 📄 89 | 39-41 📄 94-96 |
  49 📄 138 | 53 📄 169 |
  58 📄 174 | 66 📄 182 |
  74 📄 190 | 79 📄 195 |
  81 📄 197 | 84 📄 200 |
  87 📄 203 | 88 📄 204 |
  90 📄 206 | 93 📄 209
Mr. Frick & Celebrities
  🖼 35-38 📄 90-93
Mr. Frick & Snoopy
  🖼 88 📄 204 |
  100-101 📄 230-231
  ♟ 1-4 📄 232-233
Mr. Frick Day
  🏆 3-4 📄 228-229
  📄 167
Museum
  📄 83
*Pair Of Skates
  📄 81
*USFSA Museum
  📄 224
Music
  📄 17,77,82,142,146
*Good Music (by the noted
  Band leader Ted Fio Rito)
  📄 35
*Copying Frick And Frack
  Music And Maneuvers
  📄 83
*Hungarian Gypsy Tune
  📄 142
*Lilting Music
  📄 94
*MCA (Music Corporation of
  America)
  📄 38-39,77-78
*Rock-And-Roll Music
  📄 103
*Saintsaens' Danse Macabre
  📄 30
*Swiss Music
  📄 83,145
*Yodeling Music
  📄 133
Musicals
*Brazil
  📄 160

*My Fair Lady
  📄 31
*The Sound Of Music
  📄 157
Musicians
  📄 140,222
<u>Mutz</u> (Pet Name, Bear)
  📄 109,164

N

Nancy Travis
  🖼 54-56 📄 170-172
Nature
*Weather
  📄 17-18,35-36,104,126,
  143-144,146,252
*Earthquake
  📄 17,85,220,252
Negotiations
  📄 35,160,162,164,168,215
<u>Neue Zürcher Zeitung</u> (NZZ)
  📄 165,238
New York
  🖼 28 📄 69 | 34 📄 89 | 44 📄 115
  📄 11,34,36,38,76,78-83,88,
  99-100,106,110,118,124-127,
  135,143,148,156-157,160,
  163-165,215-216,222-223,
  237-238
*Nassau Coliseum
  📄 252
*New York Herald Tribune
  🖼 34 📄 89
  📄 76,88
*New York Times
  📄 118,238,252
Nikita Khrushchev
  📄 85

O

Oakland | California
  📄 36,163-164
Ocean Liner
  📄 118
*SS Normandie
  📄 32

-246-

*SS United States
 📄 118
Orrin Markus
 📄 35
Oscar Johnson
 🖼 72 📄 188
 📄 37,41,78,80,118,125,141,
    144,158-161

P

Palm Springs | California
 📄 221
Pay → Salary
 📄 12-14,17,19,22,34,36,41,78,
    85-86,94,99,103-104,106,
    119,123,126-127,136-137,
    140,145,156,159-160,162,
    219-220,252
Peanuts
 🏆 1-4 📄 232-233
 📄 4-5,141,164,222
Pearl Harbor
 📄 151
Peggy Fleming
 🖼 42 📄 113
 📄 98-99,140,143,159,216,221
Performances
 🖼 72 📄 188
 🏆 2 📄 227
 📄 220,252
Philadelphia | Pennsylvania
 📄 76,106,109,127
Phil Taylor
 📄 30-32
Phoenix | Arizona
 📄 35,148
Pilez Golaz
 📄 84
Portland | Oregon
 📄 36,119
President
 * Continental Vice-President
  📄 126
 * President's Car
  📄 224
 * President Of The Swiss Club
   Of Alexandria
  📄 18

* President Of The Boston
   Garden Arena
  📄 36
* President Of Switzerland
  📄 84
* President Of The United States
  📄 79
* President John F. Kennedy
  📄 21,75,152
* President, Rudolf Minger
  📄 24
* Vice President,
   John Nance Garner
  📄 78
Priest (Pfarrer)
 📄 13
Professor Ake Senning
 📄 110
Professor Ruedi
 📄 107-110

Q

Quitting (Notice)
 📄 41,102,140,143
* Frack
  📄 38-39,41,118,135
* Mr. Frick
  📄 109,111,162,220,223
* Werner Groebli
  📄 22-23

R

Railroad
 📄 14,19,28,99,126,145-146,
    152,224
* Pullman Car
  📄 102,145,224
* Railroad Man
  📄 11,15,152
* Railroad Roadbeds
  📄 145
* Railroad Station
  📄 11,16,152
* Swiss Railroad
  📄 40,223

Ralph Edwards
 📄 120
Ray Armstrong
 🖼 46 📄 122
 📄 119
Religious
 📄 17,20,152
Richard Dwyer
 🖼 38 📄 93 | 86 📄 202
 📄 119-120,141,161-162,166
Rifle
 📄 85
Rita Peake
 🖼 22 📄 63
River Kwai
 📄 33,77
Rockefeller Center Rink
 📄 80-82
Ronald Reagan
 📄 77,79
Ronnie Robert
 🖼 21 📄 62
 📄 41
Royal
* Buckingham Palace | London
  📄 238
* Emperor Haile Selassie
   Of Ethiopia
  📄 18,25
* King Farouk
  📄 18,26
* Princess Elizabeth
  📄 30
* Princess Margaret
  📄 30
* Queen Mother Mary
  📄 30
* Queen Victoria of Spain
  📄 30
Roy Shipstad
 🖼 72 📄 188
 📄 37,99,160-161
Rubber Legs
 📄 5,80,119

S

Sacramento | California
 📄 36,166-167,224

Salary → Pay
📄 17,29,32,34-35,94,119,
160-162,215,252
Sally Eilers
🎞 2 📄 43
Salt Lake City | Utah
📄 32
San Diego | California
📄 162,166
Sandweg And Velte
📄 20-21
San Francisco | California
🏆 3 📄 228
📄 36-37,41,76-77,84-85,103,
118-119,128,141-142,
144-145,148,151-152,156,
161,166-167,216,219,224
San Francisco News
📄 251
Santa Fe | New Mexico
📄 104-105,145
Santa Monica | California
📄 119
School
🎞 52 📄 154
📄 12-14,16-17,21,23,25,27-28,
37,40,79,88-89,101,105,
140-141,161,224
Schwyzerdütsch (Swiss German)
📄 105
Seattle | Washington
📄 36,80,102-103,127,142,
148,151
Sesame Street's Big Bird
🎞 96 📄 212
Shipstads And Johnson
🏆 2 📄 227
📄 38,79,94,141,159,217,224
* Roy Shipstad, Eddie And
Oscar Johnson
📄 37
Silver Skates
🎞 11-12 📄 52-53
📄 4-5,37,133-135
Skaters
* Figure Skaters
🎞 15 📄 56
📄 4,24-25,38,79,89,124,133,
160,221

* Ice Skaters
📄 10,17,27,87,104,117,
135-137,159,166,220,222
* Professional Skaters
🎞 74 📄 190
📄 4-5,23,31,37,80,87-88,
117-118,159,219-220
Skates
📄 9,13,17,41,76,80-82,84-86,
100-101,119,123-124,136-
137,140-141,152,159,224
* Breaking In A New Pair
Of Boots
📄 81
* Comic Genius On Skates
📄 5
* Crazy Positions On Skates
📄 80
* Funniest Man On Skates
📄 30
* Heavy Skates
📄 124
* Rita Peake On Skates
🎞 22 📄 63
* Steel Balls
📄 82,141
* Travelling With Skates
📄 124
Snoopy → Charles Schulz
🎞 88 📄 204 |
100-101 📄 230-231
🏆 1-4 📄 232-233
📄 4-5,219,222-223
* Snoopy In Switzerland
📄 223
* Snoopy's Home Ice
📄 222
* Snoopy With A Herd
Of Cows
📄 223
Sonja Henie
📄 33-35,77,83,107,133,224,252
Sonny Werblin
📄 38
Spencer Tracy
📄 33,133
Sports Writers
📄 79,215
SS Steamship → Ocean Liner

Stage Door Johnnies
📄 94,105,140,142
* Gerry Graham
📄 105
St. Moritz
(Engadin, Switzerland)
📄 25-27,29,88,94
* Puttin' on the Ritz in St. Moritz
📄 118
* The Glitz of St. Moritz
📄 25
* The St. Moritz Express
📄 33,252
Stock And Bond
📄 5,33,99,105,120,137,151,
161,165,215-217,238
Stunt
🎞 40 📄 95
📄 40-41,79,88-89,126-127,220
Suitcase → Luggage
Susan Berens
🎞 80 📄 196
Swiss
🎞 13 📄 54
📄 4,10-15,17-18,20-26,28-29,
31-33,35,37-39,75-76,79-81,
83-84,86,88,94,99-102,105-
110,117,120,125,127-128,
133,135,139,144-145,147,
151-152,157,163-165,
215-217,219,223-224
*Swiss Army
📄 13,15,25,86
* Swiss Boys
📄 11-13
*Swiss Businessman
📄 81,86
* Swiss Comedian, Swiss Comics,
Swiss Clown
🎞 22 📄 63 | 34 📄 89
📄 11,80,88,94
* Swiss Consul
📄 108,144
* Swiss Folk Costumes
📄 26,83,133
* Swiss Federal Institute Of
Technology (ETH Zurich)
📄 23
* Swiss German
📄 4,29,105

www.ingramcontent.com/pod-product-compliance
Lightning Source LLC
Chambersburg PA
CBHW081937170426
43202CB00018B/2939

3.

Title:	**Swiss Movements special edition**
Author|Editor:	Werner Groebli|Thomas Foeldi
Publication Date:	October 2016|Update July 2018
Edition:	**Paperback**
Pages:	254
Size:	8.5x11 in. (21.59x27.94 cm)
Cover:	Color Glossy
Interior:	Black and White on White paper
Chapters:	13
Pictures:	101 Black and White photos
Honors:	4
Cartoons:	3
Peanuts (Snoopy):	4
Information:	Original newspaper clippings
Printed by:	CreateSpace
Availability:	Amazon|CreateSpace|Bookshops
List Price:	$24.60
ISBN	978-3-9524638-2-6

4.

Title:	**Swiss Movements deluxe edition**
Author|Editor:	Werner Groebli|Thomas Foeldi
Publication Date:	April 2017|Update July 2018
Edition:	**Hardcover**
Pages:	288
Size:	8x10 in. (21x26 cm)
Cover:	Matte finish on the cover
Interior:	Black and White
Paper quality:	Standard Paper, 80# Semi Matte (118 g/m^2)
Chapters:	13
Pictures:	111 high quality Black and White photos
Honors:	4
Cartoons:	3
Peanuts (Snoopy):	4
Information:	Original newspaper clippings
Printed by:	Blurb
Availability & Price:	Please mail your request to: mrfrick@bluewin.ch
ISBN	978-3-9524638-3-3

Editions

Swiss Movements

An American Dream
The autobiography of Mr. Frick
Of the legendary Ice Skating Team of Frick and Frack

Swiss Movements is available in four editions:

1.

Title:	**Swiss Movements**
Author|Editor:	Werner Groebli|Thomas Foeldi
Publication Date:	April 2016|Update July 2018
Edition:	**eBook**
Cover:	Color
Interior:	Black and White
Chapters:	13
Pictures:	13 Black and White photos
Peanuts (Snoopy):	1
Availability:	Amazon
List Price:	$8.60
ISBN	978-3-9524638-1-9

2.

Title:	**Swiss Movements**
Author|Editor:	Werner Groebli|Thomas Foeldi
Publication Date:	April 2016|Update July 2018
Edition:	**Paperback**
Pages:	258
Size:	6x9 in. (15.24x22.86 cm)
Cover:	Color Glossy
Interior:	Black and White on White paper
Chapters:	13
Pictures:	13 Black and White photos
Peanuts (Snoopy):	1
Printed by:	CreateSpace
Availability:	Amazon|CreateSpace|Bookshops
List Price:	$14.60
ISBN	978-3-9524638-0-2

THE NEW YORK TIMES, SUNDAY, APRIL 22, 1973

Amazing Frick Cuts a Cool Figure on Ice

By McCANDLISH PHILLIPS
Special to The New York Times

UNIONDALE, L. I. -- Werner Groebli is a Swiss figure skater who went wrong. He lost his reputation as a youth, changed his name in shame, and has never since consented to go out on the ice looking like a swan in a tuxedo.

Mr. Groebli is better known as Mr. Frick, the oldest and richest fool in the Ice Follies, which opened last week in the Nassau Coliseum. He is the geriatric wonder of his business, having first won fame a long while ago as half of the comedy skating team of Frick & Frack.

He is a surviving relic of the age of Sonja Henie.

Yesterday the Swiss junior champion of 1934 celebrated his 58th birthday. He has been with the ice show since 1939, logging 50,000 miles and 26 to 32 cities a year, and he is heading for a mark of 14,000 performances. Just to look at him is enough to make a man angry.

Many of us were children in the nineteen-forties when Frick was a youthful-looking ice clown. Now we are fathers, and some of us are grandfathers, paunch-burdened, double-chinned and gray haired, and Mr. Frick remains what he was then -- a youthful looking ice clown.

To add insult to this grave injury to our egos, the man even has dimples. Without make-up, his face, still firm-fleshed, gives off a ruddy glow of health, as though he had spent all his life breathing Swiss mountain air instead of taping cracks around the edges of hotel room doors to keep the stale cigarette smoke out.

Health Food Faddist

He is famous for that among his comrades, as well as for a highly original health food faddism in which his idea of a healthy breakfast is coffee and "bourbon over, grapefruit." He pours a jigger of bourbon on his grapefruit the way others pour honey on it.

While others in his show are all grace and dash and speed and liquidity-in-motion, Mr. Frick is all sharp angles and tightly turned corners and jagged edges.

Off the ice he is a real estate investor, stock market player, absentee landlord, newspaper addict and pyrophobe.

"I tape doors to keep the smoke out of my room, and it will also be helpful in case of fires," he said a few hours before the show opened in the Coliseum, in a run that goes through next Sunday. "I'm really afraid of fires. I carry a hammer and chisel to loosen stuck windows. Now they're not stuck so much any more, they're permanently closed and you need the hammer and chisel to crack them open."

Mr. Frick is polite and a little formal in person and he manages to be quite funny in what he says without being even slightly jolly.

Minor Olympics

"I have a big margin yet," he says in reply to a question about how long he will go on. "I can go on, but I do not know how many more trips my suitcase will stand. I've had it 30 years. It has cost me $2,600 in tips.

"The sheer collecting of fine reviews and notices weighs me down and may force me off the road."

Of the exactions of the road, he says: "It's not the touring, it's the packing, the ever-increasing junk you carry with you."

Of the exactions of the work, he says: "Each performance is a minor Olympics."

From age 6 to 16, he did "all figure skating, with not a shred of comedy in it." Then, with his naughty next-door neighbor, Hans Mauch, he began working out spoofs of serious skating, which scandalized their families. That is a big reason why young Groebli and Mauch took up their identities as Frick & Frack.

It shocks people who remember them so well together that Mr. Mauch, who is four years younger than Mr. Groebli, retired in 1953 because of a deficiency that gave him brittle bones. The Frackless Mr. Frick has been skating, as a solo turn for 19 years now (with deft, but not comedic, assistance from others, now Jim Reid).

Before the Ice Follies, they worked with an outdoor show on the West Coast called The St. Moritz Express, which turned out to be the Toonerville Trolley of ice shows.

It got hit by "hail, rain, sandstorms, earthquakes -- yes, there was an earthquake -- heat, waves, sleet. The elements were against it," Mr. Frick recalled. "It lasted five weeks. It died with 200 people in the audience, and the owed us salary."

The team went into the Follies on May 13, 1939, in San Francisco. The pay was about $350 a week, for each man -- in the depression and the money has gone comfortably up into four figures since then.

"Is an act ever finished Mr. Frick asked?"

"It never is," he quickly replied.

"I hone and polish until things crystallize," the ice star said. "I spend sleepless nights to make it coherent routine, well-constructed -- in good timing, in good pace, in good taste."

The clown has had a heart defect since he was 17 years old that has shown up on every test since then.

He finds it necessary to be psyched up each day, to maintain that freshness.

"I cannot look old. I must look young and fresh," he said. "Young comics are waiting in the wings, waiting for the old bastard to quit."

Appendix

The San Francisco News
Wednesday, June 15, 1949

Wacky Hockey by Frick and Frack

Here are two young hokey, potentials who, to say the least, have a style all their own. They are Frick (left) and Frack, featured comedians in the Ice Follies who decided to inject a few of their original ideas into the game. Here the boys suggest a squatting technique for face-offs so that the view of other players at both ends of the rink won't be obstructed.

As every hokey follower or player knows, the game calls for a fast pace. So, Frick and Frack suggest this "resting" technique for weary forwards. While rushing down the ice the forward simply sits down on a burly defense man's knee, and in case you don't think this is big league stuff they are wearing uniforms of the Montreal Canadians.

Uschi Kessler
  141-142
USFSA (US Figure Skating)
  224
* USFSA Museum |
  Colorado Springs
  224
* USFSA Hall of Fame
  225
USS Nautilus
  64   180

V

Vacation
  12,78,121,158,216,219
* Aruba
  162
* Barbados
  109
* Caribbean
  81,109
* Lake Tahoe
  135,221,224
* Las Vegas
  120,166
* Spontaneous Vacations
  118,124
Vancouver
  36
Věra Hrubá
  133
Vicki Denton
  47   131

W

Wall Street
  33,127,137
* The Wall Street Journal
  48   132
  33-34,141
Walter Brown
  36
Walter And Irene Muhlbronner
  109
Walter Rudolf
  128

Warden Duffy
  85
Wardrobe
  83,86
Washington D.C.
  78,86,106
* Washington Paper
  86
Weather → Nature
Weight
* Orrin Markus
  35
* Overweight
  101,104
* Overweight Charges
  123-124
Weight Watcher
  139,165,221,225
Werner Fritz Groebli
  38   93 | 68   184 |
  83   199 | 99   218
  3-5,11,88,94,97,130,224,252
Werner Von Braun
  21
Who's Who
  221
Winterland Rink San Francisco
  76,85,151-152,216
Wintersport
(Touring Ice Show, England)
  31-32
Wollman Memorial Ice Rink
  222
World Champion → Champion
World War I
  9,13
World War II
  13,18,21,31-32,151,153

Y

Yodeling
  14   55
  31
* Swiss Yodeling Band
  135
* Yodeling Music
  133

Yvonne Groebli
  43   114 | 45   116 |
  72   188
  5,86,100-112,118-119,124,
  128,136,139,142,147-148,
  155-158,160-167,215-216,
  219-220,222-224,237
* Yvonne's Health
  103,112,155,237

Z

Zurich (Switzerland)
  18,24,28,97,119,116,
  119,122,123,125-129,
  137,144-145,166,180,
  192,244,251,267
* Architecture Study
  22-25,88
* <u>Bahnhofstrasse</u>
  237
* Church Bells
  17
* Domestic Science School
  16
* Kennel
  111,155-157
* Lake Zurich
  237
* Opera House Of Zurich
  237
* Respected Zurich Attorney
  102
* Sonja Henie
  35
* Swiss Federal Institute of
  Technology (ETH Zurich)
  23
* University Hospital of Zurich
  109-110

* Swiss Girls
  - 101,105,157
* Swiss Jewel Mr. Frick
  - 92 208
* Swiss Junior Champion
  - 38,252
* Swiss Junior Figure Skating Championship
  - 25
* Swiss Movements → Editions
* Swiss Neutrality
  - 32,151
* Swiss School Children
  - 52 154
* Swiss Team of Comedy Skaters
  - 76
* Swiss Yodeling Music
  - 14 55
  - 83,145,155
Swiss Club
* Swiss Club Of San Francisco
  - 145,219
* Swiss Club Of Alexandria
  - 18
Swissair
  - 110,156
Switzerland
  - 52 154
  - 4,9,11-12,14-15,17-19,21,24, 27-30,32-33,36-37,40,78,84, 97,100,102,105-107,109-111, 126,128,133,135,144,151-152,155,158,164,166,216, 219,221,223-225,237-238
* Douche
  - 102
* Frick (Town in Switzerland)
  - 147
* Kennel
  - 111,155-157
* Life Magazine
  - 79,94-96
* New York Herald Tribune
  - 88

T

Ted Barton
  - 119,167,219

Ted Fio Rito
  - 35
Thayer Tutt
  - 105,147
Telephone Company
  - 128
Texas Instruments (T.I.)
  - 107,216
The Kermond Brothers
  - 83
The Moser Brothers
  - 14 55
  - 135
Thomas Dean
  - 36
Time Magazine
  - 79
Tokyo
* Little Tokyo
  - 152
* Pair Of Skates
  - 81
Tony Bennett
  - 38 93
Toronto
  - 36,88,141,144,148,163
Travelling
  - 13,86,99,106,108,126,139, 148,167,215,224-225
* Fracks Wardrobe
  - 86
* Travelling Across The United States
  - 32
* Travelling Bar
  - 86
* Travelling By Air
  - 123-124,158
* Travelling By Train
  - 80,105,145
* Travelling Coach and Director
  - 143
* Travelling During The Colder Months
  - 140
* Travelling During Wartime
  - 152
* Travelling In Style
  - 123

* Travelling Orgy
  - 139
* Travelling With A Dog
  - 111,156-157
* Travelling With An Ice Show (Shipstad & Johnson's Ice Follies)
  - 83,94,139-140,148,158, 160,224-225
* Travelling With An Ice Skater
  - 104,111,224
* Travelling With Skates
  - 124
* Travelling With Tools
  - 148
Tropical Ice Gardens
  - 1-2 42-43
  - 32-33
TWA (Trans World Airlines)
  - 106,124,126,223
* TWA Constellation
  - 44 115
  - 106,124
Tulsa | Oklahoma
  - 144

U

Uncle (Onkel) Heini
  - 16-18

Uncle (Onkel) Ruedi
  - 13-14,18,22
United States
  - 5,32,37,75,78-79,102, 108,118,151,164,215
* President of the United States
  - 75,79,152
* SS United States
  - 118
Swiss Friends Of The United States
  - 102
U.S. Army (American Army)
  - 175-176
U.S. Government
  - 81,245
U.S. Navy
  - 151